Routes to Reading

Stories of Immigration

Published 2006 by Reading Local History Trust
www.theimmigrantsproject.org

Designed by Lift, set in Sabon Roman, and printed in Great Britain at the Cromwell
Press, Trowbridge.

Acknowledgements

This project has involved many people giving their time freely and generously and huge thanks is due to them. Although it sounds hackneyed to say it, *Routes to Reading* really would not have been possible without them.

I would first like to thank Stewart Tippett, Owen Muganda and Joycelyn Melton-Grey, who gave their time and support to the project. They undertook training as oral history interviewers and carried out many of the interviews in this book with great enthusiasm and competency. They also gave up their spare time to attend review meetings and to offer helpful advice. Thanks to Doris Ferguson-Townsend who also skilfully interviewed people and who gave me many contacts in the community.

Tammy Bedford (Arts Manager at Reading Borough Council) and Matthew Williams (Senior Curator at Reading Museum) have given help and advice way beyond their professional duty and always responded positively to requests, even when last minute.

The text for the book would not exist without a whole army of voluntary and paid transcribers. Many thanks to Alison Mackay who is also a member of Reading Local History Trust and who, in addition to spending many hours of

Trainee librarian
(Reading Central Library, 1963)
Berkshire Chronicle

her time transcribing, has given shed loads of helpful advice. Elaine Bradshaw, thank you for your transcriptions and also the many contacts you gave me through your work at Reading Library. Judith Gibbison has interviewed, transcribed, prepared text for editing and proof read, again giving much help and support freely. Christine Borgars, thanks for your transcriptions and many great community contacts.

Heather Gooding has been involved in the project since its conception and has given her time enthusiastically to it. Many thanks for your community contacts, help and support. Thanks to Natalie O'Toole for press releases, marketing advice and enthusiasm for the project. Richard Sandford has researched the contextual information, transcribed and proof read.

Thank you to Reading Local History Trustees, Elaine Watts, in particular with regard to ISBN, and Susan Spiers for her commitment and practical support in sorting out the office and at functions. Huge thanks go to Keith Jerrome, Chair of the Trust who has been active in all decision making areas and whose infectious enthusiasm for all things local and historical is definitely catching and without whom the project would not have been started.

Martin Salter, thank you for getting us started, for your continuing support and for writing a foreword to *Routes to Reading*, which so eloquently demonstrates your passion for social history and the town of Reading and its people and which is shared by so many of us involved in the project.

Matt Carey and Stephanie Lee at Studio Lift our book designers have done a wonderful job in understanding the content and translating it into a style which reflects and enhances the stories told.

The Heritage Lottery Fund, Reading Borough Council, The Earley Charity and The Co-operative Group provided financial support through grant aid. Thanks to staff at Reading Central Library for providing us with an office. The Sardar Palace kindly allowed us to use their restaurant for the project launch.

Many others have been involved in fundraising efforts or by giving support and local contacts. Thanks to Veera Gupta at the Indian Community Centre and Misha at the Polish luncheon club for making me feel particularly welcome.

Reading Museum Service kindly provided the images used in the Foreword and Acknowledgments.

It isn't possible to continue to name everyone personally so please accept my sincere apologies but grateful thanks if you are not mentioned directly here.

Finally, but most importantly, thanks to all the people who gave their time to share their lives with us and who told their stories with great candour and generosity.

Ann Westgarth
The Immigrants Project Co-ordinator & Routes to Reading Editor

Foreword

The idea for this project was slow to germinate. I suppose the seed was planted somewhere in the deep recesses of my mind sometime in the mid 1980s as I forged links with members of the diverse communities that lived and worked in the Cemetery Junction area of Reading where I was a councillor. A few years later and I had become responsible for Reading Borough Council's grants policy and attended the launch of an oral history book entitled 'Talking of Coley' which had benefited from council funding. For the first time I saw how it was possible to breathe life into history, to document the lives of ordinary people and their communities and to record for posterity their stories in their own words. The book launch brought together people who had not seen each other for many years. It was a reunion and all the more poignant for being so. In fact a couple who were childhood sweethearts 50 years previously met up that night, fell in love all over again and got married so that they could spend their twilight years together.

The socialist in me has always had a problem with the conventional teaching of history. It has to be more than the lives of Kings and Queens and the great and good. The limited study of social history that formed part of my own schooling inspired me more than any other subject. I remember being captivated by G.D.H. Coles' 'History of the Common People' and in particular its account of the 1926 General Strike and the struggle for social justice. At the launch of the Coley book it started to come together for me. Here were real life survivors of the slums known as the 'Coley Steps' – a rabbit warren of dwellings with no proper sanitation where kids slept eight to a room and

Black GI's VE Day (Coley, 1945) *Berkshire Chronicle*

families lived in abject poverty. The area had long been re-developed but the stories and memories remained. However, they would be largely lost with the passing of time unless efforts were made to record the memories of those who were still alive. That night I determined to do the same for the people I represented across the other side of Reading in the Newtown area.

In 1995 the Reading Local History Trust was established under the leadership of my old friend Keith Jerrome, a trade union officer and keen historian. Our first venture was 'Newtown – The Inside Story' which very much replicated the model of 'Talking of Coley'. To our surprise the Newtown book with its stories of life between the wars at Huntley & Palmers biscuit factory and the changing nature of East Reading proved remarkably successful and generated a £4,000 surplus. The Trust decided to re-invest this and any subsequent sums in similar projects resulting in books about Katesgrove, Tilehurst and the Reading Volunteers in the Spanish Civil War. For a couple of years the Trust remained dormant until the idea for 'The Immigrants' suddenly exploded in my head. It was a hot Sunday afternoon in July 2004 and I was rushing back from the West Country to attend a presentation of certificates to prominent members of Reading's black community by the Carson Small

Anti Apartheid March (Market Place, 12th June 1964) *Berkshire Chronicle*

Foundation. The event was held at St Giles Church in Southampton Street and I was invited along in my capacity as local MP with my predecessor Sir Anthony Durant. Sitting at the front of the church I looked out on a sea of faces, many of whom I had known for most of the 20 years I had spent in public life in Reading. There were people from St Vincent, Barbados, Jamaica, Guyana, Grenada and elsewhere. Somewhat morbidly I recalled how we were all aging fast and then I realised that unless steps were taken soon all these people's memories and stories would be lost and an important part of the history of our town would never be told.

You see, Reading is a town built on immigration. Initially from rural areas in the south of England in the 19th century as people moved off the land to work in the factories, brick kilns and mills which sprang up as part of the industrial revolution. There followed further immigration from Wales, Scotland and Ireland as workers sought new opportunities not available to them in more economically depressed areas.

The stories collected by this project, of which a selection are reproduced here, tell of people fleeing war torn Europe following the Second World War, Bosnia in the 1990's, and political persecution in Zimbabwe. They tell of people seeking security and freedom, a new life to overcome poverty or a desperate situation at home. They tell of separation and romance, some coming to join their partners, or to seek out new opportunities.

People tell of their arrival from the Caribbean in the 1950's to train as nurses and midwives in Reading's hospitals, often working long unsocial hours or night shifts to make ends meet or to care for their children. Others worked on production lines at factories such as Huntley & Palmers, Ideal Casements, Huntley, Bourne & Stevens, and Frame Clothing. The 1960's saw the arrival of immigrants from Pakistan and India and in the 1970's from East Africa. Many trained or re-trained as teachers or health workers and set up new businesses from scratch such as taxi companies and restaurants. Reading now has the largest Bajan population outside of Barbados anywhere in the world and is also home to communities from other Caribbean islands such as St. Vincent. There is a large population of Pakistani and Kashmiri origin as well as smaller Sikh and Hindu communities and significant numbers of people from Bangladesh, Nepal, China, Sierra Leone, Ghana, Nigeria, South Africa, Zimbabwe, Kenya and Tanzania.

As you can read here, most of the people who have come to settle have not been satisfied to make a life just for themselves but have been active in setting up community organisations and self-help groups to support others. The Reading Refugee Support Group is one of many such groups supporting more recent arrivals from many of the world's trouble spots including: Rwanda, Ethiopia, Sudan, Algeria, Libya, Kosovo, Albania, Serbia, Croatia, Bosnia, Afghanistan and Iraq.

The enlargement of the European Union has seen up to 10,000 workers from Poland swell the ranks of our buoyant labour market; boost the congregations of local Catholic churches and the opening of many stores stocking Polish fare.

Reading is an extremely diverse multi-ethnic, multi-racial community with a good record of race relations. Many of the people who settled in Reading after World War II are now in their 50s, 60s, and 70s and have fascinating stories to tell. Some have had to deal with racism and discrimination but also tell of the support and friendships they have forged in the town. All arrived with little in the way of material possessions but a huge amount of self-determination and a willingness to work hard to succeed. They tell of how Britain was perceived from the other side of the world and the reality of what they found when they arrived here. The agony of leaving friends, family and loved ones behind. The uncertainty and risk, hostility and isolation. Struggles with a new language and culture and trying to find homes, jobs and schools for themselves and for their families. There are stories about human endeavour, human achievement – triumphs and disasters.

This rich international tapestry of human experience is a story worth telling and with an increasingly strident tabloid media seeking to demonise Britain's immigrant communities it is timely that this book is published now. Only the most rabid of racists could fail to be moved by the story of a person like Alice Chigumira – a child of humble origins who rose to become a Zimbabwean diplomat and then had to flee her country and end up an asylum seeker in Reading, reliant on the kindness of others. She now works as an assistant social worker in Reading helping adults and the disabled.

This is what Alice told us … 'My worry is still up to now how people see refugees, their own perspective about refugees, asylum seekers, refugees - what are they? But unless you sit across me, when I'm walking down the street and coming to assess your mum and dad in their home, black as I am with my dreadlocks, you never see a refugee, you see somebody with empathy who wants to make a difference to somebody who is not from their own culture, but who values the other people's culture, the diversity of people. Diversity doesn't necessarily mean if you are British - it's Sunday roast dinner. Diversity means who you are as a person. The most important thing is I love Reading, I love Reading every time I just walk out of here…I've integrated so much… I've found good mothers here who are British who look after me like I am their own daughter. I've found families here who look after me as if I am their own child. I've found friends here from a diverse community, from the Asian community, from the White community, where I have felt comfortable with them. Reading is just a place where you say, I can come here and stay here and retire and won't feel the hassles of being in a bustle and hustle town. It's just a place where you feel comfortable in every way.'

The brilliant team of volunteers led by our inspirational co-ordinator Ann Westgarth has done a great job recording the memories of Reading's increasingly diverse communities. They have amassed an impressive archive of material which goes far beyond the selection represented in this book. Every one of the interviews collected is a valuable resource and a testament to those individuals who have shared their stories. The fantastic response has resulted in far too much material for one publication but all of the interviews will be placed on the project's website and have a permanent home at Reading Museum. This is not a scientific record nor is it an academic study. It is a collection of stories of people from all over the world who come to our town in search of a better life.

I hope you enjoy it.

Martin Salter MP
Reading West

West Indian Employee at Cornish Wafers production line (Huntley & Palmers, 1960)
Berkshire Chronicle

Preface

The Immigrants Project set out to interview people who came from all over the world to settle in Reading and *Routes to Reading* forms part of that unique record. The overall aim of the project was to capture and preserve these experiences for future generations; it was essentially an oral history project. This book is one of the ways this material is being made accessible to a wider audience. These stories are selected from a much larger and ever increasing collection, which forms the major part of an oral history archive held in Reading Museum. The recordings and transcripts will be available for historical and educational purposes and for use in exhibitions. On the project's website, additional interviews and the voices of those involved can be heard.

Routes to Reading has been laid out so that the interviews can be read as they were recorded. Transcripts of the recordings have only been edited to meet the confines of space and to maintain fluidity. In this way it is hoped that they remain as authentic to the original as possible and that the cadence of an individual's idiomatic language is maintained. The questions are deliberately highlighted to provide breaks in the text where the pace of an interview or story is altered by the intervention of the interviewer, or where a change of direction or the 'moving on' in a story occurs. Where photographs or other documents appear, these have been provided by interviewees themselves from their own personal collections to add a visual dimension to what they are describing.

Yellow vertical lines have been used to highlight the common themes that emerged from people's stories. These include, childhood, education and training, family values, self-sufficiency, community support, political situation, economic situation, jobs, community support, racism, and, where home is regarded, coupled with a sense of identity, particularly for immigrant's children. Food was regarded as significant, as Ling says in her interview 'you can change everywhere but you can't change the stomach.' Separation is apparent, either by distance from one's family and parents, or where husbands have travelled ahead to set up home or where children are left behind with relatives or close friends until parents can afford for them to join them. This is counter-balanced by a very strong sense of family unity. A number of interviewees mention their first experience of snow.

At the end of most interviews there is a short factual piece of contextual information relating to the countries people originated from prior to and up to the time they left.

Ann Westgarth
The Immigrants Project Co-ordinator & Routes to Reading Editor

Contents

Spaho Bajric

Born: 19th July 1944
Small town near Sarajevo, Bosnia

Date of Interview: 23rd June 2006

Bosnia

● Sarajevo, Bosnia
○ Slovenia
● Reading, UK

Childhood
Family Values

Jobs

Political Situation

I was original from Bosnia and I was born sixty three years ago and in a small town near Sarajevo.

Do you have any memories of your childhood, education?

I have to say in childhood I was happy child and I was growing in nice family and they give me a very good family education to respect other people, my neighbours, friends and to be honest and to work hard in my life, what I did.

How many of you in your family?

I was brought with a big family ... I had four sister ... two brothers ... but my family was quite wealthy family and they adopt one boy during the war and we call him brother and my father sent him at university at that time. He pay everything and ... he did something what I try to follow like it in my life.

What specifically did he do that you tried to follow later in life?

I try to help other people but I will talk and in my experience a little bit more later.

You spoke about the war ...

Yes ... and first I have to say where I used to work. I was Professor of History and Latin Language at Dobor College. It's Bosnian, small town about 60,000 people but about 20,000 student.

Lovely town on three rivers and I really enjoyed my life with my students, with my wife and two kids.

Everything was OK until ... May 1992 then war broke in Bosnia and Serbian people and Yugoslavian Army, they aggressive on my country and [pause] my ex-student who used to work in Bosnia police came one day and he told me, 'Professor, you must go. Your name is on list for arrest and killed?' And my son name was as well. And I had only ten minutes to take my personal things - passport, little bit money. I didn't go to the bank and I was without my, without anything but ... my ex-student help me to escape from the town. He took me on free territory to the other town where I became refugee in own country. And at that time my son was student in Sarajevo, and my daughter who was at medical college she was in other town. I didn't know anything about them. When I escaped to town Zepce, small town 20,000 people, but at the time they had about 10,000 refugees and I found accommodation in one primary school and they shared one room about sixty or seventy of us and ... local people they provide us with food and ... everybody was expecting the war would be finished for couple of days, but unfortunately it last more than three year.

My wife at that time was quite ill and when I took her to hospital they told me, 'Sorry, this is more. We can't help your wife. You have to go to the other country, Croatia or Slovenia. They will help you. They will accept you like refugee.'

But it was big problem to go out. Police, they did not allow me to go and when I took paper from doctor and show them, and they said, 'Yes, you can go.' They gave me ten days and after ten days I have to come back [pause] And all roads they are under control of Serbian soldier. It was very dangerous to go to them because they will arrest you or kill you. We had to go through one mountain and about ten of us we were travelling during the night and during the day we were hiding in the forest.

How were you travelling?

And ... they find somebody by car, they pay for that, and they were travelling by foot as well because it was mountain area and they had somebody who know area very well. And it took us about four days to reach Croatian border, and in Croatia I found my friend who helped me to go to Slovenia with my wife who was quite ill.

In Slovenia I went to refugee camp in town Kamnik and they offer us accommodation. It was one room for five people. I was very happy to pay something like that. Without money, without anything with you, you have to accept what they offer to you. My wife [pause] I took her to hospital in Ljubljana and after three weeks doctor told me she would die and ... at that time I didn't know anything about my family, about my children, where is my daughter, where my son was, and I went to Red Cross in Slovenia and ask to help with coffin for funeral. They promise me they will give everything. When I went to ... I was in Bosnian, Slovenian mosque where Bosnian people used to work and they said 'They can't help you. You have to pay for funeral service.' I was so upset that somebody can't offer you religious service and at that time I swear I will never go to mosque or church and, but after I change my mind anyway.

And I took my wife to Croatian and Bosnian border from Slovenia where she was alive and next day she died. [pause] Her relative who was ambulance driver took her body and me to small town they call Bosanski Brod and we went to [pause] grave with her body but fighting was around and bomb, shelling. We had only five minutes for funeral service. What I did I try to remember place where I put my wife and after that I had a big problem after three years when war was finished unable to find her grave.

Day when my wife died it was the worst and very unhappy day for me as well. I lost somebody that I loved but at that time I found my daughter. She was in Macedonia and in one refugee camp. She was travelling through Bulgaria, Hungary, Croatia and she came to Slovenia. A friend of mine told her about me. [pause] When she asked me, 'What's happened with Mum?' I told her 'Your Mum ... has died.' She was crying and she said 'I will kill myself.' I tried to stop her, make her calm. I promise everything be OK, I will look after her [pause] and [pause] in Slovenia I try to do something to help myself and family and I join Red Cross to help other refugee and I join council and ask to work in Bosnian school to help Bosnian people. And it was on voluntary base.

Unfortunately one day police arrest me, Slovenian police. They told me, 'You can't go out from refugee camp, you have to stay in refugee camp' and they treat me like prisoner and I was so disappointed I was looking to go to any other country to be free to enjoy my freedom. Doesn't matter which country, is it Albania, is it France or Germany. At that time Red Cross they made list … and country for people who would like to go to Germany, France, Italia, Switzerland. I prefer to go to France. At that time I speak French but both my children they ask 'dad, please let's go to England.' I didn't know anything about England and what I should do in country where I never visit before. I never speak English, and what I will do. They said 'Dad please, let's go to England.'

And five buses from Reading in Organisation of Reading Churches they come to collect about 100 something and 70 Bosnia refugee to bring to United Kingdom. And I do remember Joe Wise editor of *Reading Chronicle* was one of them and I met him. We became after that very good friends. And I was very quiet. [pause] For me I thought it will probably be couple of weeks war will be finished, I will go back to Bosnia. Unfortunately something was happening different. When I arrived in Reading after it took us about one day and night. When I arrived in Reading they accommodate us in St Saviour's Church. I spend three days laying on the floor with some other Bosnian people but …

Spaho's house in Bosnia

When roughly was it that you came here?

It was sixth of October 1992. I do remember exact date when it was. And after … one week something like that they accommodate us with some families, Reading family houses. I was with one family near Cemetery Junction for three weeks and people who brought us here they offer me accommodation. It was in Newtown one old house and this just simple furniture but the most important I was free.

What's happened after that? I didn't know anything about England. I didn't know anything about system how it works here and I didn't know anything about Social Security service because in Bosnia we did not have it. Only if you worked you can get money. If you don't work nobody will help you. And we got free accommodation and other time income support for me and two my children. I was so embarrassed. It was so unpleasant situation that I would take something that I did not earn. It was first time that I feel 'Oh, I'm guilty, I taking money from somebody who earn is not my money.' Other people try to persuade me that other people claim as well, is not shame. It is situation that I can't change anything. And after the people help me with some clothes I had only one trouser and about fifty pound in my pocket, everything was my capital. All my money it stay in bank in Bosnia and I wasn't able to bring anything with me.

At that time I was going to speak English. What I should do? I was in country … that I can't communicate with other people. My son and daughter they speak little bit English because they learn at their school and university and I had always to ask them to translate with something, to help with something. I feel that I was probably the most stupid man in world and it was funny but you can't communicate. I met one French man. I start to talk French and after that I said 'Oh I am all right. I can communicate with other people.' People who help us in church they care about us to find some English lessons and it was volunteer who start to teach me. My first lessons was in St Saviour's Church.

After ten days gentleman who was responsible for everything his name was John and he made me … shock. He brought interpretator from BBC and ask me 'Can I change my religious to join the church?' They provide and support for me and my children, they offer scholarship. I was so so upset.

Which religion you [inaudible]?

I don't know which is some sort of Christianity [both talking together]

Which religion were you before?

I never follow it, I was free man you know. But I was born … I was born like Bosnian Muslim and I was so proud of my parents' religion and I said 'Why are we change?' And I was so upset I ask for my passport to go back to Bosnia. He was so embarrassed he apologised me he will never do it again and I realised they respect me so much and they tried me to help in other way.

My children … I was worried for them. They had to find school. They have to continue with their education. My son was in Bosnia student but my

Education & Training

Self Sufficiency

Community

Jobs

Education & Training

daughter she finished two years at medical college. And what's happened when we asked for place at school nobody accept them because their English was quite … weak and first they had to improve English. My son spent one year for preparatory course at Reading University. He was doing maths, physics, chemistry and English and after one year he passed. My daughter they put her to GCSE and teacher told me she can get good result but she was so clever girl I know that the problem was English.

And I borrow money from friend of mine from Germany. I pay at private school for my children to go to learn English and after one year both of them they passed First Cambridge Certificate and after that Proficiency. My daughter start to do her A Level, and in chemistry, maths and physics. It was very rare that girl take maths and some her friends call her genius, but she took maths because you don't need much English but she was preparing herself to studying pharmacy or dentistry. For me I was learning just basic … it was couple hours per week and and … it wasn't be enough. If I need more lessons I had to pay. I didn't have any money for that but I found volunteer teacher who promised that will help and really she helped me and I start to learn more.

After six months we receive insurance number and we were able to work. What I should do I use my experience from my … I said young day because we had family business in construction industry. My older brother was a businessman and when I was student I used to help him. I work with him but I was quite good with painting and decorating and one Indian man offered me job. It was small amount of money. I was working at that time probably thirty five to thirty pound per day but I was happy that I could earn money and I can help my children for their education. I know it wasn't money for living it was money for put in somebody in their future.

My son at that time applied to go to university North London University and they accept him but student fee was quite high about £5,000 we have to pay. It was impossible for us to pay because they treat us as foreign student not home student and we sent letter to the college department and they reduced fee on £2,500. It was very good news and we were work very hard to save money and pay for student fee.

And my daughter at that time used to work at Safeway food store in Reading. Headmaster of Maiden Erlegh School find job for her. She was working after when she finishes school after four o'clock and she was working for weekend. It was enough for us to save some money and prepare for university for student day when they go to university. And both of us we were helping for my son and her brother and he was working for weekend as well in restaurant and pubs to earn money to pay for accommodation and food. And after first year he applied for and … George Soros Foundation in America and he receive help from him. But I was thinking how we can do something. We have some other Bosnian people here with student. What we can do? And we decide to organise Bosnian Youth Trust. With local people who join us we were so successful. We apply to National Lottery Charity Board and with explanation that we need money for student who are Bosnian student who are at university in Reading and they offer us at that time I can't remember

Community

Education & Training

Jobs

Self Sufficiency

probably about £10,000 what was enough to pay for fees. And when we received that we were able to support our children.

What's happen with me? I was working but after five o'clock when I finish my work as painter decorator I was attending English lessons at the Japanese College in Reading.

What work were you doing during the day?

I was doing painting decorating houses and all building work, my employer, ordered me to do. I have to do it but when I finish at five o'clock at six o'clock I was at college. And I was, I said I will not spend the rest of my whole life working in the construction industry. I have to do something else and without English I can't do anything. [pause] When I come home at nine o'clock I had to prepare my dinner. Sometimes I know I slept on sofa. My dinner was on the table I forget for that. I was so tired. And in morning I have to go again for work. But I know life is difficult. Everywhere if you to a foreign country without language without friends without family without money you have to do something.

And ... in Reading we try to improve our life for refugee and we establish Reading Refugee Support Group. And I get idea and I was supporting from ... gentleman who was mayor in my town in Bosnia and we start to do this job on voluntary base. After that we apply to National Lottery Charity Board and we employ somebody part-time and after that full time. We help all refugee and asylum seeker in Reading with interpretation, translation, to find accommodation and with education, with other needs for travelling to college, clothes, with immigration. And it just became very respectable organisation and Reading Borough Council help us on many occasion.

My son at that time he got very good result at university and ... in his second year he's got Soros grant and he was working. He told me 'Dad I don't need your help any more.' I was so relaxed that I can concentrate to save money for my daughter because she was ready next year to go to the university. She applied to study pharmacy at Portsmouth University. She got place but the biggest problem was my son was third year she was first year. I have to support two student at same times what was impossible for me. I ask her if she can leave, one year take off. She was crying and she said 'Dad, please, I will work very hard and I don't need much help' but I found very good friends from Germany. I borrow money from him and I gave money for my daughter to go to university. She was so happy and she promise she will got very good result. It's happen. Next year my son graduated at North University College in London in accountancy and he promised 'Dad, I will help my sister. You take rest. You don't have to help her any more.' At that time I was so proud to have somebody who will accept responsibility and help sister to get education. He was helping her for all three years and I told ... I was different man at that time. And I said 'My children they are incorporate in this society. I can now, they can contribute now in this society because they took something from society, they have to give it back.'

Self Sufficiency

Family Values

Self Sufficiency

Community

Jobs

Community

Education & Training

Community

I was studying my English on a regular basis and improving every day and I was looking around for job. Unfortunately all my applications were turned down.

What job roughly were, what job were you looking for?

OK. I was looking usually for simple job, not much. I was looking to do to work in shops, I was looking for work in office some secretary but when I sent my CV and answer was, 'You are over-educated for this job. One day you will leave us. We can't accept you.' And ... I changed something in my CV. When I applied for job I did not put all my qualifications. I just put simple things. And I was lucky. At Ealing Family 1997 ... they advertised job to work with refugee and asylum seeker to help with education, training, employment. It was my job, I told myself. I applied, I had interview and I got the job. I was Development Officer and ... it was my chance to help other people who were in my situation. All my clients were all over the world. I had doctors, dentists ... pharmacist. I had ordinary worker and I was able to listen to them, I was able to give good advice. I was able to help them. The first things was if somebody have to learn English, to go and study English then after that we will apply for job.

And people they listen to me. I send hundreds and hundreds of clients to Reading College to learn ... or some tutor private tutor who were helping us at that time. We established team of volunteer about twenty people who were working with refugee and asylum seeker in our project. Ealing Family they offer us office free of charge, they help us. But we help ourselves. We establish translation, interpretation service for many people in Reading here and for any borough council, for hospital, for solicitor. They need service for different languages. But what we did, we charge them for that. All money what we earn we gave to our clients. We pay for fee, we pay for travelling, for childcare, for books, and we help each other. In this project about sixty-seven clients they found job. They change their life. Many of them they retrain, they sent to ... company for training because in this country and in your own country is always something different. You have to learn from this system, how the system works, what the people need and all the people who were on training particular in housing they found a job.

But I did not stop to think about my country in Bosnia. I had letter from town where I was refugee from a hospital ... doctor send me. They did not have ambulance. They did not have any equipment, not laboratory, not bandages, nothing. They asked me if I can do something and [pause] I found very close friend who was manager at that time, in Panasonic. He promise he will do something with his friend and after a couple of weeks we raised money, we bought ambulance and they ... is full of medical equipment. They sent it to Bosnian hospital and they were able to transport people from their house to hospital.

Other things what's happened was that they had many disabled children in Bosnia. My relative was had ... director of one house for disabled people and they asked me if we can do something to help with minibus who will take

Community

children from their house to we call it disability centre where they will spend all day. And I was lucky at that time 1997. One of my friends recommend me for my work in voluntary sector ... that I was nominate for Man of the Year in Reading Borough Council, *Reading Chronicle*, and I was surprised when journalists come to see me and they made interview with me and they vote me Man of the Year. I got some financial reward for that but I thought at that time I'm giving it for minibus for handicapped children project and I ask other people if they would like to join us. They publish it in the *Reading Chronicle* and the response was very good. People donate money and we bought minibus with wheelchair and we took it in March 1997 and take it to the Bosnia. For me it was sad. I came to the Bosnian border but ... and Croatian border. I wasn't be allowed to go to Bosnia. I had wrong sort of travel document.

Why were you not allowed to go?

I had travel document, blue one. They said you can visit any country except your country. And I was looking my house. It was only couple of miles from border but I wasn't be able to go and see my relatives and friends and see my house. They come to border and we met each other. We were crying at that time. I spend a whole day with them and I had to go back to the United Kingdom. Friend of mine he took minibus to town Tuzla for handicapped children.

Community

I ask what's happened with my property ... in Bosnia. My three bedroom house which I use for weekend was absolutely destroyed. My flat in town Dobor was occupied by Serbian people and I wasn't be able to go to take it back. After ten years ... I got it. I got it. And it was impossible for me to live with people like before. When I went to college where I used to work ... it was 200 lecturer, professor, teacher ... different nationality as Bosnia is mixed country. We have Croatian Catholics, Bosnian Muslims, Serbian Orthodox and other people. I found 200 Orthodox Serbian and I ask for my document to give me back, and I was so frightened you know and somebody will attack me at that time. They hate me because I was different from them and I had to pay money to get it back. It was very sad. And I took my diploma, university diploma, and all my documentation where I used to work ... to have for my ... document.

Education & Training
Self Sufficiency

When I come back from Bosnia I had to concentrate to see what's going with my daughter and she was passing all her exam and at the end she invite me for celebration at her college in Portsmouth and she's got degree in pharmacy, but my son at that time he was doing chartered accountancy. He told me 'Dad, I have to do a little bit more' and he's got a degree as well in chartered accountancy.

Community

I was working in Ealing Family for full seven years helping with refugee and asylum seeker and when I was reached sixty, I thought it's time to be retired, early retirement. And why I decide like that [pause] I had to concentrate to do more charity work to help some Bosnian people here. I am chairman in Reading for Bosnian people. We establish Bosnian Emergency Fund. We have fifty disabled people and we have to provide service for them, interpretation, translation. We have to visit them every day. But I concentrate more to establish with other people Bosnian supplementary school. We establish here eleven Bosnian schools in different places - Birmingham, London, Manchester. We don't have in Reading here, we don't have many Bosnian people.

And now I am headmaster of the Bosnian School. And recently people elected me to be chairman for twenty-three Bosnian organisation in United Kingdom and Ireland. And I was so proud to do it but it's a lot of work. But when you start to do something like that, you will never stop. And I have now time to do it and I promise I will help other people because somebody was helping me.

I want to try and take you back a bit to before you left Bosnia. You say that your name was on the list of people who were supposed to be killed?
Yes.

Do you know any reason why you were targeted?
I know. Because it was policy of Serbian nationalist, and they would kill all educated people, doctor, professor, teacher, businessman. They will kill probably one of third ordinary people. They will take all your property, all your money from you. It was their policy. But other my reason, I used to work in military service, Yugoslavian military service before. I was captain of Yugoslavian Army and I left it. I know many things about it, but people who stay with them, who did not leave, it's happened to them. Many my friends they were killed and ... my colleague who used to work with me he was in charge with that. Now, in Hague they try to extradite him for war crime, what he did in town Dobor.

You also said that your children persuaded you to come to England. Before you came to England what was your impression about England?
I didn't know anything about England. I know about ... when I watch film. It was raining something, I said 'No, I don't like to go in this country, I would like to go sunny. And English people they look like not friendly' you know, but I was wrong. I was wrong. I have never had any problem in United Kingdom. And if I in the future have to choose any country to live I would say 'I will live in United Kingdom.' It is much better than in any other country where I travel.

You mentioned that while you were still in Bosnia you were a professor.
Yes.

Why was it difficult for you to get a job as a professor here, do you think?
In this country is not only for me, it's for all people. In this country they don't recognise your diploma from your own country, they don't recognise. If you are doctor, you can be taxi driver. If you are professor, you can't do your job and if you are pharmacist you can't work here and they are quite strict. You have to be retrained here to do something here, to pass some exam to do this job. It's not only for this for all other people who came in this country particularly from Eastern European country. And what ... I disagree. I know now here about 500, I did research what is here. 500 doctors are in the United Kingdom. If they retrained them they would save a lot of money and they would have very qualified people.

Family Values

How did you feel working in the building industry when you were a professor before in Bosnia?

For me you know I thought it was my destiny, is something what happen from God and I thought 'You have to work' but again I know that I was earning money to put in the right way for education of my children. This is not money to make business or capital. This is something that you can keep for all your life. If you have money, if you have property you can lose it one day everything but if you put something in your brain you will never lose it. It was my philosophy and I accept it. But I know that I will do something different one day, but it's happened to me.

You spoke about the fact that you were in the Yugoslav Army?

Yes.

Political Situation

What experiences did you have?

I have to say Yugoslavian Army during the Tito time was very good, very friendly. They care all other people but then people died and Milosevic came in power. They became nationalist party [corrects himself] army and all army was from Serbian people. They try to make Great Serbia and they try to … kill other people and this is what I did not accept, is why I left when I realise. But during the Tito time it was wonderful.

You mentioned about your childhood that you had a very good childhood … are there any memories that you can relate, about your parents?

Yes, I know and … my grandfather and my father they were very rich people, capitalist, and when Tito came in power they lost their property and new system, but all land what you have they give some other people but they give you only ten hectares per family, what was enough. My father hated he did not like it but I recognize something was different. I thought Tito was right. He was helping poor people, he was helping middle class. He was helping with education. Everything was free. When I was at university at school I did not have to pay anything. You have free accommodation, you have free house. You do not have to pay fee. You have a job. Everything was OK. And one day my father told me 'My son, I was wrong, Tito was right.' I was so pleased to hear from my dad who hate him in the beginning but at the end he change his mind.

Family Values

What was your mother's profession?

My mother was ordinary woman and she had very good family and religious education. She tried to teach us to respect other people, to help other people, to share with them everything. If you have food, share with your next door. Doesn't matter who is, is he Christian, Muslim, Jewish, we have to share with him. I accept from my mother everything and particular I was pleased when my mother adopt one child … what I was try to do in my life later. And they were helping poor people but what I am doing now similar.

Community

I from Reading now running one project for orphans children and in past last year we start to support children who lost parents in Bosnian war, particular children from Srebrenica. I am supporting two of them. My daughter and son they accept two - it's four. All other friends altogether we are supporting seventeen. I was in Bosnia in April this year to see my child because she was finishing with her college graduation. I was so pleased to see somebody who with my help got education and can start his own life. But everything what I am doing now I think it was influenced from my mother.

And what are your memories of your late wife?

OK. My wife … she was lecturer at same college where I used to work and she died and she was thirty-nine, very young and she had very bad experience during the war. She didn't know anything about children. She was crying every day and her situation was getting worse and worse and she died after that. And it was probably the most difficult situation for me and that I lost somebody I love so much. My daughter she never recover after that. I did not tell her all story how her mother died and … ten years I was widow. I didn't like to go out. I didn't like to make any relations with any other women until my daughter persuade me 'Dad. You did a lot of things for us. Please find somebody who is right person for you, marry somebody,' and I mention lady who was friend of my, is my wife now. She was so happy she was calling her. She make a relationship with her and when I decide to marry my daughter was witness on my wedding day. It's very rare to find and now she call my wife Mum.

You mentioned during the earlier narration when you were told to leave your daughter was not there [SB - Yes] She was in a refugee camp. Were you not living together?

And everybody was escaping with different … side. You had to find some town you say 'Oh, this town could be secure.' But I gave address of all my friends … Serbian, Croatian, in all Yugoslavia. I said this is address and telephone number. If you phone them and tell that you are my daughter or son, they will help you. It's happened to me. I have to say that my son was helping from Serbian people in Serbia and I can't accuse all Serbian people they did genocide in Bosnia. I am accusing Serbian nationalists, Milosevic and Chetnik, Serbian nationalists but not Serbian people now. They help my daughter and my son as well and … other experience … was very bad in Croatia.

I had very good Croatian Catholics who was care about my son. One day police came to arrest my son to [inaudible] him for fighting in Bosnia against Serbs. He told them 'Sorry, you can't take this boy with you. He's son of my Bosnian [inaudible] friends. Only if you kill me you will take him with you. You have here drink and food, but don't touch this boy.' My son was shaking you know. At that time his mother was in Slovenia. She was dying and he was waiting to be transported to Slovenia to see mother before she die. [pause] I had quite good support from people that I know, doesn't matter which nationality.

You spoke about living in the refugee camp and that you were eventually taken from the refugee camp. What other experiences did you have in the refugee camp?

The refugee camp … I used to live in two. One was in Bosnian town. I know it was over-crowded and only ordinary people if they help you you will have food. OK, I understand it was like that. Then I moved to Slovenia and it was like prison. I didn't like you know to live in camp and I had very bad experience from Slovenia. What's happened, you can't go out without permission. You have to, if you go to shop to buy something you have to ask for one or two hours for permit to go out. It was like prison. They treat us like we are people who came to steal something and like we are criminals.

And other bad experience it was with Slovenian ... teacher. My daughter was attending school in Slovenia. One day she come back, she was crying. One of teacher told her 'You must go from this school.' She was surprised. Why? 'You are refugee Bosnian. You can't stay and sit with Slovenian student in same class' and she was crying crying crying. And we decide that she will leave school and we will go in any other country that offer us something different.

What about the memories of your brothers and sisters?

My three brothers stayed in Bosnia. I was so scared for them. I didn't know about them ... and one of them [pause] was killed. I didn't know for them. I sent many letters to him but not answered. And ... when I sent other letter, again not answered. After six seven months I got letter from his son. He sent me letter said 'Uncle, sorry, your brother has died and he was killed in Croatian border.' And they tried to keep secret from me because I lost wife, I lost mother-in-law and I lost brother. And my older brother was in Croatia ... and he was in Croatian town, but what they did was then they force them to go and work on field ... all day for food. If you go and work you receive food, but if you don't go you don't have food. And he spent couple of months in Croatia later and after that he moved to Hungaria where it was much better and stay in Hungaria until the end of the war.

And what about your sisters?

My sisters they stay in Bosnia, both of them stay in Bosnia. One of them was

Spaho with minibus sent to Tuzla

in Sarajevo and they were in siege ... without anything, without food, without electricity, without central heating. They suffer so much. I didn't know for them for one year. And the first news what I got it was from one German doctor ... and ... who visit Bosnia and he was friend of mine but he visit my sister. He found her and I got news from him that my sister and her family stay alive in Sarajevo. They were OK at the end but you know Sarajevo was like Stalingrad - siege for one year, without food, without anything and ... About 15,000 people were killed in Sarajevo.

Do you still maintain contacts with Bosnia, now you have mentioned about the things you have done?

I'm always in contact with Bosnia people and with some project and now project is Bosnian orphans. And this is what I am so proud to do it. And I have my colleague who is professor at Tuzla University and some other teacher. They are distributing all help what we are sending from United Kingdom on a regular basis to war orphans. This is, be ... I know they don't have parents, they don't have family. They have some good people who can help them. Government does not have enough money to help all of them. In Bosnia you know all country was destroyed even in the war and now is time that people from outside will help more and more. What I doing now with my family.

You have mentioned that when you left Bosnia you thought the war was going to last for six months and it lasted for more than that [SB Yes] and you were hoping to go back as soon as the war ended. What persuaded you to stay?

It's good question because everybody expected the war to be finished in a couple of weeks because this is Europe. This is not Africa ... there you can try for many years. [pause] In Bosnia we expected a European country like the United Kingdom, France, Germany to stop war [coughs] sorry. To stop war. They did not do anything. They had embargo. Yugoslavian Army [corrects] Serbian Army I do not say Yugoslavian - [emphasises] Serbian Army. Serbian Army have everything. They have guns. They kill Bosnian people but we did not have anything and we just were like lamb who ... that you can kill any time and it was shame I would say shame for United Kingdom for France for Germany. [pause] President Clinton he did something. He strike ... he brought some guns for Bosnian people to protect themselves and war stop ... OK

What eventually decided you to stay here?

And I tried to go back but [pause] ten years I was waiting for my property I've left in town where I used to work and they sack me from college where I used to work. They employ only Serbian people and it was impossible to live in town like that. And my other house was absolutely destroyed. If you don't have accommodation, if you don't have regular income, how you will survive? It was main reason why I stay here. Because here I used to work. I was helping my fam ... my children to get a good education and I was able from this place to help my family who stay in Bosnia as well to provide basic food and accommodation some of them.

Community

Political Situation

Children's Identity & Where Home Is

In conclusion I would like to find out from you what contribution you can continue to make because you have told me about all the work you have done for the people of Bosnia and the UK society.

I did a lot of things first. When I was working I tried to help people who were in a similar situation like me. Would advise to find a job to find fee for university to retrain them. And here I educated my children here. I was helping them. Now they are full members of this society. They are incorporate. They pay tax. They're earning good money but they pay tax they pay everything. They are supporting this society. And in my free time I now helping here with Bosnian Emergency Fund all Bosnian people with interpretation translation. We care about them. We organise Bosnia school and we are helping people who are behind in Bosnia. I thought it was enough for me because I can't do much more.

Bosnia and Herzegovina

Bosnia and Herzegovina (commonly referred to as Bosnia) lies on the Balkan peninsula and was one of the six federal units which made up the former Socialist Federal Republic of Yugoslavia. The country is divided into two administrative entities – The Federation of Bosnia and Herzegovina and the Republic of Srpska. It gained its independence during the bloody Yugoslav wars of the 1990s. It is bordered by Serbia to the east, Montenegro to the south, and Croatia to north, west and south. It is mainly landlocked but has a stretch of coast measuring 20km along the Adriatic Sea. Bosnia forms the majority of the country and Herzegovina forms the southern tip of the country. It is home to three ethnic groups – the Bosniaks, Serbs and Croats. There is a strong correlation between these ethnic groups and religion – Bosniaks are predominantly Muslims, Croats Roman Catholics and Serbs Orthodox Christians. During the 1990 parliamentary elections three ethnically-based parties formed a coalition and ousted the communist rulers from power in Yugoslavia. Soon after these elections Croatia and Slovenia declared independence and the ensuing warfare placed Bosnia and Herzegovina in an awkward position. The key debate was whether they should follow suit with their neighbours or stay with the Yugoslav federation – the latter had strong support amongst Serbs whilst the Bosniaks and Croats were overwhelmingly in favour of the former. In February and March of 1992 they held a referendum on whether to seek independence from Yugoslavia – the vote was won but it was boycotted by many Bosnian Serbs. The declaration of independence led to a period of tensions and sporadic military actions with open warfare breaking out in Sarajevo on 6 April. With increasing international recognition of Bosnia and Herzegovina came pressure on the Yugoslav People's Army to withdraw its troops. They officially complied, but in reality the Bosnian Serb members of the army changed their insignia and formed the Army of Republika Srpska and carried on fighting. The Republika Srpska's offensives were supported by volunteers and paramilitary forces from Serbia and equipped from stockpiles in Bosnia, they also had logistic, financial and humanitarian support from the Federal Republic of Yugoslavia. In 1993 fighting broke out between the republican Sarajevo government and the Croatian Republic of Herzeg-Bosnia;

Spaho receives Reading Community Award 1997

by the end of the year the Republika Srpska controlled about 70% of the country. The signing of the Washington accords in March 1994 and outrage at the war crimes and atrocities committed by the Serbs (most notably the slaughter of 8,000 Bosniak males in the supposed safe zone of Srebrenica in July 1995) served as catalysts for the end of the war. The signing of the Daytona Agreement by the leaders of Croatia, Yugoslavia and Bosnia and Herzegovina marked the end of the Bosnian war which had seen some 100,000 killed and over one million people displaced. Since the end of the war about 100,000 people of all ages have left Bosnia and Herzegovina.

Rose Cam

Born: Not given
Natal, South Africa

Date of Interview: 20th July 2006

● Natal, South Africa
○ Johanesberg
● Reading, UK

My name is Rose Cam.

And Rose, can you tell me where you're from?
I was born in South Africa.

And what year did you come to England?
In a week's time, it'll be forty years exactly. On the 28th of July to England in 1966.

And what was it like for you leaving South Africa to come to UK?
It was very traumatic actually because, as much as I wanted to come to England to do my nursing, I didn't want to leave my brother and sister because they really relied on me. I was the child carer and subsequently was an adult and continued to support my brother and sister and so it was very hard to leave them.

Childhood

Could you tell me a bit more about your family in South Africa and growing up in South Africa?
I was the second of perhaps you could say five children, but the first two before me were twins so my mum had five pregnancies but had six children. And unfortunately they didn't really live long. The girl, because it was a boy and a girl; the girl died in its infancy and the boy died when he was three years old and he broke a leg. Those days there were no hospital things and the people, the local medicine men, did the best they could, but it never healed and then really it just got infection and gangrenous and he died of poisoning, of blood poisoning. He was three years old. Then there's me and then my sister, my brother and then my two ... the baby who was two weeks old when my mum died of septicaemia. He died when he was three as well, so, so, it was hard, so really this is the reason why I was a carer.

My dad did marry again, but during the time my mum died, before my dad got married, we had to go and live with my grandmother in the country and that were the best days of my life because it really was open country, and we roamed for miles and we loved, I just loved it and I learned to help my grandmother on the farm, and I learned to milk a cow and learned to thatch houses.

I used to work alongside her and she showed me what to do which was brilliant and I learned to do pottery. We used to go and collect the clay and actually pound it ourselves to get the impurities out, to prepare it for making the earthenware and fire it. So it was beautiful. I really did learn a lot in a very short space of time.

What part of South Africa was that?

That was in Natal, it's Zululand, but my family are all over really Natal area and Durban and Vryheid, then Nongoma which is really known as the Zulu heartland. And that's really where my grandfather was born, my paternal grandfather.

So you said something about nursing. You came here to do nursing. So did you start your nursing in South Africa?

Yes, I did do auxiliary nursing because I really did want to do medicine. But because being orphaned in South Africa, there were no grants. You had to take a loan bursary and, if I took a loan bursary I would've had to take a big enough loan to support my brother and my sister while I was at the university and then I would've just spent the rest of my life paying the government back and it was impossible.

But, when I worked as an auxiliary nurse, I worked in a hospital which was a white hospital. I couldn't train there but I could work there as an auxiliary nurse and it also had a coloured wing. When I say coloured, it's difficult to explain to somebody. In South Africa, 'coloured', when they refer to people as 'coloured', it's people of mixed race. So there was, there was a coloured wing in the white hospital, but they couldn't mix in the same ward and so I used to work between the white wards and the coloured wards, at the same time I was studying because I did really want to do, go to the university and do medicine.

Rose Cam (22 years old), Muhlanga Rocks (SA) 1962

Jobs

Education & Training

Self Sufficiency

Political Situation

Political Situation

It was a very big hospital. In fact they used to say it was the biggest in the southern hemisphere - a place called Addington Hospital and there were nurses from all over the world; mainly Europe, France, Scandinavia and because they could see me studying, they used to help me.

They said to me, 'Look, the way you are studying', I was doing two subjects a year, but they said, 'By the time you've finished training to get your matriculation you'll be tired of studying and then go and do nursing. Why don't you go to England?' And they used to receive Nursing Times. Then, I think there was another magazine called Nursing Mirror and they used to receive those and so they used to pass them on to me.

And so I started applying, they encouraged me to apply. I applied at St. Thomas' and St. Bartholomew's. St. Bart's said they would love to have me from what they were hearing, well we didn't call it CV then, it was just the background of my training and they felt they would really have liked to have taken me, but I didn't have enough qualifications. So, but they forwarded my application form to Maidenhead Hospital, St. Luke's.

The next thing I heard from St. Luke's giving me directions to go to the British Consul in Durban to get a work permit because, by that time, South Africa, although we were in the Commonwealth and we were part of the British Commonwealth, we were no longer allowed to be in the Commonwealth because of Apartheid. South Africa was kicked out in 1961 so we'd become a Republic and therefore I had to have a permit to come here, whereas before we were British Protectorate and in the Commonwealth. So I went to the British Embassy to get the, well we call them British Consul and I got my permit to work, permit to come to England and eventually came to Maidenhead.

And then I was very disappointed because when I came there were so many black people in Maidenhead. I'd been told that there would be nobody and I was really pleased to see black people and a lot of Asians as well from East Africa. But nobody from South Africa. I was just the misnomer - everybody used to say 'How did you get out of South Africa?' And I don't know how I got out. I think somebody up there was with me because I had known men who had applied, black men applied for passports to go away from South Africa and they were promptly arrested, because if you indicated at that time you want to leave South Africa, you were immediately called a communist and against the Government. I think what helped me was because when I did apply for a passport I already had a work permit, I already had a job going to …

I had to go to a place where the immigration people to give me permit to go and they still grilled me. 'What are you going to England for?' In fact, one of the Africana women was so horrible. 'Are you going there for the process of, for the …' what did she call it? 'with the view to be a prostitute?' which was really infuriating. I just chose not to answer that because I'm not going to go down to her level. But, and also, you had to just be grin and bear it, otherwise they wouldn't give you the permit. But I got it within six months.

Pages from Rose Cam's passport

What age were you then?

I was twenty.

So when you lost your mum...

I was four and a half when my mum died. And I was twelve when my dad died.

So that affected your schooling?

It did. I used to go to school before ... in fact, when I was ten I left school to go and work and then went back the following year. And then left again and went ... But then I decided it was too much of a hassle, but, it just helped me that I was a quick learner and had a good memory and in fact the second time I left school, I left in Standard two and when I went back I didn't go back to Standard three or Standard two and they pushed me straight to Standard five. And ... and, that really helped because I caught up with my peers who had carried on at school.

In the end I passed them as well because some of them left at that point and I carried on because I loved education and I knew what I wanted to do. And, then of course, after that I just thought it's just too much of a hassle to keep leaving school and going back. I'm now going to do everything by correspondence, which I did.

So when you came to England at twenty...

I was twenty-one and a half.

So did you come in the wintertime or the summertime?

July was the summertime here, but it didn't feel like summertime. When they told me it was summertime and I looked at the sky and I thought it was so cloudy and so cold and I was still wearing a coat.

Tell me something about your first winter.

My first winter actually wasn't bad because I was expecting the worse. I hadn't known anything else so everybody kept saying 'Oh, you wait until ...' So I was waiting for the worse, but the worse never came that year. But the following year, it was 1967, it snowed and it was awful. So eight months I spent in Maidenhead and then I came in Reading in January 1967 and I was in Pendragon House. But the first two months I was at Prospect Park just working on Evelyn Ward and by this time another African girl joined from Ghana so we teamed up together, and because we'd been there the longest when PTS started we were really lucky. We had private rooms. Everybody else shared.

So you didn't miss your family?

Oh, I did. I used to write letters every night, and ... but then it was overwhelming, because when the replies came there were just so many. Some of them I never did go round to keep regularly reply because I was just ... I had a calendar every month I used to tick the day one day down, one day down and I just missed ... I dreamt, I still do now, dream about home so much.

So you had a plan of when you wanted to go back?

Oh, yes. I was, as soon as my midwifery had gone I was going back home and of course people often used to say to me 'But you're a political refugee.' I said 'No, I'm not an asylum seeker. I've come to do my training and I'm going home.' And I didn't run away from Apartheid. The only thing that made me come away was that it was so difficult for me to get into training as a nurse 'cos I didn't have matriculation and I couldn't train at Addington although I was already there and the nurses used to say 'You know, Rose, the way how much you know', because I used to learn alongside the old, the white nurses that were training and they were really lovely. In fact I used to say to people if you went to Addington straight from the airport and went to Addington and then out again you would completely deny that there was Apartheid, because we all worked together. Those blacks that worked there, they, I mean I worked at both theatres, the surgery and orthopaedic theatre and I was an auxiliary nurse, but when we were all dressed up and scrubbed and they treated me as if I was one of them and I as if I was a trained nurse 'cos they knew I was interested.

Racism

Did they treat you as a coloured or as a black?

Well, coloured 'cos my grandmother was half Scottish and so that's how I got in. Unless you had a background of a white relation you couldn't get into Addington Hospital.

So the Apartheid experience. How was that for you then compared with the …?

I just went as a Zulu. I didn't care. In fact I used to be an embarrassment to the other coloureds who wanted to distance themselves from black people and I just used to ask them one question. Where did coloureds come from? Why are you called coloureds? If you want to distance yourself from blacks because you're coloured because you're mixed! So, I used to … and in fact Miss Cork who was in charge of all the coloured workers, she was Irish. She was a Sister. She was lovely and the very first day I went there she asked me who was your next of kin and I said I haven't got parents but my next of kin is Nicolina Zungu. She said 'That's a Zulu name' and I said 'Yes.' And she didn't say anymore, but I'm told that she said 'I admire Rose because she does not try to be what she is not.' And I used to see some of my colleagues refusing to speak Zulu to black guys because, if you were coloured you were closer to whites and you … And I used to speak Zulu and they used to say I was an embarrassment and I thought well, I'm afraid that's my mother tongue. I speak both Zulu and English. And that's how I grew up in my home because of my grandmother.

Jobs   Self Sufficiency   Old Reading

Did you take a trip back there during your student days?

No, I couldn't afford … In fact, I worked my socks off. I used to work at the cinema, at the Granby, but again, they were lovely people but now when you look back they really did exploit me. They were paying me one pound for four hours.

What year was that?

1967 to '69. For four hours I was paid one pound and they knew I was doing that job because I wanted to go home. I just could never have saved anything like that.

Education & Training

This was in addition with your nursing work?

That's in nursing and also going to college because I wanted to learn as much as a could before I go back to South Africa. So that's why I was at Woodley Hill House. On my days off I used to go and do my, I didn't have a day off to go and muck about like other girls. I used to go to college to do my nursing. To do my English and Maths and chemistry. 'cos I still felt, after my nursing I want to go to the university to do medicine. And so that's what I was doing.

Old Reading

So, what happened with your plans?

Well, in 1969, I was on Rushey Ward. I was in my second year actually, the end of my second year, above the maternity unit. Maternity unit moved from Battle Hospital to where it is now and we were the first, myself and my other colleagues, first intake to do obstetric nursing. They moved in December 1969. I was just in my third year, in fact, just at the beginning and we went there to start my three month obstetric because I thought I don't want to do nursing, but I will do obstetrics. I'll just get an insight into midwifery and do obstetrics and then I'll do the rest at home. I was that determined. I thought I'm not staying another year longer in England.

There was a lady, she came in for hysterectomy. She was lovely and she happened to be in the ward. There were four bedded cubicle, four and six bedded cubicles and I … that's when they were experimenting with smaller wards and I nursed her and we really became very friendly and one day she said to me 'Are you married Miss Cox?' I said 'No.' She said 'because I've got a cousin I'd like you to meet.' I said 'I really don't want to meet anybody at the moment because I'm so close to my exams, boyfriends waste your time. If I have a boyfriend that means I've got to have time to go and see him.' I said 'No, I'd really would rather not.' And she said 'He's really lovely.' Anyway, the ladies in the ward said 'Cowardy custard.' They kept teasing. But I said 'Alright I'll meet him once.' And of course I met him. I think he was as scared of meeting me and also I thought I really don't want to meet a white man because, if anything develops then I can't go home.

This lady was a white lady then?

Yes, she was a white lady. I thought 'No I really don't want anything … something that will stop me from going back home.' But in the event that's exactly what happened.

So you liked him at first sight?

Yes! Ten months after we'd been going out he proposed. Up until that point there had been no agreement that I was his girlfriend and he was my boyfriend.

So he proposed to you then in ten months?

Yes. Yes and I just felt no I'll wait. I said 'No, I really have to think about this' and I did have to think about it. I did have to speak to my sister in South Africa and she, and my uncles, they were alive then, and my uncle said 'Do you know Rose. You know our views. We don't interfere if you love somebody you go with your heart.' I can't go back home and my people are left in Apartheid system and I'm away from it and free. And that did trouble me and I think that's why I used to have nightmares. I used to really sleep, I didn't sleep well at all for a long time.

Was the Apartheid system still going then?

Oh yes, in 1976. It's funny, we …

Rose Cam as a nurse, 1969

Political Situation

You got married in 1976?

No, we got married in 1970, but I went home in 1976. And in 1976 we went in March and came back in April and then of course in June that's when everything blew up. When the children decided they will have no more of Apartheid.

In Soweto?

In Soweto and all those areas.

Was that near to where you came from?

No, I'm from Natal, Soweto is in Johannesburg. So ... and that's really why I'm in England.

So, have you got a family yourself?

I've got one daughter.

Political Situation

So, the transition and meeting new people helped you to settle down?

It did help and I think the ability to go and do studies when you want and where you want and not be told. And I actually had a culture shock. I thought it would be easy because South Africa, especially Durban, is more English because that's where the English first landed before the Afrikaners. And I thought 'Oh, it's more English, South Africa.' But I had a culture shock because I hadn't bargained for the fact that everybody can go anywhere in the shop. I was constantly looking up to see which door I was going to get in and it was awful, it really was. It took me a long time to get used to it.

Education & Training
Self Sufficiency

So what happened to your career after you got married then?

Yes, so I switched from ... well concurrently with nursing I decided when I retire from nursing, 'cos everybody was doing nursing degree. I thought 'No, where will that take me when I've stopped nursing? I'll develop something that I know can carry me on.' And I'm glad I did because I then, in 1992, I went to a summer school. I was already teaching, I started teaching music.

So you learnt music then in this country or ... ?

At home I used to be in the choir. My parents had, we had a piano at home We didn't have formal lessons, we used to just sit at the piano until we'd get the tune that we know and really play it. And when I came to England, at the Royal Berkshire, because the piano was in the same room as the television, unfortunately I couldn't always play but I always thought 'Well one day I will really play the piano.'

Self Sufficiency

I started learning and then a friend, he was Nigerian, he was doing his doctorate in Reading and he said 'Well, will you teach me?' I said 'Well I'm not a teacher.' He said 'Surely you can help someone who is starting from Grade One?' I said 'Alright.' So I started making lesson plans and I really felt like I can do this. And he did extremely well. And then he told his friends at the university so I started getting enquiries really by word of mouth.

Education & Training
Self Sufficiency

Jobs

I did the Trinity College Certificate of Teaching and then I've done the Associated Board Certificate of Teaching and then the Open University diploma and degree in music with humanities with music. And it's building up now. I'm hoping that's going to carry on. 1992 I had nineteen pupils and I was still working full-time. And then I went to a summer school which was run by Hungarians and they've got a different, unique way of teaching music. So I got into that. So I've done their diplomas.

So are you retired yet?

Well, I'm still doing the three days for the health authority, but not health visiting this time. I'm doing primary mental health work. It's just seeing the children with difficult behaviour, children and young people. And it's been an eye-opener. It's not dissimilar to health visiting in that I visit people in their home but it's got that mental health element more highlighted in it than health visiting.

So, you did mental training as well or just part of health visiting?

I'm just doing the in-house and I'm just transferring my skills that I've learned along health visiting because I was also a community practice teacher, teaching health visitors so that has helped.

I hadn't asked you at the beginning how old you were? How old?

Now? Me? Now I'm 64.

So you're not ready to retire yet?

Yes. No. No. I'm feeling I've got bags of life in me.

Old Reading

So in terms of how Reading has changed then 'cos you've been here since 1960.

Oh it's changed so much. The Butts Centre wasn't there. When I came there were nice Tudor houses. I can still see them now, two of the houses on the side of Broad Street on the side of that road that goes down to join Castle Hill and I remember coming, walking, 'cos I used to love walking, because I just wanted to walk and get as much information about the area so that when I went home I didn't want to appear not to know about the area I lived in. So I walked a lot and I used to go to the library to read the history of Reading. I even found out that there was a woman who used to be a childminder and they called her Baby Farm and she used to drown the children in the river in Caversham and one of them lived in Kensington Road not far from where the chippy I worked with was.

So, you say that there were Tudor houses now so you think that Reading …

Yes, and I can remember seeing old ladies with lovely gardens. Not big, you know, the gardens that terraced houses have like in Oxford Road, little ones at the front and I remember seeing old ladies sitting there, you know, outside their house door, and I saw it being bulldozed. It all happened in 1970 and I remember I went to school talking to children about how Reading has changed. One of the little boy looked at me said to me 'You sound as if you have been alive for a hundred years!' I said 'It feels like it!' 'cos I was telling them about things that no longer there and some people don't even remember them.

When I remind them, where the Inner Distribution Road is, it used to be an ambulance service where is now The Oracle car park. Ambulance service was a little hut. That road was a two-way road and on that same road were houses and one of my friends who befriended me, she was a nurse, she did SEN and she was on Benyan Ward when I first came and she befriended me and really looked after me, they lived there in those terraced houses but they had long gardens backing onto London Street and I saw it all being pulled down.

You were saying about your parents was in business. What sort of business?

Oh, my dear, they've had so many businesses. My dad was a tailor by day and then he was also a motor mechanic but working at night as a night watchman as well with other people. And they had other jobs as well. But also my mum was a, she was a seamstress. She used to make dresses for people and they had a smallholding and they had two taxis and a bus so they gave a lot of employment. We had people looking after us, but my mum would not allow us to call them nannies. They were just my sister or my grandmother. And she didn't call them servants. They were just the people she knew at parts of the family, part of extended family and she, so it's nice to look back now, yeah, I wonder if my mum didn't die if I would've come to England actually. It's just amazing how one incident could change your life. I don't think I would've come to England.

So it was easy for your transition to come into a purely sort of a white, working with white people ...

Oh, it wasn't a problem because, my dad being a tailor, and also he was in business with people so he was a tailor for white people as well. 'cos we didn't live in the city at that time, we lived in a mining town.

He was black?

My dad, yes, yes. But he was tailoring for everybody. This is what I was saying. If you came to that part of South Africa and then left again you would not have believed that Apartheid was there because people just ignored it and carried on with their lives, black and white. And the police were not nearby to see, to try and enforce their, you know, draconian rules. But then, as Apartheid got deeper and deeper it spread into the country. It's worse in the country now, because they started uprooting black people from the country because they wanted the land for themselves and carving the land.

So, but, my dad sewed for everybody. I mean, all the colours of the rainbow used to come to us, our home to be measured and then I worked in a white hospital with white nurses and it really was not an issue to me. But I remember in Maidenhead one of the sisters I worked with on a ward called Desborough Ward turned to me, she said to me 'I'm surprised that you're from South Africa.' I said 'Why are you surprised?' She said 'Your attitude is so different. You don't seem to have a chip on the shoulder.' I said 'Well, why would I have a chip on the shoulder?' She said 'Well, you just, you can talk about black and

Childhood

Childhood

Political Situation

Racism

white, you don't seem to have any anxiety about it.' I said 'Well, I'm black. It's true. So, what's the problem?' And she said 'No, but sometimes some people when you talk about black they don't like it.'

Do you think it was easier 'cos you didn't have an African name? You were Rose, Rose Cox did you say?

Yes, but I used my grandfather's name. My paternal grandfather's name, if I wanted to I used to use that a lot. People they'd say 'What's your name?' I'll say 'Rose Mthethwa'. So it was no big deal to me to have that name. It's not a big deal now. It's just a name. I'm me.

Krystyna Szopis

Born: 6th February 1931
Lwow, Poland
Date of Interview: 16th May 2006

Poland

● Lwow, Poland
○ Sverdlorsk, Siberia
○ Druma, Uzbekistan
○ Taran, Iran
○ Ahvaz, S. Persia
○ Ghazir, Lebanon
● Reading, UK

Can you tell me where you were born and when?

I was born on 6th February 1931 in the most beautiful town of Poland called Lwow.

And can you tell me what your earliest memories are?

Well just living in my home town. Tremendous memories of town. My last flat where I lived and which I had been lucky enough to visit six years ago. Yes I was lucky enough to be allowed in and my school, my church, my mother's sister that lived in the same town. I do remember quite a lot even though I was taken out of the town by Russians when I was eight.

Tell me about that.

Oh, in 1940 when the Russians occupied the site of Poland they decided they wanted to take us out of our country and gave us a free ticket to Siberia. So on 28th of June in 1940 they just arrived and knocked at our door and told us that we have half an hour to pack a few things because they are taking us to the police station which we knew perfectly well wasn't right, so you could imagine how little one could pack in half an hour and there was a lorry outside of our building and they packed us there took us to the station shoved us into cattle trucks about sixty people per truck if not more and that was that. I do remember it was a very hot day. I have, we have, my mother and father and I we had I had a Chihuahua dog. We had taken the dog with us but being so hot and stuffy in the cattle truck which was completely locked but for a tiny, tiny window the dog had fainted so my mother let it through the window and asked a workman to take it back to my mother's sister which unfortunately he'd never done but what I heard later on from aunty the dog must have run away from wherever he was in two weeks time and arrived at aunty's flat.

So and since then we travelled for, I don't remember, I think it was six weeks and arrived in Siberia … The place was Sverdlorsk but beforehand we have arrived in the little village town and then with all our possessions which was almost nil. I mean it wasn't just us there were quite a lot of people in the same position. We had to walk through the huge forest, to a place that was simply cut out in the forest, and once upon a time there were some kind of prisoners there but when we came it was unoccupied. There were huts made of wood and they had they just tell us that we had to share a room with another family and in the place I can't tell you how many people there were but there must have been 300/400 people.

We've lived there till … um God knows … that would be 'forty-one something, something 'forty-one, nearing the winter but winter there was most of the year. We only had spring summer and autumn lasting about two months and the rest was just sheer winter with the temperatures going up down to minus fifty centigrade. Well that's more or less you know in a quick session as we managed to be there in 1941 as the Russians started the war Germans started the war with Russia and immediately we were told that we could be free if we wanted to get out of there. They tried to persuade us to stay but certainly everybody had started to move out. At the very same time we know that somewhere down south in Russia, a Polish army was being formed. It means that all the men out of prisons and camps were released and the army was being formed so father, my mother and I and a funny little cat, that I somehow I don't know who gave it to me, how did I manage to get it in Siberia, we went to the nearest station, got into another cattle truck [laughs] and arrived in ... I wish I knew ... Tashkent. And actually it was Samerkand near and settled for a while in a small town called Druma and Druma in Polish is one of the most serious illnesses.

There we found quite a lot of Poles already there mostly from the prisons and from camps as we were, very ill, typhoid and so on and people were just dying like flies. My father was very ill but then after he recovered a bit he said that he would go and try and join the army ... he went to ... can't tell you the name of the place. Anyway he joined the army but we hadn't heard from him for the last, for about three or four months and probably that is a bit of a sob story, where the state we lived, it was Uzbekistan and with, what do you call them, the Uzbeks in a small, small room, but there was nothing to live on beside occasionally, occasionally there was centre where they were cooking soup for all the people and so on, but my Mama she had the last ring that she still possessed. She had a wedding ring an aquamarine ring and she went to sell it. She sold it to a wife of a high ranking KGB officer. I still remember the lady and on the very same night my father came already in the uniform ... and

Deported Polish women in labour camp

said to mother, 'Well'. She said 'I've sold all these' and that was that. The lady came and somehow she became almost a friend of my mother, always begging not to tell her husband and my mother said that my father came back and we are going away. So she said 'Probably you want your rings back' and she gave them back. That's my mother's ring there. My daughter has the aquamarine ring and I've got the wedding ring.

We went to ... Mmm where to? With father we went to Turkistan where the army was being ... there was a centre of, you know some kind of army centre. We'd been there for a while then moved to the south.

By this stage it was 1942. In 1942 we ... went to, yes we were allowed to be moved with the army as the families of the people that had joined the army, to Persia ... Iraq, Iran sorry. Today is Iran. We went through Krasnovodsk. It's the port in Russia, across Caspian Sea into Pahlavi. From Pahlavi, well in Pahlavi there was a huge camp of really, well you can hardly call them huts. There were mats placed on top of wooden poles just to shade us away from the sun. Well it's no good saying most of the people were sick, very ill, I had very, very bad malaria and so did my mother but we were not the only ones and eventually ... Eventually we were taken to Tehran. Again we stayed in the camps with ...

Was your father still with you?

At this stage no, father had already gone with the army. So from Pakhlevi to Tehran, in Pakhlevi we met father and then he went to Iraq with the army and we went to Tehran with the families.

Krystyna what was it like as a young child going/having this experience?

Probably it wasn't half as bad as it would have been for my mother being worried about the child. I don't know you just get used to everything. We were free we had food so this way we were happy. We were given some clothing, be it that it had never fitted you, and the funniest thing that happened to me when we came to Pakhlevi, quite a lot of girls and women were infested with lice and I had very long plaits and as we were, we came in and were told to go to have a shower and so on and there was a gentleman waiting with a plate or whatever to cut the hair off every child hair, and Mama said 'No you won't touch it' and he said 'But they're all infested with lice' and mother said 'No she isn't and I'm not?' So they looked through my hair and I wasn't, and I was an odd child out not being bald because I had long plaits and I had them up to the age of nineteen and eventually I decided that I wanted short hair [laughs] so ... you know it was so, it was different, we were free we were not hungry. Well as I child I was so very ill but it didn't matter. In Tehran there was a Polish school where I made friends.

Were there a lot of children in similar situations?

Well yes there were thousands of us there. By the time we reached Tehran where the Poles, there were one, two, three, four huge camps around Tehran and I mean thousands of us. I can't tell you for sure how many people were deported to Russia but there were thousands, or hundreds of thousands of

Poles because Russians just wanted to get rid of intelligentsia of everybody and just push their people into our places.

Can I take you back to where the Russians came to take you away. You were eight years old at the time. What was your father's occupation?

My father was working for the Polish railway and Mama was an accountant. I mean mother worked till I was born and then she stopped working.

Any did you have any brothers or sisters?

No I was an only child.

And what about your grandparents, were they there?

No both grandparents were one lot, my mother's parents were living down south in Poland and Father's parents moved from Lwow when Granddad retired into a small place outside. So that's more or less what I remember of them. I do remember my mother's parents because we used to go there for holidays many a time. I did go and visit Dad's parents, I do remember Granddad very much, very much indeed. He was a very tall, very straight man and very gentle. The opposite to Mum's, Mum's father was stocky and very dark and I think I was afraid of him [laughs] I don't know why ... because he was so very dark.

Did you have any other cousins, aunties and uncles?

In Lwow there was my mother's sister. She had an only son but he was much older than me. He must have been about ten years older. I do remember him but he was no company for me.

Were they all deported?

No the others stayed. They were not moved. We were deported, the Russians came. We were deported simply because my father fought in the first war and they did know everything about him. When they arrived and they told him and asked him some questions and he just looked at them and said 'Look you know it all so why bother asking me questions ... '

So moving on then, you were in the camp in Tehran, your father was away ...

Yes well he was, then he was in the army.

And what happened next?

From Tehran, well Dad, after joining the army and so on and so on he was stationed in Egypt and he was a tutor in a mechanical school and we were moved from Tehran to Ahvaz in Southern Persia, not far from Basra. Well a lot of people from the camps went to India, Africa, etcetera, etcetera ... there was also a Polish military school for girls and boys in Palestine, Israel today, and I wanted very badly to join it but unfortunately I was too young so they wouldn't have me and we were, Mother and I, were very fortunate because we were moved to Lebanon. From 1944 till 1947 we lived in Lebanon outside of Beirut in a place called Ghazir.

Where did you live there?

In Ghazir well it was the first time ever since Poland that we lived in a well normal house be it only had one room but we lived in a house not in a hut not in a shack not, you know but, that would have been the happiest time because Lebanon is a beautiful country. People were tremendously friendly towards us, not saying that people in, that Persians were not because they were really, really friendly towards us, but Lebanese people were marvellous. Tremendously clever people because within a year you could go to any shop and speak Polish and they knew it. The main actually language was French because they were occupied by France for a while. Through Tehran and Ahvaz and Lebanon I went to school because in every place there was a Polish school on every camp and so on.

Were these set up by Polish people?

They were set up by Polish people. So by the time I came to Lebanon I was already transferred to a grammar school and I managed to do three years there and in 'forty-seven ... sometime in June/July. In July we were told that we were going to England. We went through Egypt where my mum found her sister, her younger sister and her husband. We stayed with them so we were not moved immediately. We stayed with them on the camp for all of it was camps, if not army camps civilian camps, for about a month or so outside of Port Said and then in 'forty-seven September/October probably we came to England.

Who told you you were going to England?

Well it was all arranged with the army. Don't forget we had nowhere to go back to. That our country was cut in two during the war and then my place, my home town was somehow given away to Russia because our eastern part of Poland the Russians couldn't give back. They gave us some places on the western side from Germany but my home town has never returned to Poland, and it's not in Poland now it's in Ukraine now. So there was nowhere to go. England had accepted refugees and then from England we had a great choice, there is no way about it, we could go to America, to Mexico, to Southern America, to Australia, to anywhere we wanted to and they would have transported us and hopefully given jobs and so on.

Somehow England was the nearest to our own country and we always hoped that one day we will go back which has never happened. Well probably some people did go back but Poland, Poland's government was so communist that a lot of people who went back were just sent back to Siberia and there was no, we had nowhere to go. Our home town, our home, the house, everything was in Russia.

So we stayed, my parents stayed on the camp outside of Reading. Well we actually arrived at the airport and my father was in Kingswood Common Camp outside of Reading. There was still army camps, they were still in uniforms then, so my mum went to join him and I was fortunate to go to the school. At this stage in England there were four grammar schools, two for boys, two for girls. They were supported by Polish Education Committee [sighs] well I can't tell you for sure but there was some money that belonged to the Polish Government before the war and don't forget that in England we did have Polish Government in exile which was situated in London, and it has existed quite a longish time, but then you know politics are politics and that has ceased to exist even though we did have one to the bitter end, till Poland became really free and independent as it is now. But the money for the schools, at the beginning, was the money that belonged to our country. Then later on probably the English Education Authorities has taken over. But I was fortunate to be there go as far as to Higher Schools Certificate, so called Matura, in Polish. We did first we did some kind of GCSEs and then higher. By the time I have reached lets say the sixth year we were told we have to sit English Certificate of Education, was difficult because in most of our lectures lessons were in Polish some we have tried to learn English language but is not an easy way to learn a language, you know, being surrounded by Poles. Anyway we did our best. And so my year was the first year that had to sit English GCSE and at this stage you had to do five subjects. If you failed one you couldn't repeat it, you, it was nullified. You had to do it over and over again and fortunately enough I've managed to do it and then we didn't, what year that be? 195…1. I went, in 1951 I went to Leicester, City of Leicester Teachers Training College.

What was it like living on the Kingswood Common Camp?

It was an army camp. Well I didn't live there I used to go there for holidays, was full of lovely young soldiers. [laughs] So it was OK! Even though I was only sixteen/seventeen. But I thoroughly enjoyed that. [laughs]

Where were you living then, at that time?

Well there were huts all the time you know army barracks. Have you ever seen a Nissan hut, well our school all was in Nissan huts … It was OK, it was as cold as hell during the winter, as hot as anything during the summer but you know it was the freedom, being fed, not too well in school, but being fed. Being surrounded by your own people. It was OK. I don't grumble. [laughs]

Did you visit Reading town centre?

Well I used to come to my parents for my holiday and Reading was as dead as dead could be, I do remember. [laughs] This time you could see people on Saturday nights or on Sunday, were the people that went to the pictures, nothing else. It was a tiny, tiny, dead place but now have a look at it now. Mmm.

So did you go to the pictures?

Oh yes I did [laughs] and being here you know there was some boys in the Kingswood Common Camp. [laughs] Yes I only did go –

Which cinema did you go to? Where was it?

It's funny. It's the Odeon, is it still where is the cinemas, I don't go to cinemas any more. There was Granby, Granby on Cemetery Junction and there was one somewhere Shoot Lane on the side and one going down almost towards Oxford Street. Mmm. But I can't remember the names anymore. I know it was Odeon and Granby the other side that I remember. I'm not a picture girl anymore.

Old Reading

So you went to Leicester College and what did you do there?

I went to study sciences and I was accepted for science and my notion was I'm going to teach secondary children because I for my A Levels I did all the sciences. Anyway I was accepted and a month into the first year at college the Principal called me and said 'Look, as my policy is that all the foreign students', and she did have some Polish girls before me 'have to take English literature and English language.' So I said 'What about my sciences?' I said 'Look I have been accepted for science. I don't like languages. I don't like literature. I'm going to fail' And she said 'No Polish girl had ever failed so you won't.' So I can't say I loved it, I didn't like it and they had given me Chaucer to study. I couldn't understand the girls, how could I understand Chaucer? [laughs] But I've managed. [laughs] By hook or by crook I have managed to finish it. It was quite a tough college.

What was it like leaving your family and going to Leicester?

Well I left my family to go to the Polish school, it was outside of Cheltenham so actually from the age of sixteen I was a boarder and I did go home for every holiday. Being in college, being in school, and probably in the beginning when I came to England, each time I had to go back to school maybe I shed a few tears. But altogether can't say it was bad. It was OK.

How would you describe yourself as a young person?

Naughty. [laughs] Constantly smiling. Full of beans. A person that could get on with people. Being in trouble in school many time for whatever reason but, but I was never rude. I was taught to be polite to people, respect people. But I never was told not to do any pranks or be in trouble this way. I was always quite a jolly person, hopefully still am. [laughs]

So from Leicester College where did you go then?

To Birmingham. My first school was in Birmingham in Harbourne and it was, I do remember I was accepted by Birmingham City and but then given the address of the school and it was St Peter's C of E School. So I came and I haven't had a clue what C of E meant. It was Church of England. Just next door to St Peter's was St Mary's Roman Catholic School. Nobody wanted me there probably I don't know. [says, laughing] Anyway I've been there for two years meanwhile I got married and I was married at, wait a second what would it be, before the end, yes I was married in March and I've decided to carry on teaching in Birmingham.

What year was that?

[laughing] Don't ask me. Fifty years ago I see 'fifty-five. 1955 and at the end of it all my headmistress came to me and said Krystyna I will get a supply for you if you have a job, to move to Cheshire, because my husband lived in Cheshire and we decided we would start, we will live there, well simply his parents were there and so on. So I moved to Northwich in 1955 in, May probably and taught there in St Wilfred's School, for the next seven years.

Where did you meet your husband?

I met my husband in Lebanon, actually in Persia first time because then he went to the, to Palestine, was in cadet school but his mother lived in the same place in Lebanon as we did and he used to come for holidays to Mama. Then I met him in England. It was a romance on and off, on and off and finally he managed to catch me, I don't know how. [laughs] So I been there till 1961 [mumbles thirty years] 1961 and he went as a mature student to college.

The camp we used to live in Cheshire was being slowly demolished. His parents were given a council house but I had a child and work, and with him going to college, well my money was badly needed so we moved to my parents down south, to Woodley actually we bought a house in Woodley. My parents joined us and my husband was in college for three years in Alsager in Cheshire or is it Lancashire now I don't ... and I stayed in Woodley with my parents and immediately got myself a job in Woodley, and since then I haven't moved from Woodley and it's a long time you know.

Where did you get the job in Woodley?

In school. I'm a teacher. [laughs] Yes it was Beechwood Infant School. Then my career went from Beechwood Infants to St Dominic's Primary. I was Deputy Head there ... from St Dominic's Primary to William Grey Primary and then I have applied for headship at St Dominic's and I was a head for ... [sighs] oh God seventeen years, something like that, it might be a bit less. Because my daughter had a child and somebody had to look after a child. I was given early retirement, stayed with my granddaughter for two years. My daughter gave up her job. I was free which I didn't like and I went back to teaching. I supplied, first I supplied in any primary infant school round Woodley and there are eight of them and then I supplied in Hugh Faringdon Comprehensive for two years and then back in Beechwood, till I was sixty-five. Probably I would have gone a bit further longer but Education Authority doesn't cover a teacher beyond the age of sixty-five and there was no insurance. I did go occasionally you know just to help out but that was that and so I had taught from, God forty-odd years ...

Did your daughter marry a Polish man?

She actually married a boy what from a Polish family, you know, born here. My daughter was born here. Yes and they do live, they do live in Reading, Lower Earley. They haven't done it for the last year because they had the notion of moving to America. Unfortunately my daughter couldn't take it, couldn't stand it and they are coming back home, so they are going back fortunately didn't sell their house. They'll be back within a few months. My granddaughter is in Liverpool University, has just finished her second year of veterinary studies ... so that's my life story ... What else do you want to know?

Is there anything else that you haven't told me that you would like to say?

Probably masses of things. [laughs] Not really.

You're involved with Polish community now.

Always have been. Always have been yes. When we came actually when my

Community   Political Situation   Children's Identity & Where Home Is

husband finished his college we came here and we've always been very active, very busy, in the club, in the community, still are and hopefully still will be for a while.

And are there many people who came when you came from Lebanon that you still know?

From Lebanon here in Reading. Funnily enough not a lot of people I do know from my home town ... but

Oh yes you were going to tell me you'd been back.

Yes, I've been back. Yes ...

What was that like?

I've been there for four days. I cried most of the time ... the town is still beautiful. It's the most beautiful town architecture wise and so on. Very neglected because it was under Russia till Ukraine became independent country ... I did go to my flat but unfortunately the flat was divided into two and on one side they allowed us in the other side didn't. I went to my school. They've been very kind, very nice to me but the Head wouldn't come out to see me only the deputy head. Well the school it, I didn't remember a lot of it but I did remember where there was the Head's office and I thought I know where my classroom was, but you know I wouldn't be sure. I did go to the cathedral where I was confirmed just before Russians took us. I was simply, I went to the First Holy Communion in the morning and I was confirmed in the afternoon because everybody know there is going to be a next transport of people were going to Siberia for a jolly ride.

What else, well I did go to the huge cemetery where because of, you know, in 1920 there was a war and Poles, well Poles from Lwow, the Poles were fighting Ukranians unfortunately and masses of them were just young boys, young girls from schools and there was a huge cemetery where my father was fighting. So I did go there. It was still in a very, very sad state but I hear, and I hope to go this year, I hear that everything is forgiven and forgotten and so on and the cemetery has been beautifully rebuilt.

When it comes to churches of Lwow, well my parish church unfortunately is not a Roman Catholic church anymore. Where I went for First Holy Communion but very fortunately it was being redecorated or something. Inside, you couldn't get inside. That would have been a very, very deep emotional trauma for me. Oh I did go to the theatre in Lwow. It's a huge opera house. That was very emotional simply because I did remember being there with my parents.

You've travelled in many countries.

I've been everywhere. [laughs]

Krystyna Szopis today

But you've lived here for a long time.

Most of my life, 'forty seven, it's got to be sixty years next year, sixty years.

Do you still feel very much Polish?

Oh yes, Oh yes. There's no way about it … you do, I remember the first time ever I went to Poland. Well I couldn't go to my side of Poland but I went to my mother's sister. When I came back some of the teachers asked me how do I feel, and I said I feel I don't belong there at all but it's still my mother, the country is still my mother. I said this country is the best foster mother but the other is a mother. You can't change. I've brought up my kids. They feel they're Poles. I mean all of them speak Polish even my grandchild. We are different there's no way about it, we are completely different from the people from Poland now. Are we better are we worse? It's for whoever to judge but we are different. We've been through bad times, good times. We do respect this country that given us a chance to get educated and I hope very much that the country realises that we have given something to it … I don't know, I've given forty years of education to it, which must have been, must have been quite good [laughs] yes.

Jan Patyra

Born: 14th April 1921
Kraznystaw, Poland

Date of Interview: 30th July 2006

○ Kraznystaw, Poland
○ Siberia
○ Iran
○ Iraq
○ Egypt
○ Italy
○ Liverpool
● Reading, UK

Childhood

I was born in the middle of Poland not far away from Lublin. My, my, town was Kraznystaw and I was born in a village near there. My father was a, well at the moment he wasn't a farmer but then gradually he got himself a farm. We had a big family, seven of us, five girls and two boys. And, well, we were quite happy.

Did you always live in the same area?

No. All over the Poland and then last one he was in eastern Poland, now it's in Ukraine but then it was in Poland. And from over there all the trouble started. Anyhow, when I finished school I just only, I went seven years to school and after that I didn't want to be a farmer; somehow it didn't appeal to me.

Did you help your father on the farm?

Oh yes yes.

What sort of things did you grow on the farm then?

Well, see I was a youngster only fourteen, fifteen so whatever the father asked me to do I used to do. Looked after the horses, do a bit of ploughing in the fields and things like that. But not a lot. But, as I said, didn't appeal for me and my friend, I had a friend, and he brought me in touch with the army band up north of Poland near the German border. He wrote to me once, he said 'Would you like to … join the army? The band?' because I mean if you ask fourteen or fifteen you couldn't sort of go into the army but as a musician, so that's what I did. I applied for it and I went into the army.

Which battalion was that?

It was thirty third er how do you call it – it was never battalion - it was bigger than battalion – unit – infantry, thirty third infantry.

Had you had any musical background at all?

No I didn't really, no.

Did your brothers and sisters or you parents have it?

No no. See my mum wasn't very keen me going into the army. But, I didn't want to be a farmer. Really I would rather be a painter because I'm painting now different things. But the painting school was far away and we weren't rich, we were pretty poor. Our father couldn't afford it, sending me to the, you know, the school.

Jan Patyra joined the Polish army at just 15 years of age

Demobbed in Reading 1947

Polish legion Rememberance Day Parade Reading 2000

Childhood

Could you tell me a little bit about your mother?

Oh, my mother she was a religious lady.

Countrywoman. Very good with the children but, she – in those days we didn't have a radio or television so the people had a lot of children. No cars, no electricity, nothing like that, those days you know it was very, very primitive. So my mum used to go to church on Sundays and I don't think that she could read, she couldn't read or write because I never ever remember writing to me a letter or reading anything. What I used to do in the winter, mother used to do that, I don't know what, somebody who could read – they used to gather together in somebody's house and somebody read their – mostly the life of some saint or something – that's how it was. But, she was a lovely lady and going back.

See when I was arrested, my mother cried. Arrested by the Soviets, my mother cried and he said to mum 'Don't cry, we not taking away, he only going to show us the way because we are strangers here.' But my mum knew better. And I was arrested and I was away for twenty-two years.

Political Situation

Why were you arrested by the Soviets?

I was, I joined the underground, you know.

This was during the war?

Yes, well, during the war, the war, well Poles were finished. We'd been occupied by Germans and Russians. I was on the town where the Russians were.

So, after twenty two years, Stalin was dead and we decided, well we could have a little bit of money, my wife and I, we decided to go to Poland. I wanted to show her and we go to where my mum used to live and she was w.., she knew we were coming, she was waiting at the station all day. And when we came, my wife said 'Look! That's your mum'. She recognise her from the pictures. So, I ran to my mum and I said 'Mum, I showed them the way.' Even after twenty two years, because we said to me 'No, we not arresting him. He's going to show us the way.'

To where? Where did they want to go? Where did they want you to show them the way? The Russians.
Well, I don't know, that was their sort of excuse.

For arresting you?
Yes.

Did they arrest other people as well or was it just you?
Yes. There ... Because we all, we had a group, ten of us, see there was organised in ten so it would come out, so you couldn't tell about anybody else only your ten.
OK. Well we can come back to that.

That's fascinating, that's really interesting. Can we, you – you're 15 years old, you want to become a musician in the army.
Yes.

On the German border?
Yes, Prussian really, it's Prussian.

It's Prussia. Can you sort of tell me what happened from then? With your army career and music etc?
Well, I, eventually you know I was, from the beginning I was homesick, you know, but because it was my own doing - I wanted to go. So I said I'm going to stick it. And I learned, er instrument, trombone; trombone and I was very happy until the war started during 1939. I was just eighteen at that time. War started, of course as you know maybe we never had a chance, we keep retreating, retreating and I was retreating to the eastern Poland because Stalin, he was keeping quiet, he didn't move. We knew there was something happening but – so I said to friend of mine that was other musician 'Listen, I reckon our war is over, we'll try to get to the Romania' because it was still free country, Romania, and from over there you know you had a chance to go to either to France or to England. But half way through on the 17th of September Russians went, you know from their side and they blocked the way to Romania. So I said to my friend 'Well we haven't got no chan.. choice.' Because my father had a farm not far away, I came home.

And after a while of course it started, getting arrested, the intelligentsia, officers and whoever. Eventually I don't know whether you heard there was a massacre, oh, so many Poles, thousands of them. A friend of mine said that 'Well we have to do something'. He said 'Why don't we form the band?' That was it, in Russian occupation, he said that there was the Germans and they went back to Germany and they left instruments. So we took the instruments and I went to the Russian headquarters I said 'We are going to, we would like to form the, form the band.' 'Oh, that's lovely' you know they said its lovely because you know they like a lot of propaganda. And so we get some Poles, some Ukrainians, local fellows who can play or are willing to learn. And we formed a band.

It was just before the first of May, first of May. And 'Oh' they said 'goody goody. Can you play when we are marching?' I said yes, but we didn't have the music. I did find the book, music book, and it was a march over there but that was a march was composed for the 1920 when the Poles defeated the Russians. It was a very patriotic. I said 'Well, there was nothing else.' So when it came the first of May, those Russian soldiers formed and started to march and we started playing the very, very patriotic Polish song. I was playing and I was, I couldn't stop, you know inside I was sort of, I said 'Well that's my first victory over you Russians.' But they, they didn't know.

Did you, did you play at different venues to entertain the Russian troops or German troops at all?

No no we only Russians.

Russians?

Yes. I never had anything to do with the Germans because I was on the side of the border which did belong to Russians. Well …

Also I think you were in the Polish Resistance as well?

Yes. Well I was in the Polish Resistance. Yes and now, see so happened our commander, district commander, he was a double agent, he worked for us and he worked for the Russians. See and one day it was, we been sort of arrested hundreds, even the priest because we had a priest he used to give us a, you know, when we joined the resistance. And of course there was the interrogations, interrogations for two months, beating and kicking and goodness know what and eventually we had a –what do you call – trial. Yes. And I got fifteen years hard labour. See because they all the resistance they wanted to know whether I had any arms or something, rifles. And I said 'Well I haven't got one but if need be I'll find one.' So that saved my life because all this from the resistance from my ten, huh, admitted they had a rifle, they been shot. Five, six of them had rifles and you know they had, they shot them. I know that, because after the war when we are released from the prisons, from the camps, none of them came back, because they'd been shot.

Anyhow that commander who was double agent, eventually 1943 or something Polish Resistance did find out that he's a double agent. He had a trial and he was shot. In Poland. So, because never knew, we said 'how did come, how did they find out about us?' See? But then when I read it in a book after the war that he was a double agent, I knew. Anyhow, so I spent two years in a labour camp.

Whereabouts? In Poland?

Ach no, ach no in Russia, in Siberia. It was terrible. I don't know I weigh more than about seven stones at the end, skeleton.

Now one day, you know because the war started between Hitler and between Stalin, and one day when the Germans were advancing they were near Moscow so Stalin decided to let us out, it was an amnesty. See, so one day one of the commandant of our camp, he used to call us the Polish goodness know what, he spoke to us he said 'Citizens of Poland' I couldn't believe my eyes you know he said 'You're going to be free' the Polish government is in London, Sikorsky, General Sikorsky he had a chat with Stalin and they arranged it and they let all the Poles, ex-soldiers, let them out.

So were you let out to join the army to fight against the Germans?
Yes.

There was a Russian army or a Polish army?
No there was a Polish army. Because we said. And as you see from the beginning we didn't have uniforms but English you know their convoy, north convoy they brought all the uniforms, so we did have a uniform, and Stalin wanted us to fight he said 'Well, why don't you fight over here with us in, against the Jerries?' And we, but we said no, see we didn't trust the Soviets. So eventually we left Russia, I went to the Middle East, see that's our chaps in the Middle East.

Whereabouts in the Middle East did you go first?
Iran and then from there to Iraq, up north we were. From over there we moved to Palestine.

Were you fighting through ... ?
No. No we been still, we been all skeletons, we did have to learn, well get some strength.

I see.
Then we got a British armament and with training, and at the end they send us from Egypt to Italy, and we started to fight and we did fighting all the time to the end of the war.

Where did you first see action?
Before Monte Cassino.

In Italy?
Yes. Yes. It was terrible. I mean we had our own band, we had sixty-two men. When the marshal who was our commander, eighth army commander came to see us after the Cassino we didn't have anyone, it was only twelve of us, so our commander he said 'I'm not sending you fighting any more'? That's Cassino, terrible. And I was very lucky I wasn't even wounded at the Cassino, bruised and goodness know what but survived it.

Jan Patyra on top in the Polish army
German border

Did you meet any of the other troops at Monte Cassino, the Indian troops and the American troops?

Oh that's all the troops were with us, yes, French, Americans.

See because I, on the desert I didn't have nothing to do I tried to learn English, from the book, but I never sort of heard any Englishman talking, so I don't know I used to say something in English, but did it sound like the English, I don't know, see nobody spoke English.

See. So they used to send me, they said 'You go and interpreter to the French army.' I go over there, they are French Moroccans, ha ha, I knew few words in Arabic you know so but that's all. That was the same when we came to England, later on, see when we came to Liverpool.

So you..

After the war

So you went through Italy, helped with the liberation of Italy

Yes. Well, see what it was really, yes. Churchill and Roosevelt they didn't want to upset the Russians so they said 'Right we are not going any further we are not going to Poland or Austria and Poland because there'll be a trouble.' See, so we stayed in Italy all the time and after the war we came to England, 1946.

All right, what by ship?

Yes, by boat to Liverpool, all our army. And from Liverpool they again, my commander said 'Well, you speak English, you supervise to unload our boat.' We had instrument there, armies and all that.' I said 'Right' So after that when we supervised and we put everything out, my commander said 'Right you finished. now you go from Liverpool, you go to Wallingford', gave us the tickets, train tickets, because I had twelve men with me. Liverpool, Wallingford, where the hell is Wallingford? I didn't know anything. 'Oh, yes' they said 'You change at Bletchley, and later on at Didcot and you stop at, well, near Wallingford there's a little station' 'All right'. So Bletchley, Bletchley, when the train started I kept looking, I don't see the Bletchley, I see Bovril, I see Biro I say 'No, it's not Bletchley yet' because my men was asking 'is it Bletchley?' I said 'No'. So we got out at the next station we stop, I looked through the window because during the war, I don't know whether you remember, there were only little names of stations because there was a, you know, Jerries. And I see again Biro and Bovril and Lux. Well, that's a funny country, they got all the same name.

Adverts. Why Wallingford? Why were you sent to Wallingford, was it an army camp?

Yes. There was all, our unit was already there. See so you go to Wallingford.

Holding trombone (right-hand back) with army band Iraq

So you got ...

So I said to myself 'Well there must be something funny,' I've seen the train conductor and he said 'No, no, no, it isn't, the Biro and Bovril isn't the name of the station'. He said 'I'll let you know when it's Bletchley?' So I said to my men, I said 'That fellow, he's going to tell us when we get to Bletchley'. When we got to Bletchley, we unloaded and eventually we got near the Wallingford, a little station, forgot that little name, funny. We waited and waited, mind you from there it was only about six miles to Reading, to Bletchley, to Wallingford. And there was only about two trains a week, a day. We waited and waited and waited and there was only one fellow at the station because it was a tiny little station. They said, my men said, 'Go and ask that chap, when is the train coming to Wallingford' so I go and in my broken English I said 'Could you tell me what time the train comes to Reading, to Wallingford?' And he must have been the local one, he spoke Berkshire accent, a burr, you know so fast I couldn't understand a blinking one little word of what he was saying. I said 'Pardon' so he said again. I could see he was getting sort of bitter. I said 'Are you talking to me in English?' and he blew his top. 'I'm talking English, what about it, I'm talking English, why can't you understand what I'm saying?' I still couldn't understand anything. My chums said 'What did he say?' I said 'Don't ask me I don't know'.

After the war, after years, I met a girl from the station, I told her this story, she said 'Do you know, that chappie, he was local one, he died a few months ago, he was ninety-four.' I said 'If I knew I would like to meet him again'.

So you were demobbed at Wallingford?

No, I wasn't demobbed, we were there and that was our headquarters.

So you had, your headquarters were.. and you were still playing in the band, yes?

Yes, and then they started demobbing people. But I stayed in Nettlebed, Wallingford.

OK. What was at Nettlebed? Was that camp or..

Camp, yes.

What, for demob soldiers?

Well. That was a used to be a American airmen, used to live there.
See, so after the Americans left we just went there. Still a soldier, over there. And from over there we start forming a small band, you know because a lot of our chaps went to Poland, or somewhere else, you know the band wasn't the band any more. So we formed, sort of like a small dance band.

What sort of music did you play, mainly American or Polish or … ?

Well, see, music, it's international, see whatever it was in England we played.

Played whatever?

Yes. Whatever it was. And so from that we went with the Polish theatre all over England, Wales and Scotland. So we travelled and because there was Polish camps everywhere, civilians, army camps and all that. Yes, that's me. And eventually I was demobbed in 1946.
After I was demobbed they gave me clothing and I got a job at Huntley Palmers in Reading.

That was your first job in Reading?

Yes.

So you got the job. What do you do at Huntley & Palmers? Tell me something about Huntley & Palmers

I was just ordinary labourer.

Right. What sort of things did you do?

Biscuits. First of all I was mixing the dough and then in the oven and goodness knows what and that's when I met my wife. See I was on the first floor and hanging on the rafter, just like a Tarzan, and she was just passing by because she used to get the different paper to different offices all around – it's a big place – over 2,000 people used to work …

And you know I started to talk, I said why it's a nice little girl, I know that, started to talk and talk more and that's what it started, you know. And I knew her and I liked her, she liked me, I was her first man and let's hope the last one. And I'm very, very lucky, I couldn't wish for any better wife.

Jan Patyra today

Jan Patyra and wife Dotty

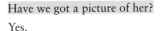

This went on?

It did. She is so good. I did have a Polish girl, in Russia, you know when we were in Russia. There were, because we had the soldiers and we used to have army families with their children and we had schools, you know they used to go to schools and goodness knows what. And there was a little girl Vanda, I fancied her, you know she was a nice-looking, she was very young, fifteen, no more. And her father was a sergeant and her mother was in Poland because she was taken to Russia on her own as a little girl. And so when we moved from Russia to Persia we stayed at the Caspian Sea – very romantic and I said to Vanda I said 'Listen', first time I never, we never had any sex or anything you know, I just loved her. I said 'Listen' to Vanda 'I love you. I don't know where I'm going to be, what's going to happen, where we're going to fight, but I shall wait for you' and she said 'I'll do the same' because she was with her auntie, civilians. And they stayed in Tehran, and one day I had a letter from her saying 'John, Jonny honey or something, we are moving from Tehran to … ' because everything was censored so I don't know where she was going but I believe she was going to the East Africa, because there was a lot of Poles over there, in East Africa. You know, our families. And that was the last letter. And I didn't, I waited and waited and waited and still waited for her, you know that little girl. Till I met somebody and he said 'You know, that's the one, that's Vanda'

Have we got a picture of her?

Yes.

Lovely picture.

Well that's a Russian she took it in Russia. And she said, we were on the way from Persian Gulf, we were going to Africa, East Africa, Uganda or Kenya, somewhere there and she said she developed dysentery, very bad dysentery and she died on the boat and they buried her at sea. So that was the end of it I never heard any more about it.

Sad story.

Yes, but there again I wouldn't meet Dotty, my wife.

So. I see. Kismet isn't it?

Yes. Yes.

Could you just tell me a bit more about, you know, when you came to Reading, how you, you know how you saw Reading, what it was like, etc, you know, working at Huntley & Palmers?

Well, I still lived in the camp.

All right, so you travelled?
Yes.

But how much did you earn when you went to Huntley & Palmers?
Five pounds a week.

And what year was that?
'66, 1966.

That's when you first started work there?
Yes. And that was ordinary. If you were lucky you earned a little bonus but sometimes I didn't earn any bonus, you know the. And I used to have a letter from Poland that said 'Jonny, we haven't got such a medicine, could you send us,' so I did, I'd go short but luckily I was in a band, so at the weekends very often we used to play so there wasn't much, I used to get perhaps two pounds fifty or three pounds for my band, for dance.

Whereabouts in Reading did you play with your bands?
All over.

What venues? Can you remember the names of any of the venues, where they were?
Yes. Well, we used to play the Town Hall, that was Police dances mostly. And then different organisations, you know we used to play different bands, different places. And our piano-player, he was an Englishman from Henley and he knew a lot of it, so we used to play Benson airport, you know for the airmen, and Polish dances for all these camps, and everywhere, we used to play there. It was a good band, very good band we used to have.

Was there a favourite piece you played?
Well, not really. We used … *In the Mood*, you know American Patrol and all that.

So you settled in Reading and had a family, yes?
Yes.

What hours did you work at Huntley & Palmers, what were the hours?
Well, we used to work seven days, six days, Saturdays as well.

What time did you start?
We used to work eight o'clock to six I believe. We used to work all day.

That was a picture of your band.
Yes, that's our band …

Is that you on the trombone?
Yes.

Jobs

Community

Self Sufficiency

Jobs

So how long were you at Huntley & Palmers for?

I must have been there about ten years. See our son was born but it was not enough money for here so I got myself a job at the power station, Earley power station there used to be. Oh it was work, hard work, hot, dirty, but the money was much much better. See I worked there, then I moved to the Caversham, we used to work, cork factory.

On the river?

Yes and after there I loved swimming I was everyday, dinner time used to go swimming.

So was the cork factory, was it like a mill? Because they had ...

Yes.

Can you describe it to me?

Well, there was a mill where they mixed the rubber and cork everything because cork used to come from, not from Spain, from other countries and then when it was all mixed and pressed we used to bake it, you see you have to bake it. and then when it was done they used to cut it and slice it whatever they wanted for the cars. That was very good but again very hot, see. So I worked there and they got fed up and I went to Theale which was refrigeration, we used to make the fridges and things like that.

Prestcold?

Prestcold, that's right. And I worked there till I was retired, till I retired. And I retired at sixty-five and my wife got herself a little job at Marks and Spencers and I was getting fed up being at home not doing anything so she said 'Why don't you apply?' I applied, I was sixty-five then, I applied and they and I got part time job. It was lovely.

So, coming to England and living in Reading, I mean making a life in Reading?

Yes. I mean we did travel to the Cornwall and good knows what, Scotland, but I still I like this place the best. I said to my wife 'If I won any millions on the lottery I wouldn't move from this house because we've got lovely neighbours' and its quiet over here as you can see. What else do I want?

Ok. Well, Jan thank you.

I am very very pleased. I tell you my life. I experienced, seen so many different countries so many here and there, so if I died today I'd die a happy man because all my dream came true. Now really when I had a heart operation you know I was so bad I didn't want to live really but my wife came to hospital 'Don't give up, Jonny don't give up. You always keep saying to the grandchildren that Patyra's never give up' and she was crying. I said to myself 'I'm not ready to give up' and I survived. See, so I don't know how long we going to be together but I love it. See if we belong to the Marks and Spencers retired lot, we go in different places. Now we've got a millennium, Polish millennium it was very very nice. So we are in a choir, we sing, my wife sings in Polish with a Berkshire accent. Ha ha. but she's very good, you know.

Is that the church, Polish church?

Yes, near the hospital, yes.

In Watlington Street.

Lovely. It was ruined when we got it but we got it. I mean that was my wife's church, Church of England and she was christened there and goodness knows what, but one day she said 'Do you know, I want to change to the Catholics.' I've never pressed anybody to change their religion, no matter what you are; they're all the same, really. I said 'Do you really?' We knew the priest very well, so he used to give her lessons. They used to argue and I said to him, I said 'I wonder who is going to convert who Catholics or [inaudible] Church of England?' but she wanted. I said 'I know what you wanted because you want to be the same, once I'm dead, to go the same place.'

Polish Church today, Reading

Old Reading

Poland

The Republic of Poland is located in Central Europe. It shares borders with Germany, the Czech Republic, Slovakia, Ukraine, Belarus, Lithuania, Russia and the Baltic Sea (over which it shares maritime borders with Denmark and Sweden). It lies mainly on the lowlands of the North European Plain but is also home to the Carpathian Mountains, many lakes and rivers as well as ancient forests. Over the course of the past thousand years the territory ruled by the Republic of Poland has varied and shifted. Poland was the second largest state in Europe during the 16th century and at other times Poland has disappeared entirely from the map. In 1918 Poland regained its independence from its neighbours, but the borders were once again redrawn after The Second World War. After the Napoleonic wars the victorious allies divided Poland with the eastern portion coming under the control of the Russians. Eventually the Russian Czars annexed the country through the erosion of Polish freedoms. At the end of the First World War Point 13 of Woodrow Wilson's Fourteen Points (the restitution of Poland) was implemented. Poland managed 20 years of relative stability until it again caught the eye of its powerful neighbours. In 1939 the Nazis and the Soviet Union signed the Ribbentrop-Molotov non-aggression pact which effectively provided for the sharing of Poland between the two states. On 1 September 1939 Hitler ordered his troops into Poland, 16 days later Soviet troops invaded and occupied most of the eastern part of the country (which had been home to many Ukrainians and Belarusians). The Polish formed both an underground resistance movement and a government in exile in response to the invasion. It provided the 4th largest contingent of troops to the Allied forces and also suffered the loss of the highest percentage of citizens of all participants in the war. Poland was witness to some of the worst atrocities of the war. About 6 million Polish citizens were killed by the Germans, but the Soviets also committed their own atrocities: these included the deportation of 500,000 Polish citizens to the Soviet Union (many to gulags or concentration camps) and the slaughter of more than 100,000 in Galacia and Volhynia by Ukrainian nationalists. At the end of the war Poland slid westward on the map – the Soviets insisted on keeping the territories given to them under the terms of their earlier pact with Nazi Germany and part of Weimar Germany was given in compensation. The former territories now form parts of the Ukraine and Belarus; the new Poland emerged 20% smaller with its eastern border now lying on the Curzon line and its western border on the Oder-Neisse line. Cities such as Brest Litovsk, Pinsk and Lwow were now under Ukrainian control. This redrawing of the borders has forced the migration (both internally and externally) of millions of people including Poles, Germans, Ukrainians, and Jews and was left a small minority in neighbouring states like the Ukraine, Belarus and Lithuania.

Elvio Fappiano

Born: 4th September 1941
Italy

Date of Interview: 20th July 2006

● Italy
○ Reading, UK

My name is Elvio Fappiano, date of birth is 4th of September 1941. I was born in Italy.

Can you relay to me your experiences as a child?

Well as a child I was born during the Second World War and then after the war it was a hard time for everybody, almost all of Europe, but Italy was badly affected because people even if you had the money or whatever, there was nothing you could buy, everything was destroyed was rationed. We used to have a booklet with rations, you were allowed so much things a week, so much bread, so much sugar, so much of this and once that had gone, it didn't matter how much money you had there was no, no way you could any more. That was it, so people who had a bit of land and things, they used to grow their own things to sell to people, the more land you had the better you was doing, you grow more your own things, you had something extra, some other people didn't have any such luxury and we carried on.

Then in the '60s, there was the '50s, the '60s, there was a huge immigration. The Italians they was trying to emigrate wherever it was possible, mainly to Belgium, France, German, Finland, Australia, Canada, you name it, wherever you go you find Italians. I was nineteen then and I had the opportunity, I thought to myself, well I want to go somewhere, because in Italy there was a compulsory National Service, the army and it was two years you had to do, but there was no pay or anything, it was very hard life. So I said to myself I'm not going to waste my two years of my life there, and I start looking for somewhere to go. I see this opportunity to come to England because there was, the '60s was a great demand for English people from people from abroad of any kind of trade or experience.

At nineteen I didn't have any full time qualification or anything but I had a lot of interest in the catering. I saw this job going as a domestic in a private house, so I applied for it and within a couple of weeks I had my working permit to come here to England to work as a domestic, which was allowed only to work in the private house or schools or hospital. You had to be resident and for four years you had to, every month we had to go to the Police Station to report our stay, or just say no change or if there was any change. If we had moved job or address we had to report everything, and then after four years you apply to the Home Office for permanent stay and, unless you had done something silly or you had a criminal record or something, no one was rejected.

So it was approved and I decided to stay here. My thing was, maybe I stay here a few years, make some money and go back home, but things change in your life.

Jobs

I stayed four months in that private house, which I came for, as a chef and I was treated very well, there was very nice people, rich English people that was in Woolhampton, it's about ten miles away and they treated me very well. I had a driving licence, from the first day they gave me a car and they gave me anything I needed and I was doing everything, but I was, I was the chef, I was a gardener, I was taking the children to school, take the dogs for a walk, which was one thing I didn't like. Anyway it was good, but it was one thing I was a young boy, you know I want a bit more time free, looking for girls or something, so there was a college nearby there called Oratory School, I don't know if you heard about it in Woolhampton. I said to the lady of the house, I said 'Look I'm, I want to go back to Italy because this job is, it doesn't suit me, you know I've got nothing to complain about your, the way you treat me but it's in general I miss home.' She was ever so nice, ever so kind, she asked me 'Look if it's because you want more this, more that, there is a college here and there is some other Italians who work in there, if you like you can go and work there,' and I said 'Do you mean it?' because she had to pay my way to come and she said 'Yes, yes, I'll tell them, I'll go there and you can have a job but, if you don't mind, sometime when you have a day off or sometime, can you come over and cook some Italian dish for us, for the children?' I said 'That's fine' and I, as again, they was the nicest people I had met.

She went to the college and within two days she had got me a job in the college as a cook and I went there, there was about thirty girls there including my wife, that's where I met her.

Anyway I stayed there one year at the college there and then I was always looking for something better if it was possible. I wanted to open my own restaurant and things but there was no way because if you didn't do the four years you wasn't allowed to do nothing after then, but I had a few jobs, privately in restaurants and there was some Italian restaurant, some café in Caversham, which now is all changed. Caversham Road, it's just up from Friar Street but now it's all changed because of the DIY and things and I had a few jobs like that and then I found a job at the University of Reading as a chef. I stayed there for about a year and a half and actually there was a job going at the hospital, which was slightly better. The only thing was they had no residential thing but I went and applied for the job and as, with the help of the District Catering Manager at the time, she could put a good word for me, so I got the job without being a resident and the only thing she said to me 'You've got a very good reference and you've been doing as an assistant chef, we haven't got a job here, we got a job as assistant cook, if you like to take it.' I said 'Yes I'll take it' because it was still better than there, so I took the job 1964 at the Royal Berkshire Hospital.

Within one year I was promoted to assistant head chef, then I stayed there another year and I was promoted to head chef and I worked there for for, er thirty-nine years, then I took early retirement essentially. I took, the place, the kitchen at the Royal Berks, for a few years we won awards for cleanliness, best food in the region, in the hospitals, you know all things like that. Just before I retired we managed to get three star, when the hospital was awarded with stars, we managed to get three stars for the food and things so I left good reputation behind me.

Self Sufficiency

Old Reading

Jobs

Old Reading

Self Sufficiency

Community

Self Sufficiency

Jobs

Unfortunately they didn't manage to keep it, it's still going okay, but it's been a bit, a shame.

Anyway during my lifetime of work, and as I said to start with, I was, my aim was to go back but things changed, I met my wife and 1963 we got married and we had children, we had a set of twins, so we had a big family within a year and things changed and as I say, well I'm going to settle here. I managed to buy the first house, those days I mean, I know it sounds silly now, but in those days I mean my wage was £5.00 a week. I managed to get a house in Caversham for £750.00. It was a bit you know damp, but we got it, I got it and spent some more money on it and make it happen and stayed there for about ten years and we sold it 1971, there was at the time that the price of the house was going up by the seconds. I sold mine for two thousand three hundred and fifty and I couldn't find anything else, then this one came around, it was five thousand two hundred then, but it was in a state. The insurers they came in to see it because they had students in for a couple of years or a few years and I don't think any of them ever washed the place or anything, it was everything disgust. I thought to myself well I got to do something, I've got,' the price was reasonable, but like I say was needed a lot to do, but I did go through with it, put an offer for five and took the two hundred off and they accepted and slowly I did what I wanted to do with it.

During the time, as I was working in the hospital, we done, there were quite a few things, like in 1965, we created an Italian club, an Italian community. What I done I went, myself and one of my friends, we went around the house to house of the Italian people, they put 50p each, each family and we made a nice party, we hired a hall and made some food, being, my being a chef and so on, we made some food, we had a nice dinner dance more or less you know because 50p a family and everything else was free, that was all the 50p they pay we managed to cover everything, for drinks. From that day we carried on, we get more organised and more people got involved and we created a community. We never managed to buy our own place, but we used the Christ the King Hall in Cressingham Road, we used that for quite a number of years you know. We still, going on, like I say, not like what it used to, but that's remained and it's all down to me to create that community that we could met all, because in Reading there's a lot of Italians.

Then I used to, on my own time, apart from the job I had at the hospital, on weekend or my day off and things I had a continental mobile shop, which had my own, I didn't have to go and ask oh do you want anything, there was steady customers. Every second week because I used to do Reading and Basingstoke, one week in Reading and one week in Bas, every second week or weekend I used to say I knew more or less what they want, by the way I had steady customer, so and so and so and so, I'm here, what do you want. I did that for about ten years or so then, as I say I couldn't carry on full time job and do that and I was getting great demand so I had to stop.

Then I done a few private functions, weddings, mainly for friends and family and things, they used to come to me, oh my daughter is getting married, I'd say 'yes fine, what do you want you know, what do you want to get done and we'll do it.' It was not a thing like I was doing it for a living, no it was more a hobby than anything else, helping people and obviously I was getting some little cash for myself, but just for the expenses and what everything else and people was very happy because I was charging them nothing actually, just what it cost. We carried on a while, then in 2001, after thirty-nine years in the hospital I took early retirement and then do nothing. Pass my time with my grandchildren, which I've got eleven of them.

Before you left Italy what was your impression about England?

Well the impression about England before I left Italy, some people who had been here, some, all the people who had been here before, some of them was war prisoner and then they come back to Italy, they used to say that England was nice country to stay, people was okay. English was a bit hard to deal with but then again it's the same in everywhere, you get good people, bad people in everywhere you go. When I came here I found it very nice with the people I went to work with. In England is opportunity for anyone to achieve their goal, so myself personally I settled down and said, well I want to raise my family up, give them a good education, own my own house and be happy, get what I needed, the essential, without them struggling, that was my goal which I achieved and very happily so. I've got four daughters, which they all, as I said they had a good education and all done well and I pass my time with my eleven grandchildren.

What do you remember, in particular about your childhood as you were growing up in Italy?

Well I remember most everything. I think I said, mentioned in the second interview that soon after the war it was a hard time for everybody, I remember was going to school but I was eleven when I left school because I could see that everyone was struggling to get on. I said, well I can write, I can read and that's enough for me so it's time I'm getting a job and then from that age I went as an apprentice for a blacksmith, like a shoe horse and stayed two years there and then I took it, I still am confident that I can, I could make horse shoes and shoe the horse if I had to.

Then things was going on and you could see that horse was coming to an end because there was the revolution of bikes and push bike, and motor bike and as I say, well I think I got to change for something more. So I left that and I was an apprentice for a bicycle, bicycle shop, which again I did well, when I was put my head on something I was always achieving and again now if I had, if I get old thing, all the equipment, I can build a bike from a pipes, buy the pipes, cut it to measure and build a bike, I'm confident I can still do it now, provided I get the right tools and the right things.

Then I see well what's coming round, the motor bike and the car, I say well the push bike could finish as well, I took one step forward, upward, and mechanic and I did about six months of that and say well it's good, it might be good in a few years time but there is no money at the moment, I need something now and I started to mess about with fruit and veg … managed to get myself a three wheeler scooter, to go from one village to another selling, get the things that this village had too much, the next village didn't have any, I used to go and sell things and had my own little enterprise and was very happy

Family Values
Education & Training

Jobs

Childhood

Childhood

with it, but as I say I was getting older, always better idea coming for work and that was the idea of coming to England and there we are.

Do you sometimes go back to Italy?

Yes every year, sometimes more than once, like last year I've been three times so we, we got our own place there, so we go whenever we wish to and my children, my son-in-law and the children, they all like there, so they all coming, they all going every year as well, still got our relatives there, my sisters, my nephews and so on, long lost cousins, so we do go every year, yes.

What do you see your role in England now as coming from Italy?

Well my role in England and I know I'm Italian, I come from Italy but I've been here now for, '61, almost fifty years, so I'm settled and I think it's great. England is a country of multicultural things, people and religion and things, it's not easy to find an English person any more. I mean you get people, including my daughters, yes we're English, we're British but you go back to the origin and everyone, oh my grandfather was French, my grandmother was Italian or my Uncle is this, you know it's always got, to find a typical 100% pure English is very, very hard. I'm one of those people who adapt to what what's going on, now I obey the English rules and things, I do some traditional Italian, there's some tradition you keep for the rest of your life, but I use that in my own house, not when I'm outside, when I'm outside I do what the British law is and I obey to that.

And did those bad experience of leaving school early and having to work help you in the, in the long run?

Well it did help me give me experience of life and how to earn your living and appreciate it, it's nothing put on, because there's nothing worse than things put on a plate for you without knowing where it's coming from. I believe if you own things you appreciate much more, as Tesco say every little helps and my in-laws as well, when I was growing up, when I get married and I want to have a family, if my goal is possible to give my children the education they need which I have achieved that, and thank god for that and pleased with it, proud of it, that's it.

Shirley Graham-Paul

Born: Not given
Kingston, Jamaica
Date of Interview: 6th June 2006

Kingston, Jamaica
Reading, UK

My full name is Shirley Graham-Paul.

Can you tell me when and where you were born?

I was born in Kingston Jamaica in October [year not stated]

And can you take me back now to your earliest childhood memories.

My earliest childhood memories are beautiful, brought up as an only child. My father was a sea man so he was at sea and come home, you know, in his leaves, so it was poor mother who had to cope with me, and I had lots of cousins so, then I had other children to play with as well but it was beautiful absolute bliss.

What age where you when you started at school Shirley?

... In the junior in the baby school I call it, we call it kindergarten, I could have been about four-ish, three four-ish and that's when you paid privately ... and then when I was five I went to ... no it was seven you went to the older school, the big school we call it and ... then ... the private education carried on. When I was eleven I was transferred to the senior school.

The educational system was really good and the teachers weren't like teachers today, they were very strict so you had to do as you're told. Also ... the competition between children, now they don't want you to compete, but in our time ... we competed with each other. and there were three of us, no two of us, a boy and myself, I remember vividly, we were counted as the best writers. So every Friday all the notice from the school would be given to us and we would write up and put it on the notice board ... And as an incentive of learning or ... you know being strong in your education ... at the weekend we offered it the best of my class, we got a prize. So it could be anything. It could be a book, it could be rulers, pens ... whatever, but it's an incentive to encourage each of us to do well.

Was it common for people to have ... continue having lessons, these private lessons you talked about after school?

It wasn't but I was fortunate. You know, my mother made sure and of course daddy ... was away but he looks after us.

Where did you live?

In Kingston, Jamaica.

What kind, what sort of place was it?

It's the basic. Just basic home. You know, but it was good ... And Mama had a helper who'd come in and do the ironing ... and she would do the cooking cause she enjoys cooking ... but all the washing and ironing would be done by this lady.

And how often did you see your father? You said he was away.

If he was away for ... three months then he would have shore leave and then he'd be home don't ask me how long cause I was too glad to see my father ... and I was spoiled rotten I can tell you, I was absolutely spoiled. I still have things that my father used to bring when he when he's coming back off the ship. He had these men at the ... at the pier that have a cart and daddy would shop for just about everything. This cart, including even material for making my school uniform came over. ... Handbags, my swimming costume ... everything. My mother, she had the same and then this chap would know exactly where we live and he'd deliver it so about the time daddy get home we would have it and I'm excited cause I can't wait to see daddy. And he was six foot three tall, well-built and this little girl adored my father cause he was a wonderful man.

So did he talk about where he travelled as a sea man?

No ... strangely enough. He was a very quiet person. And I think I've inherited that from him 'cause people say 'You're so easy going and so quiet.' He'd be whistling away, you'd hear him coming up whistling away or singing. And ... loves his newspaper, so he's sitting in the rocking chair reading away. And then my little job, which I loved when daddy was home was to go and get the ice, cause we didn't have fridge and freezers at that time. So you'd go to get the ice and bring it home and then my mum would make my father's drinks. So I enjoyed that.

Where did you have to go for the ice?

Just across the road. There was a shop that sells things across the road so you just go and get it.

Did you buy it then?

You had to.

What did you carry it in?

In a bag. You just get it in a bag and you bring it back.

You talked about going to school, coming back in the evening doing more studying. What did you do in your sort of leisure time?

The studying after school ... it was, it sometimes is there in the school so you have, say an hour what we call private lesson, one hour private lesson and that was it. So school would finish at three thirty then you have an hour to four thirty and you come home. So when you get home ... you know, the things also as ... what you wore to school had to come off and be hung up and then you have your plain clothes or your ordinary house clothes ... and then you'd meet with your friends. ... But then if there is homework ... mum would make sure you do that before you go playing [laughing] you see. So we had to do that as well.

And there were different [pause] types of ... clothing. Even now, I go to church and they say 'You are always so smart.' It's a custom; that clothes you wear to school it's totally different from the ones you come home and play in. And that's totally different from the ones you wear to church ... And that's how it was. You know, the same with Christmas. At Christmas you have, because it's sunny and it's bright, and in my time you had what we call Christmas market. So ... you would have a pretty Christmas dress and new shoes at Christmas market, which you would have worn to church anyway, and go down. And then ... on Boxing Day you'd have another dress but you have the same shoes. And then New Year's you get a nice new shoes and new dress again. So everybody looked forward to be dressing up. And that was really nice. I looked forward to that.

You were at Secondary school and you were studying there. What happened next? How long were you there and what did you do there?
We did what you called a ... what you called GC, GSE or GCC now ... was what we called Junior Cambridge and Senior Cambridge. Because ... they were

Shirley receives book about Jamaica from the Mayor of Kingston, 1960

Jobs

marked from England, Cambridge University so … you had Junior C and that's what we did.

When did you leave the … Senior School?

I left school, so then I started doing [pause] private work as well as shorthand and typing, we call it stenography at the time. And then because my friends were coming over to England and they said to my mum … by then my father had passed on. [pause]

You were just telling me Shirley that your father passed away and that your friends were … talking about coming to England. Why were they talking about that then?

I think it was to further our education. Because when you get to that age then it's very expensive for education and I didn't have a father. … And mum never worked you see … so this is why I did that. My aunty she came over as well … and yes, after he'd died, because he was with the shipping company for so many years, mum had the widow's pension and was compensated very well.

What age was this? How would you be about, then?

I remember now … about [pause] seventeen. Seventeen, eighteen.

So … did you say you had an aunty here?

Yes, but she lived in London, in Stoke Newington.

And did your mum … did you discuss coming over together or … ?

Oh yes … that would have been discussed with the two aunties and my mother. It wouldn't be me just making a decision.

So tell me what happened next?

So yes, the decision was taken and I came over. So I came to Slough.

Were you travelling alone?

Yes. I came by plane. People were coming by boat and we'd hear so many stories of what transpired on the boat and my mum said 'No, you're going by plane' and that was a long haul. Because those days the flight stopped in Newfoundland before we got to England, I think it could have been about nineteen hours flight or something like that … with the stop.

So where did the plane take off from?

From Kingston. It was then the Palisadoes Airport. It was not Norman Manley as is called now. It was the Palisadoes Airport. And … I remember not wanting to look out … because … and then classed as stoic, I just didn't want to see anyone to start crying … so I looked out and they could see me and they waved but I was sort of … holding back.

At a friend's wedding in Jamaica *1958*

Experience of snow *1962*

Racism

… just the things that I would need. I didn't need a lot cause I could
sew so I made my suit. I remember that. I went into town and
got beautiful material and made a lovely suit. And … again got a
lovely pair of shoes and those days you had to wear your gloves.'
'Cause mum would say 'You're not fully dressed if you haven't the
stockings, and your gloves and your hat' you see. So I had my hat. A
friend, who is a milliner, she made the hat for me and I had this navy
blue suit … and the gloves were light blue and the shoes was navy
blue and the hat was navy blue. I remember that [laughing]' cause it
had to be right and it had to match.

Slough.

It was rented accommodation. 'Cause in those there was still racism
going on. If you looked black it wasn't easy to get somewhere to
live. And it mainly the Asians who'd rent you somewhere … So …
that's how we had to make do. It was a difference from what I left at
home. Like a culture shock? … what you left at home to be coming
here … and being that way. And … it was all different islands lived
in the place. But we all got on very well. So it wasn't a problem.

What I meant is … is the way people are sort of … they look at you
and because you are of … you know, different colour … then it's
strange for them. I remember I was being, I was being naughty, I
remember going … to the shops cause this friend, very dear friend
she became, she was showing me the ropes. Her name is Linda. Her
son is now a big opera singer here. And … she said 'Come on, I'm
showing you the town, showing you where to shop' and so on. So we
went to the high street and … poor dear me in my innocence, went in
the shop, it's like a delicatessen, but at the same time it had another
bit of shop, so I wanted cheese and I wanted different things …
And I am in the queue and this woman kept serving everyone else
and leaving me right there. And then when everyone else was served,
then she came and she looked at me and she said 'Yes' … so I said
'OK, I too can play this game'. So I … pointed at some bacon down
the end, I pretended I didn't understand English so I was dumb as
well … [laughing] and pointed at some bacon, nice choice bacon and
she sliced it and I pointed at the cheese I wanted and she cut that and
I pointed at various different things … and she brought them and
she, you know, went through the till, and then she's told me how

Racism

Old Reading

Jobs

Education & Training

Racism

Education & Training

much it was you know, and I said to her 'Fine, now you can put them back because I don't want them' and I walked out the shop. [laughing] That was my way of dealing with her racism. And I walked out. And I felt good about it. [laughing] Because that was … you know, that was really telling me that she really didn't want me in the shop.

Then I remembered, … no, we came to Reading then Cyril and I came to Reading and … I remember the days of looking out the window, because the lights … they were gas lit so these men in the suits, even those ones who cleaned the street wore suits … and they would come at night and evenings and light this big pole and in the mornings again about six o'clock you watched them and they'd come and put it out as well. And I'm thinking … 'This is interesting?'

Can I just take you back…So Cyril was your husband?

Yes. Children's father.

Anyway, got here and … started to go to Reading Technical College … and … I wanted a part-time job, cause I had my youngest baby then. I didn't want to leave her so … when he's home and I could go … and do a part time job, when he's home I can go to college in the evenings. So I went to Boots. Boots had advertised for [pause] [coughing] an assistant … and I went and asked for the manager and this very smart man came to the door and 'Yes'. And he wouldn't even ask me in. So I said 'You've advertised in the paper for this assistant … and I'd like to apply. He said 'Actually, the job is taken'. I looked in the paper again and it was in the following week. So I went back and I said 'You're still advertising for the job' and he said 'Oh I'm sorry, they didn't take it out but it is taken.' Then I thought great, no problem. 'Cause the way I was brought up and that's me, my father was a man of principle, you develop a lot of the upbringing.

And then another friend, she were going to college and she was here and I said 'You know something, I would like to do nursing, I want to go in the nursing profession.' She said 'Are you sure' and I said 'Yes, … they need nurses, they won't say no.' So I applied to do a nurse training and yes, I went for my test and what have you and passed. So … when I was in what we call PTS then, you know, Pupil Training School. And one day I was going into Reading and I went and then I asked to see this manager again at Boots and I had my uniform on … and I said to him 'Thank you for not letting me have that job because I'm now being trained as a nurse.' He never said a word. [laughing] Yes, just let me go back and show him. He did me a favour … I thanked him.

Where were you doing your training?

It was a mixture of Wokingham, Taplow, Peppard … and the Berks 'cause you seconded to different places at different times.

Awards and memorabilia from Shirley's career

Education & Training
Self Sufficiency

And was this a full time training?

Yes, yes. But then it was shared … it wasn't agreed between my husband and myself and by then my mother was here. She came over a year after. So she was here to take care of the children. And … when I'm off, we are devoted us, one thing, we are devoted to our children, my husband and myself.

How many children?

Three girls. Three girls. So … that was good. And thankfully, … I studied and passed my exams so then I went on further and I was qualified. I wanted to be a midwife because that really was my love. And I applied and yes, … in those days it was part one and part two midwifery. So I did my part one midwifery in the Canadian Red Cross … in Taplow … lovely and … oh what dedication in those teachers and tutors and nurses and we were just one big happy family. Yes, so …

How long did that training take altogether?

Eighteen months. Yes, eighteen months. And of course I wouldn't stop … so I decided to do what we call, it was then called, 'special care babies' course. But working on the ward, I found that very frustrating because we were so busy and you couldn't give the patients the time that they needed. I decided to come and work in the community, where it was my time … even if I'm late, I was not leaving a patient unhappy. And that's what I wanted to do. So I worked in the community as a community midwife. That lasted … twenty nine years. Because I loved it. I was being paid for my hobby. I just love children. So … I then did my short teaching and clinical practice course so that I could have students as well in the community.

Community midwife *1971*

Shirley holding Mary Seacole book for
Black History mural

Community

Have you seen many changes in midwifery over the years?

There are a lot of changes … totally different to when I was
midwife. But then it's today's world. Modern science and technology
have taken over. And therefore, you know, we have to accept the
changes because we're never going to go back to those days … so
it's just learning how to adapt them and work with them. And for
the patient's benefit as well. [pause] So, I am quite open to science
and technology and I'm not one of those who say 'no' to anything.
[pause]

How old where you when you finished your community midwife?

I was examining in the surgery and one patient couldn't get off the
bed, up to sit up so I helped her. And of course her weight pulled on
my shoulder … and I injured my shoulder. Now, I didn't … those
days was where you don't want to let your colleagues down because
you know if you go off they'll be short. And I carried on working
until it started to hurt a lot.

In the meantime, as I said to you, one of these that was for ever
doing something community work, I was … being trained … I was
doing the neo-natal bereavement counselling for mums who'd lost
their babies. I was also studying with Lifeline pre and pregnancy
abortion clinic, counselling … I've finished these off. During that too
… I've trained in those I've decided … my marriage is going to part
anyway, and I thought … let me do something different. So I was
… doing evenings … evening study at Wokingham … Counselling
Service. One and only black counsellor in training. And I did
counselling for three years and got my certificate.

Now … it's like … constantly pursuing my own … educational
challenges. And while I was working at the hospital also there
were … quite few sickle cell thalassaemia patients. I never stopped
doing community work. So I was then involved in the national
organisation for sickle sell anaemia research. So once I'd come to
a meeting I said to them 'There is a need in Reading … and there's
one consultant haematologist seeing these patients. They might not
be as many as Birmingham or London or what have you, but she's
on her own and I feel that we should have a group supporting.' And
they said 'Shirley, if you think there's a need we'll support you. Get
it going, set it up and we'll come down' and so I did. And that's
where we started. Reading had their own organisation for sickle
cell anaemia. And that carried on until we had our first counsellor.
I was trained and she was trained and another lassy was trained as
counsellors.

What year was it when you started that?

'Eighty, I have the form … I have a thing in there but I haven't got
it off hand. It's still going on cause Trevor is now, he's one of the
longest founder member and he's still carrying it on. I'll remember
the date and get it and tell you anyway. So that is still going on. The

programme was very good. We had our first conference at the Civic Centre.

There was another young lad who … the whole family had the issue … and I, because of confidentiality, I never ever mentioned anybody's name. I would go and see them in private and so on. And this poor dear wanted to be a mechanic and [pause] can't do that because he's ill. So I knew of two guys who owned a petrol station and car repairs and I went to … and I said 'You know something. I am going to ask you a big favour. This young man … it's not something that you can do … but because he wants to live out this fantasy, do you mind employing him and … ' one of them had a wicked sense of humour and he said 'Shirley, you're always asking me for so much'. So I said, 'Well …' And he said 'ok, bring him along.' And I took him over there. And he was doing little bits … and of course it got to the stage where he couldn't do … you know, so they called me and they said 'You know something he won't be able to.' And I said 'Fair enough. At least he's had a taste of this fantasy and you've been good to help him to live that through.' Unfortunately, sicklers at that time didn't live very long. So he passed on. And … We had from the organisation a fund [pause] to sort of set up a trust. But because I'd moved on from that I honestly don't know. And his father who was a sickler only died two years ago as well.

Tell me about your involvement in other projects in Reading?

You know the black mural, the mural along the wall. When you drive past and you see the nurse holding Mary Seacole? … that's me. [laughing]

Tell us where the mural is exactly?

It's [pause] as you're coming over the IDR, on the right hand side, where all the black historians are … Marcus Garvey, … Queen Nefertiti, Mary Seacole and a lot of history's on that wall. At the moment they're wanting it down because you know, the place is closed. I've got the video of the launch of that mural, I still got it at home if you want to see it.' And it was the days when Tony Durant was then the MP … a hard working man. So he's on the video as well. So she was very pleased … So that's … I had … been working hard on Mary Seacole as well.

Tell us about that.

Mary Seacole is [pause] she's a lady of colour. She was mixed race. Her father was Scottish, her mother was Jamaican and … her mother was also a … nurse looking after the soldiers. And she … wanted … she helped her mother so she wanted to do this in the Crimean War. And I've got the book actually and I'll give you the book so you could well, let you have a read so you see the history of it. Yes, she … funded herself and went off to the Crimean War. She was in the front line nursing all these soldiers and … mixing up her potions from what her mother taught her and helping the soldiers. And then being … the person, the business person her mother was, she set up her own little things of buying things and selling the soldiers to make them comfortable and what have you. And … in that time … she … doing everything she got broke. No money. So she came back to England and tried to get some more money and when she went back … by then Florence Nightingale was the known the person, but she was in the … background you see. Mary Seacole was in the front line. And she applied to … be trained with Florence Nightingale which wouldn't even give her an audience. And … they refused because she was of colour, but that didn't stop her.

Can you imagine in those days somebody being so strong? So … she came back again and it's a very long story. But … she died here … and actually they did a bust commissioned by one of the royal family's cousin. And that's in the book as well. She … Well two ladies were doing their PhD in black history and they started researching Mary Seacole and they found her grave in Kensal Rise Cemetery. So … they did a book similar to her own book Many Lands of Mary Seacole. We used go every year to the service and once we've found the grave. Now this grave was really … was … not cared for. And … Connie Mark, myself and Val Laurence and we looked at each other and we said 'You know something? Something's got to be done here. Now that we know we've got to do. Bring her name forward'. So that's how we started. We started off as the Friends of Mary Seacole. Then this year, at the service it was our twenty fifth anniversary of forming, we've changed the name now to Mary Seacole Memorial Association.

Well, that's going on still. Having done all that … Shirley couldn't stop. So Shirley … decided [pause] she's going to [pause] she's going to do … some other type of counselling. Cause I feel that's one of my gifts. So I was the first black counsellor in Reading again for doing … Relate training. Marital counselling and couple counselling and so on.

This was voluntary work that you took up, was it Shirley?

Yes, you had to be trained for four years. And then you'd give them back the time because they pay for your training. So after you've done the time then you've got to give them back their time and then you start being paid. So I started doing that voluntarily but, our folks abuse the situation, it's free so they come for a little while and they feel good and they don't even tell you they're not coming back. So you're sitting there … wasting an hour and I thought no, I don't know if this is what I'm meant to be doing. So I left that.

You were telling me recently you were involved in the carnival. How did you get involved in that? In the West Reading Carnival.

Yes, … this new committee that has been formed, I was also one of the trustees for the Barbados and Friends Association. I thought … now they … after we had the Mary Seacole the big year last year, … a lot of the members from that, the committee members are with the carnival committee so I was invited to join them. So we had a Mary Seacole float for the carnival … it was just a beautiful carnival this year. It's first we've had so many floats for a long time. Although it was raining and the weather was up down, up down, you had sleet, you had snow … sleet and you name it … rain. People were enjoying themselves and … yes it was very good. So we had our … sort of what we call … postmortem meeting on Friday and the majority of the feedback was so good … so we're heading for a better one next year. We're also now in the planning stages of another Mary Seacole event … for Black History Month again, which is just … we've just had one meeting with one of the people that are going to help us.

This is a local event. The Black History Month, in October?

Yes, and we're hoping to do that every year now … to … make Mary Seacole awareness known. And also other black history, historians in other words. [pause] I've got, as I said I've got the video of the mural, I've got the Mary Seacole Black History Month Video that we had, last year. I've got a photograph and the mural and the video of the children last year at the Battle Library and the Oxford Road primary school. Those children … the teachers are fantastic. They were so well informed that they were just answering those questions from the poet, we had a poet there from Slough. And he did all this teaching and poetry and different things. And those children was so … well informed. And as you know, I don't know if you know it, but that school has a lot of mix multinational children. It was really, really interesting.

You said that you actually appear on the mural painted on the central club wall. Did you have to pose for that painting? How did that happen?

Yes, the young man who did that work, he was then … lecturing, I think he's in Leicester or Birmingham. He's on the video so I'll remember his name when I see the video. And … yes, he … we wanted just Mary Seacole's picture on it, but it wasn't big enough and he said to me 'Because you're a nurse, why don't you come down, hold the picture and then we'll take a photograph and then put it on.'

In between that, again, I was a member of the Board of Visitors at Huntercombe Young Offenders Institution that's in Nettlebed, as I said before, children are my focus. Teenagers are my focus. And we are so fortunate that you say 'There but for the grace of God, our children are fine'. A lot of the children that are youngsters that are in those institutions, they just need parenting. Or they've got in the wrong company. So … most times my rule was being like a mother. It doesn't matter what race, what colour, what social class.

You've been involved in lots of different community work and you work in the community as a professional midwife. Over the years where do you get your energy and drive from?

Only the good Lord knows. I don't. Having just finished this one and finished the Carnival and … now embarking on the Black History Month, October to come. But my time of leisure is … plants, gardening, going for boat rides, I just get on the boat down the river … and it's peaceful and is calm. I will go up to Goring and I just sit there, on my own. I'll go for a nice long walk. That's my time. I do meditate a lot. I do get involved in my church a lot. That keeps me going … definitely. I do a listening group in the church as well for people who have needs. I do that too. But they're ways of having time for myself. I call it 'me time.' So I haven't got to be steeped in it all the time.

How long have you lived in this country?

[pause] about [pause] nearly fifty years.

And do you ever go back? Do you go to visit Jamaica?

Yes. But I haven't got any relatives there. They're either here or in the States. But … two years ago … I didn't tell you that one either, I'm involved in a Jamaica Diaspora, you know the links with England and Jamaica. So two years ago, I went to that conference there … There's another conference coming up in the next … two weeks … which some have formed the Diaspora group as well here in Reading. So that is up and running now as well.

Did you ever feel you would go back to live in Jamaica or did you always feel that you made your home here?

I have no ties there. To say, my children are here, my grandchildren are here … so this is home. I have no reason … to say well, you know, it means making new friends, it means having new people around. Where here … and there's me and I'm accepted as me. [pause] so this where I feel, you know, I … I belong. But it doesn't stop me knowing I was born there. It doesn't stop me going back … and … not only going back there but I see myself as a Caribbean person too. Cause I visit the other islands. I get involved in things with the other islands. Because … the world might look large but it is very small. If we take time out to love each other and to care for each other … it's a small world.

Jamaica

Jamaica is an island nation situated in the Caribbean Sea. Jamaica is the fourth largest country and the third largest island in the Caribbean. The Blue Mountains of Jamaica lie inland and slope down to a thin coastal plain; as such most of the major towns lie on the coast. The capital is Kingston which is on the south eastern coast. Kingston faces a natural harbour which is protected by a long sandpit called the Palisadoes. Palisadoes connects Port Stanley and Norman Manley International Airport (formerly Palisadoes Airport) with the rest of the island. Kingston took over from Spanish Town as the administrative hub of Jamaica in 1872. The majority of the population (about 90%) are the descendants of African slaves brought to the colony by the British in order to work the sugar cane plantations. By the start of the 19th century slaves outnumbered their masters 20-1, this led to a series of slave rebellions on the island (Jamaica was home to the highest number of slave revolts in the Caribbean) until slavery was abolished in 1834. Jamaica gained independence from British rule on 6 August 1962 but remained a member of the Commonwealth of Nations. Before that date it had had a degree of autonomy and since the mid 19th century there had been the emergence of a new middle class from the wider populace. The new found prosperity of the middle class took a serious blow during the Great Depression of the 1930s – indeed all echelons of society felt the repercussions. In 1938 there was a revolt by dock workers and those in the sugar industry, this led to the emergence of a competitive party system and an organised labour movement. Two main political parties came into existence within five years of the revolt – the People's National Party was founded in 1938 and the Jamaica Labour Party (who provided the nation's first prime minister, Alexander Bustamante) in 1943. In 1944 the first elections were held and Jamaica thus gained a degree of local political control. In 1958 Jamaica briefly joined nine other UK territories in the Federation of the West Indies only to withdraw in 1961. There is a large global Jamaican diaspora. Emigration from Jamaica has historically been heavy. During the late 19th and early 20th centuries many Jamaicans went to work in the banana and cane fields of Cuba, the Dominican Republic and

Central America. A popular destination during the 1950s and 1960s was Great Britain, primarily because of historical ties and Commonwealth law. When Great Britain tightened immigration controls in 1962 an increased flow of immigrants from Jamaica was seen in the United States and Canada (however, Canada saw its first Jamaican immigrants as far back as 1796 when Nova Scotia's small black community was augmented with Maroons from the island). The expatriate community still has a significant part to play in the Jamaican economy by sending remittances back home.

Ling

Born: 15th December 1972

Anhui, China

Date of Interview: 15th September 2006

China

● Anhui, China
○ Nanjing
○ Lancaster
● Reading, UK

I was born in An Hui province which is in countryside, which is quite poor. About the age of six, 'cause my dad was working in the city, so, and my grandma was living there, they brought me to the city, to be educated.

So, what would be the name of that city?
Nanjing.

Nanjing? Where abouts on the map of China is Anhui?
The territory of China is like a chicken or a hen. Anhui is somewhere in the belly. It is in the south, ye, the south east. And Nanjing is in Yangzhou Province which is more … developed, more developed and more advanced. So lots of people go in the city to find jobs. This is still going on for decades.

Do you remember the journey to the city at all?
I remember vaguely, 'cause my mum was not used to the cars, coaches. It was kind of coach sick. I can remember that she was sick on the pavement. My mum sent me to the city, brought me there.

Tell me about your family.
I have two brothers and I am the youngest one. [laughing]
My mum, my dad, my dad is my mum's second husband. In my, how to said, in my childhood, they always arguing. 'Cause my dad is eleven years younger than my mum. So they were always arguing, quarrelling, you know, that kind of thing. I have, I lived with my grandma for quite a while.

Tell me about where you lived, in the city.
'Cause my, how to say, you know my experience is very break down for quite a few steps. As far as I can remember, my childhood from the age of six or seven. 'Cause, you know in China, we count child's age when they still in the womb. By the time of child is born, she is, he is one. After the Chinese New Year, she is two even she is only a few month old. So, I can't really remember, in the Chinese style, calculation of age about six or seven, in Western calculation might be 4 or 5, that age. I can't really remember where I lived before that, then I came to the city. I live with my grandma. It was … not a bungalow, it was kind of a shed.

Childhood

Education & Training

Shed?

Yes. At that time, everyone is not that rich. Not like China now, there is huge gap between the rich and the poor. So that was the place I lived.

Was it just one room?

Ya, I lived with grandma, so that is only one room, and there was another, I don't really know. It's kind of, how to say, there is a small room. Outside its extended a little bit. So that's the kitchen. We didn't have flush toilet at that time. So everyone have a kind of pot. I don't what that is called, pot or, you know, you did things there, in the morning, took to the public toilet and empty there and wash it. I stayed with my grandma about the age of, when I almost start my, when I need to go to the secondary school. I don't know. It's complicated. Because, I have to go to the rural area to pass, my high, no secondary exam entry. Because that is my root. There is one thing called Huko which doesn't really exist here. I think only in China they do this kind of thing.

Huko?

Huko means that when we were born, we are attached to there. Although, you go anywhere, but when you … get married, pass your, when you want for the further education, you still need to back there, to pass the exam, or to get the bureaucratic papers, these kind of thing, you know.

Tell me about what it was like in the rural area. Was it different than living in the city?

To honest, I quite like there. Although it's not, it's not … as convenient as the city life, but … I think the people are very nice there. They are genuine, open, frankly people. In the city, I probably, I remember when I first entered the city, that is the memory I still remember that. I was in a shock because I have never seen so many cars, at that time not as many cars as it is now. And everyone close their door. I remember I … because I spoke the local, the rural dialect, and I, my parent put me in the primary school, I felt very lonely, nobody understand me. People from the city treat people from rural countryside, regarding you as ignorant, something like that. Not a very nice, not a very nice feeling. When I go back to the countryside, although I missed the convenience of the city life, but I found myself very, very happy there. There is one thing I have to point out, because I still missed the city, its convenience, something like that, but I was still lonely when I came back to the rural area, because I've spent so many years in the city.

So, what about friends?

I had one, I still keep contact with her. She is my first friend when I came back … came to, not came back, when I first came to the city. We were in the same class. She was … she is, how to say, she has the same experience, but not as, you know. She is a very very nice girl. In the Chinese Culture revolution, kind of, her parents, her mum went to the … because Chairman Mao asked the graduates, sent the graduates to the countryside to educate the farmer or the peasants, they don't have the chance to read and write. So Chairman Mao sent these graduate and student from the city to the to the rural area to teach the farmer to learn read and write. In a way it is good. That is way, although China was very poor, had a very low GDP at that time, but the illiterate rate, compared to African countries, the illiterate rate is still, is still OK.

So you were saying about her mother.

Ye, her mother went to the rural area.

As one of these graduates?

Ya. But you know, because she was brought up in the city, she found difficult to settle in the rural area. That's where she met her father. Her father was, a kind of the director of the, of the county, the village of the Communist Party. He helped her to go back to the city. Because she wanted to go back to the city.

You met her in the primary school?

Ye. I met her in the school. She was brought up in the country, in the rural area, but because her mum back to the city, and her mum split with her dad. So she's a bit lonely, we were very close.

Tell me about what school life is like in the city there when you met your friend the first time?

The schools … I think the teachers are very strict, compared to, you know, the children here … We had to, it is a different pedagogy, the teaching style. We have to listen to what the teacher says … to … and have to respect the authority. I am still doing now. Respect our teacher and some, anyone above me which I think I have to change. You know … The children are quiet,[pause] in that time we started our English lesson in primary school, about third year, in year three in primary school.

Do all the children learn English in school in China?

Yes. Nowadays, they even start from the kindergarten, nursery, which I don't like. I think for the children, I am not that kind of, how to say. We are, we need to respect our root first, you know, to learn our own language first, and then adapt to the other, second language. In China, if you can speak a very good English, and you get a degree, you can get a very good job. That is why the parents are pushing their children at very, very young age to learn English.

And your language is Mandarin?

Mandarin, Yes.

So you went to primary school and then you went back to take your exam for the secondary school. And you then came back to the secondary school in the city. What was that like?

I had to pay a lot of money [laughing]. Because, in China we call it Jie Du Fei. That means that you are not belong to the catchment area, you are from other places. If you want to stay this secondary school, you need to pay. Kind of contribute to, make a contribution.

Is it free to go to your own, if you went to the school in your own area? Is it free or do people still have to pay for this?

It says free. In China, we have Nine Years compulsory education, but you still need to pay ... other fees.

Ok, so how you did afford this? You said you have to pay. How much did you have to pay, for that education? Was that because you wanted to go to that particular school?

Yes. It is difficult for me to put it into dollars, into pounds because ... that was twenty years ago.

How much was that in Chinese currency, do you know, then?

Then it's about 500 Yuan. 500 Yuan for a year. That was still a lot of money. Well, my dad worked very hard. Like every Chinese parent, even grandparents they work hard for their children, for their children's education.

What did your father do?

My father is a craftsman. He taught himself to draw, you know, painting, craft this kind of thing. He is very clever.

Draft?

Crafts, craft, crafts.

Craft is making something.

Ye. Making something. He can make table, chairs. Like carpenter, but like cabinet maker, we might say. He design things and draw things.

Did your mother work?

No. She worked in the land. But after that ... you know, she doesn't work.

So he was able to afford to send you to this particular school. What was the school life like there?

It is like a water, I mean, doesn't have so many flavour, but you have to go through that, have to take it [laughing] ... I can't really remember what kind of particular exciting things.

Did you like school?

At first I didn't. I did it because my parents worked so hard, and just like every Chinese, you know. If you bump into a Chinese student in the UK, ask them, you know, do you like to study here, they will probably say, my parents work very hard to send me here, I have to do, have to do, you know, perform my best.

Childhood

You lived a lot with your grandmother, did you have much contact with your brothers? What was family life like?

My two brothers are quite older than me, much older than me. We have contacts for the Chinese New Year ... mid August, like Moon Festival, you know, big festivals.

Moon Festival. What is the Moon Festival?

Moon Festival, it's ... has a legend. In ancient times, there were ten suns in the sky. There was a hero, he just shoot, nine suns. There was one sun hiding underneath beneath the sea, so he didn't...then the goddess wanted to award the hero and she gave him the thing, take, kind of medicine. If he took it, he will not die. But his wife wanted to try first, she took it all and she became light and she flew to the moon. On that day, the mid August, the Lunar, Chinese Lunar Calendar, she and her husband can meet, but because she is kind of, up in the moon. On that particular day, if you want to have a relation with someone, you pray. [laughing] That is Moon Festival. Everyone, so, on the day, everyone is ... on that day the moon is bigger, brighter. If the weather is nice, you can see, admire that moon. It is kind of reunion, the hero and his wife. Like Chinese New Year.

Sort of romantic time as well.

Yes.

Education & Training

So, regarding your family then, did you, tell me what the typical day would be like at home or when you come back from school, what would you do?

In school, there was lots of homeworks, that one thing I should mentioned before. Lots of homeworks. With heavy bags, the bags full of books, text books and exercise books. It's a long, lot of homeworks. Because, you know Chinese people the emphasize on the education, that come from Confucius theory. So you have to, in order to, in order to promote yourself, you have to work hard, study hard. Because of Chinese educational resources were limited, so everyone try their hardest to get to the best school, get to the best university. Very, very competitive.

Do you have any social life, as a teenager?

[pause] We go out in the school holidays. But in the school holidays, sometimes we still need to work. Work hard, during the school time we can go to friends' houses, visit, stay there for lunch, or something like that. I didn't travel a lot. I really wish, in China, there is song saying when you have time, when you have the time, you don't have the money to travel; when you have the money to travel, you don't have the time to travel. [laughing]

Describe the landscape for me.

In the city?

Childhood

Yes.

Grey. Not so many greens in this country.

Do you mean no parks, or ...

There is some specific park, but it's not like here park everywhere and every ... what else ... lots of shops. You go every street, I think you go every street, if it's big, main street, there are shops on the ground floor, and the flats upstairs. And with the flat, in the front of the flat, you can see lots of clothes hanging outside.

What is the climate like there?

Climate. Nanjing is very hot during the summer. It is one of three stoves in China. I think because in the, because of the geographic location of Nanjing city makes a bit difficult for the cool air, a bit difficult to come inside.

Yangtse river goes cross. I don't know why it's hot and humid there.

Education & Training

OK, what age do you leave school, the secondary school?

Secondary school, about 18 years old. Because of my, my grade wasn't high enough, or I am not good enough to, 'cause the universities have second class university and there is first class university. I didn't go to the first class, I am in the second class college. I studied English. And just the kind of teaching English.

Jobs

And how long were you there?

I was there three years. And after three years, I got a job just to teach at the primary school. At that time, English, English education was booming in China. So that, the place I worked is privately owned ... college, kind of institute of languages, just teach children and adults in the evening and on weekends.

Education & Training

So there is state education, and then there are private schools and colleges?

Yes, that was the first, I think was the first one in Nanjing. Yes.

So you will have to be, have quite a bit of money for your child to go there, would you?

Yes, you have to pay, pay a lot. But you know, as I said before, Chinese parents will do everything for their children's education. So they pay quite a lot. You know, in my own, I only worked in the evening and on weekends, I earned enough money for me to get to another, second, another diploma course.

Self Sufficiency

So you were study in the week, and working at this school. How long did you do that for?

About three years. About three years until I met my husband and then I came here. How to say? He graduated after he got ... his Masters degree, and then he stayed in the city and then worked there. He was employed by an engineering, kind of translation and interpretation of the engineering and construction industry. I worked part time, because they need someone to type, at that time, not everyone has computer and know how to type. Because I earn quite a lot of money through teaching, taught in the school, taught English, so I bought myself a computer and learnt how to type. He actually, I typed his translation.

So what happened next?

We were out, not out, you know … kind of dated for a few months, about 8 months. And then he found, one day he told me that, he got, a scholarship from Lancaster University. And he said the 'I want to study there.' Well, in a way, I wanted to say: 'no, please don't go.' [laughing] … but … because I quite like him, although we didn't really say 'Do you want to be my boyfriend? Do you want to be my girlfriend?' we were not like that. But I said: 'Well, congratulations', that kind of thing. But he said: 'Well, what do you think? Do you want to go with me?' you know, that kind of thing. I said: 'Give me a week.' [laughing] So I shut myself up. I do not, He knocked my door, he phoned me, but I don't want to, I said: 'Give me sometime, I will to think about it.'

What were your thoughts?

[pause] In China, at that time, we think that somebody go abroad, it will get him corrupted, [laughing] in a way. It is not corrupted, but, you know, he will be a different person.

How do you mean? Explain that.

Different person. Well, I think, the foreign education and the foreign experience will make you different. Your thinking and the person you loved before maybe not the person, you know, love few years later. This kind of thing you never know. I was a bit worried at that time. My friends said: 'Well, you can go with him. Married him and go with him.' But in way, I want … I don't want him to think that marrying him just because he's coming abroad, you know. I don't want that. Then the other day, I told him. I said, 'Well, this is the thing you want, you want to do, then you should go for it. But I am not going to, you know, go together, you know, go to England with you. I want to, I give you two years. After two years, if you do not come back, then we, just a kind of finish'. Which is very generous, two years. He said, 'I will not let you wait until two years.' Then he came here to study, and worked very hard.

He went to Lancaster?

Yes. He went to Lancaster. Then about 18, 19 months later, he phoned me. He said that about Easter time, he had some holidays. He came back to marry me. Because, you know, in China, it is difficult for … the unmarried couple to, I have to get married in order to, in order for me to get to a visa to come to England. So he had two weeks off. And everything is shoo, shoo, shoo, doing paper work. Go to the authority to approve, for my boss to say: 'yes, she is allowed to get married.' [laughing]

Your boss at work?

Yes. My boss at work had to say she is not married.

Family Values

Oh, I see. Through the official demonstrate that you were not already married. What about your parents' attitude to marriage in China? What is, do they have any influence over who you marry or ...

I think because of, because I am always very independent from them. They kind of, whatever, whoever I marry, as long as I am happy, they are happy. We get married on the 20th of April 1998. And in July, I came to ... I came to England.

So you travelled to the UK. What were you thinking about before you made that journey?

Before made that journey? ... I would, thought about ... to meet, to live with the person that I never lived together before [laughing]. It is kind of exciting, and at the same time not very sure, but you know ... about England, I didn't really think more about that. Because I think it is the person that attached to the place that matters, it is not the place that matters.

So where did you fly from in China?

From Beijing. Beijing airport. Beijing to Manchester. Yes. Yes. At the airport, I had to go through lots of, how to say, the control, Immigration control. I waited there. The person is very nice there, people is very nice there. After everything sorted, he said: 'Your husband is waiting outside for you.'

Jobs

Education & Training

So when did you come to Reading?

Two year, Two and half years ago. I lived in Newbury for four years. After my husband graduated, he got a PhD degree, he found a job. We stayed there four years. During the four years, I had my, well, in Lancaster, before left Lancaster, I had my daughter. And then we came to Newbury and I studied in Reading University.

What did you study?

In education. Master in Organisational Planning and Management in Education.

Jobs
Racism

Jobs

When you first arrived in the UK, early on you'd been worried about him going and being 'corrupted', that's the word you used, how did you find life in the UK?

Life in the UK. It's ... compared to ... I don't really think it's a better life for me. It's difficult for me to get a job that fully developed my potential, use my ability. Lots of, you know, when we in Lancaster, lots of Chinese, you know, my friends, there were doctors, there were teachers. But because of the language barrier or something else, they couldn't find a job that really, really to use their knowledge. It's very difficult.

Community

So you came, when you came to Newbury, you had your first child. And your husband was working and you then, you began to study at the Reading University. Tell me some, tell me more about the life in the UK, and your thoughts about it.

I think because I have a child, the health care and ... the health visitors, kind of professional, they kind of very caring, very professional. Also, there are lots of toddlers groups. With child, you can easily make friends. So in Newbury, we, formed MOSAIC, that is an international group, we got funding from the West Berkshire Council. For the, you know, the people from every different countries, they got together, sharing things once, every Saturday, the first Saturday of the month. Sometimes we need people from the same experience, come together, to give support to other people.

So this is kind of multicultural group, of people from?

From Japan, China, Vietnam, Malaysia and Korean, we got people from Korea, Africa, Indian. And I am the ... event co-ordinator for that group. I am the committee member of that. I was very keen on it. I don't know what is ... [pause]

Tell me more about the support that you feel about that gives to people.

I have a one lady who was very ... I think it's a misunderstanding ... [pause] It is because of the cultural thing, she doesn't really say, communicate with her husband. She had a little child. She needed support, but her husband, you know, she doesn't really, she felt not very, she doesn't want to give another burden to her husband. Because she thinks sharing her problem is a burden to her husband. She was very, very stressed and very depressed. So we, me and another friend just to go to her place, to chat with, to talk with her and her child can play with my child. And just something around her.

If there isn't a group providing an important support mechanism for people, what happens?

I think would be very difficult. I have been through a very difficult time myself. So I relied on a different source to support me which it couldn't give me enough support. Like I relied on my doctor and my health visitor. Because at that time I had a very bad Post Natal Depression. [pause] So I relied on them, because of the cultural, again it's a cultural difference, I don't know whether I want to say, but ... I said, 'I love you' to my GP, which is a man, who was a man and he was panicked, he thought that I am going to have a relationship with him. But actually that is kind of gratitude of thanking for being there to support me, but that 'cause enough ... He said, 'Well, I can't look after you any more.' I was, What? I was collapsed in his room. It is like he was my last rescue, I tried hard to hold on you. Because I said silly things, you just, you know, that kind, in a way, I shouldn't do that, but at that time, I can't, I was desperate to hold on someone. So, and then, I found it is very important for us to have an own group, we support each other, we know each other.

So now you are in Reading. Is there a similar support group or friendship group that you are involved with?

Here, there is Chinese Christian Fellowship. There is a Chinese community here. And I am involved with teaching Chinese, which is voluntarily to help, you know, teaching Chinese for the people, the Chinese people's children, here, in Reading. We have funding from the Borough Council. And ye, I am involved in that.

Community

Education & Training

Jobs

Food

Racism

Where does that take place?

Caversham. Hill down School?

Highdown, Highdown school. Are there many children who attend?

Yes. Because Chinese … is Mandarin and Cantonese. They all say Chinese, but it is different dialect. Chinese and Mandarin, Mandarin and Chinese. So altogether about, I think there are more than a hundred students.

And why is it, why is the school there? What is, it teaching the children Mandarin? Is it because they are not speaking it at home?

Like me, I want my child to learn Chinese because that is my cultural and also because China is more and more developed, economy, become a superpower. I don't really want to say 'superpower', but the … the economic growth couldn't be overlooked by the world. So it is more and more important, for my child, to know the cultural and the language. Not only because that's my root, but also, you know, good for them. Even now, the British government and elsewhere know the Mandarin is, the Chinese, on the whole is an important language for them to learn, even the youngest generation in England to learn Chinese. So I think that is very important for my child to know that.

Now you have two children, so one is at school and you have a two-year old boy. How does your daughter find going to school?

She is happy there. She is, she is very happy. Because I was educated, you know, very strict, very pushy. I try not to do that to my children, but, in a way, I push him, push her very hard. I teach her Chinese at home as well as ask him, ask her to attend, take her to attend the Chinese school in Hill, Highdown school.

What do you think of Reading, as a place? Why did you move to Reading?

Because my husband got another job and also I got a job. It is easier for us to come here. But gradually I quite like here, because I got a Chinese community and even a Chinese supermarket. [laughing] Near Reg Vardy. I don't really know the name, but I know where it is. [laughing]

Why is it important to you?

In China, we say, you can change everywhere but you can't change your stomach. [laughing] You know, I am fed Chinese food for so long, it's very important for me to get, you know, that kind of ingredients, to cook real Chinese food.

How do you find mixing with English people?

I think the people are the same, you know, everywhere. You can, you get some nice people and you can get some nasty people, even in my country. Some people will say, well, being discriminated; you know that kind of thing. But I wouldn't think that. Here I met some lovely lady, very very beautiful person. She is English. But you get … I met somebody even in the, on the train. When I was travelling from Newbury to Reading on the train. Because

I was pregnant at that time with my second one. I wanted, I felt very hot, very dizzy. So I wanted to open the window. And there was a lady who was very nice, you know, she saw me opened the window and she moved from the seat to elsewhere. I felt, I said thank you. There was a gentleman, he stood up and closed the window up. I said: 'well, I need some fresh air.' He said: 'no, I don't want the breeze coming to my face.' You can get the people like that. You know, if you are lucky, you get some good people.

How do you see the future now?

I want to, I want to because ... a counsellor. Just to help, people from other, like, coming from, like immigrants, you know, help them ... to find, you know, to think positively about their life here ... I probably will go back to China for a few years, or, that's depends on my husband. But I will definitely will go back to China, you know. It is a, it is like the leaf from the tree, it always comes back to the root. Maybe when the children get a bit bigger, I don't know.

Have you visited China?

Yes. There is a version, a word of re-cultural shock. Re-cultural shock. When you go back, you come from there, and you spent a few years outside there, when you go back there, it is a shock. It is the development makes me shock. And I think every society has a dark side, you know, I don't really want to say which society is the best and I am not going to say England is better than China. The society is different, but in one particular aspect, I would like to say, I found England is much easier. It is an easy life than China. Because everyone has to, in China, has to very competitive to earn money, to get the social standards, you know. Here you can live your own life, you want to be, whatever you want to be.

China

The People's Republic of China is arguably the third or fourth largest country in the world. It is in East Asia and shares borders with Afghanistan, Bhutan, India, Kazakhstan, Kyrgyzstan, Laos, Mongolia, Myanmar, Nepal, North Korea, Pakistan, Russia, Tajikistan and Vietnam. Its capital is Beijing and its largest city is Shanghai. Since 1949 the Communist Party of China has led the country under a one party system. On the 1st October 1949, at the end of the civil war, Mao Zedong declared that the people of China had stood up and the People's Republic of China was born. The Communist Party of China took control of mainland China and the Kuomintang (Chinese Nationalist Party) retreated to Taiwan and some of the islands off of Fujian province. Mao led the country through a program of economic and social reform which was called the Great Leap Forward. The aim of the Great Leap Forward was to move away from the primarily agrarian economy to an industrialized communist society. The plan has been seen as an unmitigated disaster, leading as it did to millions of deaths and a fractured economy. As a precursor to the Great Leap Forward peasant farmers were coerced into collectives to maximise production and at the same time social reforms were implemented which outlawed religious and mystical institutions, replacing them with political meetings. In 1956 whilst the Party propagandists declared that the harvests were high much of the general population was plunged into famine. In 1957 Mao launched the Hundred Flowers Campaign which supposedly allowed free speech and criticism of the Party; in reality it was a ruse to out dissenters and nearly half a million people were eliminated. Between 1958 and 1963 The Great Leap Forward saw widespread implementation of agricultural collectivism in rural areas coupled with the utilisation of cheap labour to drive forward industrialisation. Huge people's communes were created and private plots were outlawed – the communes didn't just focus on agricultural production they also incorporated light industry and construction projects. Steel and grain production were the main focus of Mao's plan and in 1958 he visited a backyard steel furnace in Anhui province (at the behest of provincial first secretary Zeng Xisheng), he was so impressed with what he saw that he encouraged the widespread use of such furnaces. This project in fact produced low quality steel and also diverted workers from the fields; so the harvest of 1958 was largely left to rot in the fields. Between 1958 and 1960 China became a huge exporter of grain, but many peasants were left to starve. The following years were followed by a pattern of droughts and floods (including the Yellow River flood which claimed approximately two million lives) and famine was widespread up until 1962. These policy mistakes eventually led to Mao being replaced by a more moderate leadership (who were willing to listen to experts unlike their predecessor). Mao and his allies launched the Cultural Revolution in 1966 which sought to remove the moderate leadership and mobilize the general populace in support of Mao's ideology. This led to further social and economic problems and real change only came about after Mao's death in 1976.

Abduhl Sheikh

Born: 10th March 1942
Nairobi, Kenya

Date of Interview: 24th May 2006

Kenya

● Nairobi, Kenya
○ London
○ Birmingham
◑ Reading, UK

Can you tell me what your earliest memories are as a very young child?

Well basically living in an area where we had about three houses, one immediately next to us, no two next to us, one about 500 yards away, the next house was about a mile and a half and the other houses were towards the … river, come stream, I would say, during summer time it would of sort of become a stream and during rainy season, short rains and long rains, it used to become a river.

Apart from that it was, I would say just plain wilderness, not forested wilderness. I mean Nairobi is not built on where there are forests. You get maybe some odd trees, and lots of game which occasionally used to pop into our yard and eat up any flowers or vegetables that we had grown, I mean no sort of wild animals like lions. We used to get the odd hyena but mostly gazelles, birds, guinea fowl … an animal we used to call, we still call actually, Yellow Necks, resembles a partridge, smaller than a partridge though with a yellow patch underneath its neck. Very tasty bird, extremely tasty, size of a capon, more or less.

I mean in those days we were not, as you can imagine yourself, rich or something and there's no entertainment apart from once or twice a week the dancers used to come in dressed in the native costumes like, I wouldn't call them grass skirts, but skirts made out of either reeds, grass and with feathers around the waist and the headdress was that of a … I can't recall the name of the bird, black bird about a foot long and the tail itself was about eighteen inches long, beautiful tail and they used to have a lot of those.

Radios came in later but only to those people who could afford them. Our family was one of them which was able to afford a radio and I've still got that radio it's a very old Bosch valve model, still works, that's right yes, it still works, in excellent condition. The programmes in our own languages used to come in the evenings for about an hour or half an hour with songs and news, brief news, the world news and people used to gather outside in our courtyard and we used to listen to the radio.

The kids played, not English games … It's a game called gulli danda, it's a Punjabi sort of word. Basically it's a bit of a round stick which is about inch and a half this which is tapered towards both ends and a long three foot, four foot handle or a stick, ordinary stick, round stick. What you do is you dig a hole, a slight hole and then you sort of put your rod underneath it and you chuck it as far as you can. The idea of the opposing team is to catch it, if they catch it you're out and the next one takes over. If you don't catch it then it's up to you to go as far as possible.

Childhood

Could you spell the name of that game?

Well it's Punjabi word … gulli, pronounced as goolly not gully and danda which is a rod, is danda. I mean there was another game which is played, I mean in mostly the Asian countries and you can see from the television sometimes even now it's call Kabaddi. If you imagine yourself in … a small version of a tennis court with a line drawn in the middle and then you have two teams, I think there about six in each side. The idea is … one team, the first team to take a deep breath, hold the breath in and speaking the words 'kabaddi, kabaddi, kabaddi' continuously, go to the opposing side, touch somebody and then come back in to your side. If you succeed in doing that whoever you've touched is dead so he has to leave the area and sit on the side lines and if your team succeeds in getting everybody out, kill everybody you've won. The opposing team one person only, not all of them, whoever you touch, tries to hold you back so you have to breathe in. Now if you break your breath and you breathe in you are dead.

In the evening you listened to the radio, where would that be broadcast from?

In those days the station used to be called Cable and Wireless, in the western side of Nairobi. I'm trying to remember the names now. They are Swahili names you see and called, it used to be just after the Westland area, is still known as Westlands just after that there used to be an army base and next to it, because they used to have the armed forces radio and attached to it was the normal civilian radio. It used to be the English early in the morning then in the afternoons, and then in the evenings they used to split, the Asians used to get about an hour between six and eight I think. As time progressed, they split and we had our own station, English had their own and there was also a Swahili station as well but that was quite a while afterwards.

So going back, tell me, you were born in Nairobi, when did your parents come to that place and why?

… I can't tell you the exact year my parents came but I would imagine that they arrived there in mid-thirties. Reason of course being the problems in what was India at the time. They used to live in Lahore, the actual – you know where Lahore Fort is, the old city, my grandfather used to have a house over there and I think basically it was to, sort of get away from family problems. He got in touch with my wife's grandfather who used to live in the same area, and they then invited him, and they also helped him out in getting him a mechanics job. A company known as OMT, it was very, very famous in Kenya, a motor trading company, very well known. Eventually he opened up his own business, a garage in partnership with another man who used to work in the same company and that was very successful as well.

So tell me about you going to school. What was that like?

It was basically three hours, reading writing arithmetic, geography and all that, you know there was no calculators. We were not allowed anything. You must learn by heart. All the tables you had to learn by heart at least up to twelve.

You had to learn about history, the English history, Kenyan history and as well as the Asian side of history. Basically, generally speaking, the world history you had to learn.

Who were the teachers there?

Mixed. The higher you went the more mixed you became, but in primary basically there were the Asians because they could understand the languages and if somebody didn't, English was of course the official language. You had to learn, you had no choice in the matter and then you had a choice you could either go for your native language, either Gujerati, Punjabi, Hindustani or Urdu. It used to be known as vernacular. So you had to choose which one to go for when you, just before you went into the secondary education which is your GCE or in those days it used to be known as the O Levels or Cambridge, examinations, you know the University of Cambridge used to control the secondary education over there and the criteria and curriculum used to come from this country.

You said you had to pay for the schooling.

Yes.

East African Safari, c.1964. Abduhl second from the right.

Abduhl Sheikh on a hunting trip, 1969

Education & Training

So do you know how much that was?

I think the primary education used to be five shillings a month. A hell of a lot of money in those days ... and of course you had to buy your own books, You know the exercise books. The textbooks used to be supplied by the school and if you damaged it you had to replace it. That's about the only thing the school used to supply and when you got into the secondary education they used to supply you with ink. Powdered ink and you had to mix it with water. I've still got a small tin left upstairs. I'll show it to you later on. You just mix it with a little bit in there, it's blue-black ink. You had to use either a pen, with a nib and a holder, we used to call it nib holder or a fountain pen and in those days there used to tubes in it and a little lever. So you press the lever out and you would dip your pen into the inkpot and you would press the lever back and it sucked it up. Those were the things we were allowed to use. No Biros, pencils ... yes, coloured pencil, yes.

Childhood

What about the rest of your family. You were there with your mother and father, brothers and sisters?

Yes, I have five brothers and one sister in total and it's only recently that I've learnt that, I knew that a child elder to me, older than I was died in its infancy and I think it was only this year that I learnt that the first born child was a sister and she died as well. I've no idea how, what her name was.

So how would you describe your childhood?

… Nice. Very good memories, some sad, but … I would describe it as free, no restriction, no sense of danger, no fear of anything, secure and safe. Family life I would describe as very turbulent but most family lives are, you know, amongst the brothers and sisters. There were quite a few, sort of, I wouldn't call them fights, among us and of course most of us got a few clouts around the ears, you know, 'shut up' and all that, you know, children are there to be seen and not heard that sort of attitude, 'go out and play' but it came down to occasions the kids were there and whether you liked it or not you had to be there and the reason given that if you don't sit with us and listen to what's happening you will not learn what life is about so 'shut up, sit down, look and listen.' My father used to say a very wise word 'God has given every person two eyes, two ears and one mouth and the reason for it is to listen more, see more and talk less.' Very sound advice.

When you left school when would that be?

I was, I think, about eighteen. Fifty-three. I think it was either 1953 that I passed my GCE or the O Level, Cambridge. It used to be called the Cambridge exam with three or four O Levels and went straight into the civil service. Joined the Police Force and the fun started then of course.

What sort of things were you involved in?

Mostly it was … just general patrol in the car. We were armed of course in those days with 38 revolvers, very strict rules, extremely strict rules of when to use. In fact if there was a riot or something the first thing I did was to take the bullet out of the gun just in case somebody else acquired it, very strict rules. Robberies, but basically it was drunks burglars, people like that I mean in those days crime there was not crime like in this country.

How long were you with the police force?

Until I got the order of the boot. Got kicked out.

So how old would you be then?

Twenty-seven, twenty-eight. Around that time. 1970. September. First of September I think it was. Sometimes in September, I can't really say.

And what happened then?

Well we had six months to get out and of course in those days there was lot of problems in this country. This was the only country I could come to. No other country would have me. It wasn't my choice, I'll be honest with you, to come to this country. But because this was a British colony and I had a British passport I had no choice. Had to wait for a voucher system. I've still got that passport with me. One of the good or bad habits is that I tend not to destroy paperwork. I must have a clearout one of these days. I've still got that voucher business. My daughter, myself and wife, we came here in September.

So when did you get married?

'63. No we got, Kenya got independence in '63 … Yeah, yes '63.

Kenya got independence, I got married just after independence actually, in August 21st.

This was in Nairobi?

In, well the wife was in Mombassa and I was in Nairobi so we travelled over there, hired a house and of course our weddings are rather elaborate and took place over the weekend and then came back and that was it, I mean.

Was this an arranged marriage?

Well it depends on what you call arranged. I know my wife before we were married. Although there was no interaction as it is in this country, but the culture is such that in our sort of society we don't take liberties. We respect each other. But it was, the marriage was in agreement with me, I had to agree and I agreed and she had to agree and she agreed. We know each other. It just happened.

So then moving on to, you were saying you had to leave. How did this come about?

After independence, the Kenyan government decided in conjunction with advice from the British government that the civil service would be, what they called 'africanised'. It was run by … The people from this country, the local Asians who were born and bred there and Africans. And all of a sudden Jomo Kenyatta decided that everybody must be replaced and everything must be taken over by the African. When I say African, I mean black in colour. Those were, I consider myself, being born over there, I considered myself as an African as well, but a lighter shade of pale so to speak. But in their eyes I was an Asian. So the British government gave assistance to all the whites who were there. They were called expatriates. So they got their compensation for losing their job and all that. They got assistance. They went straight back very, very quickly. because of the international pressure that the British government said enough is enough. As a result of this Africanisation programme and because nobody advised me at the time that I should, had to apply for a citizenship, a Kenyan citizenship. One would assume automatically that if you're born there you're automatically a citizen. My wife is still citizen of Kenya. I wasn't. Why, nobody can explain to me. Nobody told me. So one day I received a letter saying that you're not a Kenya citizenship, you are given six months notice to wind up and go and that was it. No use fighting or doing anything.

And how did you travel here?

Flew. Oh they allow you enough money to fly. And there's £300 of your money the rest is mine. That's the attitude, so literally came in here with two suitcases, three bags, three boxes and it's only recently that those three boxes I sort of chucked out. I still had them up there. I don't know why. Just a sort of reminder, you

Abduhl as Senior Prison Officer, Brixton

Family Values

Political Situation

know. One contained a sewing machine, she's still got her. One contained my trophies, animals that I had shot. I used to be a good hunter there as well. Not for pleasure, for eating. I think there were four or five trophies. Some animal skins. I've still got them and one was crockery that had been given to us as our wedding present. Still got that. Three boxed, two suitcases, £300. That's all I had. No friends. Strange county. Cold miserable weather.

So you land at Heathrow. [yeah] And what did you do?

My father's partner had a cousin living in London, used to be a bus driver and fortunately he was there to pick us up from there. No we landed at Gatwick actually not at Heathrow. He picked us up and we stayed I think with him for a while. We tried to find a job. The police wouldn't have me. Nobody would have me with job. Got no money at all. £300 did go quite far in those days actually ... I applied literally every day. Got no help from the government or the social security, absolutely nothing ... Then I applied for the prison service. Sent in the application. I remember it was Birmingham. I went to Birmingham prison to attend the test and all that, passed the test, I was accepted and they said we'll let you know what happens next and then the bloody post office went on strike for three months, I remember that. No letters, no nothing and I was really, you know. I used to go round the local Pakistani shops over there. Clean their windows, clean their cars so I could earn something because that money was running, you know, running out. I could have bought a bloody house with that £300 if I had a job here, straight away, but one had to. She managed too because she likes sewing, she's a seamstress. She still does a lot of sewing. She managed to find an old sweatshop where she went down to sew anoraks for Marks and Spencer's so there was about £3 to £4 a week coming from there. No more than that. I managed to make about, what two or three pounds a week. Which is just about enough to pay for the weekly rent and to keep us in food and me in cigarettes.

How did you feel at this stage?

Awful. Depressed. That was the first time I'd come upon the racial prejudice that was in this country and the pressure was immense. People used to spit at you. People talk of racial tension here now. They know nothing of racism. Absolutely nothing to what I had to face. I got attacked. Spat at. Couldn't go into a shop, people wouldn't serve me ... there were times when I should pick somebody up and kill somebody. Dogs used to be set against us and I couldn't understand why the people called me Paki. I'm not a Paki. Why do they call me? I'm not black. Why do they call me black? Are they colour blind? I can't describe the feeling. I mean you've got to suffer this sort of harassment day in day out. Even kids used to come down and kick you. You couldn't do a thing about it. We go to the police. They threaten you. So what do you do. No friends. No nothing. It was something which I won't forget, but I learned a hell of a lot from that experience. I'm a person, if I decide to do something I will do it and I will prove that I'm better than you. This is the reason that I was the first prison governor, Asian prison governor in this country. The first one. Because somebody gave me a challenge as well, but we can speak about that later. But that time was tough and then of course, came the news after the strike was over and this letter came and would you report to Wakefield, er ... prison training school with a travel warrant, instructions and everything and what to carry what not to carry. So I spent three months there being trained.

Where was your wife?

She was in Birmingham. She stayed, and that is the only person whom I still consider as a very, very good friend. No relationship, but he offered her sanctuary and he still remains good friend and I don't forget people who help me. I never do and never will. That's something that stays with me till I die. I used to get salary and every month we used to be allowed, you know, three days back home. So I used to bring my cash salary with me and say here you are life's a bit easier for you. So things started to get easy. Even during the training, it was quite obvious that the instructors, apart from one or two who, sort of, took interest in me. It was a strange phenomenon, you know, different culture person coming in to join the prison service. Something new. I was the first trainee Asian prison officer, to join the prison service. Something unique, if you know what I mean and there was a lot of prejudice, a hell of a lot of prejudice amongst the students. There was some good ones there who became good friends, but I would say about ninety percent didn't want to know, didn't want to associate.

I passed with quite high numbers actually and I remember my tutor telling me that he was extremely surprised that I'd passed. He was very surprised I'd passed and I got posted to a prison called Coldingley in Bisley in Surrey. At that time it was the showpiece of the country. All electronic. Electronic open doors. Cells opened electronic.

Where did you live then?

In the quarters. We were not allowed to buy house in those days. You must live in the quarter next to the prison in case there's a riot. They had a big alarm in the quarters and if that rang you went. You know, in those days, very bad experiences in there, initially. Especially with the neighbours, with people coming down and threatening my wife when I was at work and things like that. It was tough days. But there were some very good people here as well. We made friends with one particular family. The wife met her. He was a prison officer as well. Brook, Len Brook, very nice man. The wife met his wife because she used to take the daughter to school and became friends and there was another person called Harry Drain, Dennis Johns, George Wayne. I wonder if they're alive. Some very nice people there as well, who eventually, you know, started to make me, as they grew to know me, they trusted me more.

So you're at Bisley and then how long were you there?

Eight years. But this is where I got my first challenge. A person, RC, I remember that bastard, sorry about the word. Came in from Wormwood Scrubs, one of the worst prisons in this country even now. He came in as a principal officer, and he became a training officer. He was the biggest racist I've ever met ... we were supposed to pass an examination, the principal officer's examination before you could apply for promotion. So I said I'll go and attend

Community

Jobs

Education & Training

Racism

Jobs

Racism

Self Sufficiency

training classes. He said 'I'm not having you in my classes and as long as I'm in here I'll make certain you never ever go above the rank of an officer.' So I told him, I said 'Listen Mr C, I will pass the examination without your help and I will get promotion without your help and then I'll come and see you.' And do you know, of the fifteen people that he's supposed to have trained, not a single one passed and I passed and I was second in the country with my marks.

Two years later I got promotion without his help. I became a senior officer. I was posted to Brixton. Didn't have much else choice, didn't want to go there, which is again one of the worst prisons, still is to a certain extent although it's better than Wormwood Scrubs. Ten years there and what I learnt in Brixton was good and by the time I left there wasn't a single person who didn't respect me and I was the first senior officer Asian in there. Got promoted in Brixton.

From Brixton, because of the overcrowding, the Ashford Remand Centre or Ashford, now was it a remand centre at the time? It was young persons prison near Heathrow, Middlesex. It was closed down so I was given the task together with the number one governor of reopening it manning it, to take the overcrowding our, because its hell of a lot of money, and closing it down. Those three years that I spent at Ashford was the best in the prison service, as far as I am concerned. They were excellent, I'll never forget them and neither will the staff. They still occasionally drop me a note saying thank you because the staff were brand spanking new from the school.

When did you actually move to Reading?
… '87, I think.

And where were you working then?
I was at Ashford so it was easier for me to sort of commute from here. About half an hour to Ashford in Middlesex, near Feltham.

So when did you finish at your prison service? What year was that?
Do you know, can't really remember. I think about three years ago. I know I was, I'm 64 now. It's more than three years ago, I retired when I was 60.

Your own children, we didn't talk about them. You have one daughter?
Just one daughter, yeah. She's a civil servant in the Ministry of Agriculture or something. Again, perhaps it's within in my bloodline or something, she was the first Asian female to be an executive officer in the civil service. She's part-time now. Her choice. Comes every Friday with the grandchildren. Always look forward to that.

How many grandchildren do you have?
Three.

How do you see the future for them here in Reading?
Bleak. Worrying, extremely worrying. The laws of this country bend backward to encourage criminality, lawlessness, disobedience. What happened to the religious values or Christian values? That is what's worrying me and indeed

it worries my daughter, sometimes she does, sort of, talk to us about this and I said well, you keep reminding them of good and bad and then trust your maker. That's all you can do in this country. Future is not very bright for us people and I'll be honest with you, if I didn't have any family, if I didn't have any daughter, I wouldn't be living in this country. The minute I retired, I probably would have gone somewhere in North Africa. Bought a house over there and spent the rest of my life over there.

You said before you felt you were African, so do you still feel that way.

Yes, I still do and that will never go away. I've lived in a sort of cosmopolitan society. I've been brought up in society where you've got every religion, every creed, every type of person that is in the world in that country. While I was in Kenya, never ever did I feel that I'd been discriminated against. I'll be honest with you, been here since 1970, that's about thirty-six years now, never once have I ever been made to feel that this is my country. In fact, every time you switch the television on you get a message, a subtle message that this is not your country. So how do you reconcile that with the fact that the legal requirement as well as the moral requirement of this country is that you should be allowed in this country. How can you be loyal to this country that it's telling you openly, covertly, we don't want you. 'Specially after the invasion of Iraq and all that. It all got worse. If any country wants its people to be loyal then it should treat them as its people.

I mean, have no doubts, if there were say an emergency outside now, a house fell down or a flood came in I'll be first one to be out and helping out. In fact I do go and help out in various charities. Only last week and in this weather I was up in Reading park making up baskets, free baskets they sell for East Reading and all that and I had a lot of excess spare plants that I didn't want to throw away from my garden. We sold them over there for charity, still do. There's no need for me to do it, why should I? But I still do it. That's because it helps other human beings.

Kenya

The Republic of Kenya lies on the east African coast. It shares borders with Somalia to the east, Ethiopia to the north, Sudan to the northwest, Uganda to the west and Tanzania to the south. The Indian Ocean lies to on its southeast border. Its capital is Nairobi which continues to be East Africa's primary communication and financial hub. Ethnically, Kenya is a richly diverse country which has led to tensions amongst the diverse groups. There is a very small non-African population (1%) which consists of Asian/Desi, European and Arab peoples. The majority of the population is Christian but there is a significant representation of other religions with 10% of the population following Islam and another 10% following traditional African religions. Kenya has a long colonial history. The Portuguese had a colonial presence there in the 16th century and the explorer Vasco de Gama visited Mombassa as early as 1498. The Omani Arabs took control of East Africa between 1730 and the mid 19th century when the Germans and the British took key ports along the coast. Germany held power until the late 19th century when it relinquished its coastal holdings to the British in 1890. At the turn of the

20th century work commenced on the Kenya-Uganda railway which opened up the interior of the country. There was tribal resistance to the construction of the railway. After the railway came more European settlers who earned large fortunes through farming coffee and tea. Although in the minority these settlers had much political power owing to their positive influence on the economy. With this political power came the exploitation of local labour which in turn precipitated a large internal migration to the cities. The Legislative Council was biased toward settlers (although ultimate power resided with the Governor), the first steps toward recognising the African populace were taken when Kenya became a Crown Colony in 1920, although it was to be another twenty-four years before Africans were admitted to the Council. In 1944 a multiracial legislative council was created in Kenya by Britain, this gave rise to African nationalism in the state as many Africans rejected the colonial notion of multiracialism. On 11th September 1952 the Mau Mau rebellion broke out in opposition to British and Colonial rule, the following year a state of emergency was declared (it was finally lifted at the end of 1959). The loss of land by the Kikiuyu peoples to European settlers had been one of the main catalysts of the rebellion, but there was also a general discontent over government regulation of peasant farming. The Mau Mau rebellion was a bloody conflict but it eventually led to African participation in the political process as British policy makers attempted to alienate the insurgents and their supporters. In 1964 (a year after achieving independence) Jomo Kenyatta (an activist who had been imprisoned during the Mau Mau rebellion) of the Kenya African National Union party became Kenya's first president (having formed a government just before independence). During the latter part of the 1960s many Kenyan Asians fled Kenya because of laws which prevented them from making a living – many left businesses and lost their wealth and homes because the then government refused to issue work permits. Tens of thousands of Asian Kenyans left the country and over 100,000 took up the chance to get British passports.

Shabana Sheikh

Born: 1950

Pakistan/Kenya

Date of Interview: 11th May 2006

We moved to Africa because my dad was in the army, the British Army, in the second world war, and he was in Burma and I think when the war finished he was retired in Kenya. He came to Pakistan, got married had two children and he went back, and we stayed there with our mum till he was ready to call us.

What were your earliest memories of your life in Africa?

When we got there, like, my dad, when he started with the army, he started working for railways, East African Railways and he was a stationmaster. He had a job in Kajado it was called, it was about fifty or sixty kilometres from Nairobi and it's a jungle absolutely jungle with all the lions and giraffes running around you know. Our memories are, getting in a big Land Rover sitting with dad and with his few friends and just going for hunting and we used to scream 'Oh there's a lion coming' that's all our memories and we used to really enjoy that, and Mum used to be sitting home waiting, she never used to like going she used to say I don't like this killing.

How old were you then?

I think we were like five and six but because we, that's all we saw as soon as we came to him and that was his lifestyle. When he used to do the hunting, the deer he used to bring it home and the servant used to clean it up and they used to barbeque with it. We just grew up like that and there was no schools there nothing, the shops used to be very, very far and it was just like the girls running around in the fields

It seems as if you had a lot of freedom?

Oh yes it was.

Did you feel a sense of danger with these quite large animals?

No, not at all because I think as soon as we got there that's what first we saw and like you know when children grow up with the dogs in the house or cats you just get used to it. We were there for a few years and then my dad moved to another place called Athi River and that was right next to the Kenya National Park. We would go running to the river and you could see big crocodiles coming out. One day we were playing with this sand you know, they take the sand out of the river and they make big mountains of the sands, and we were jumping one day and we just saw a crocodile outside by the river. It was a big green, dark green, you know dark with green lines on it and when we saw it crawling further we ran from there.

House across main Mombassa Nairobi railway line, where Shabana used to live

Wedding at 15 years old in Nairobi, 1975

Newly arrived in Reading, Melrose Avenue, 1966

Education & Training | Childhood

Tell me about the rest of your family

Well we stayed there in Athi River there was no schools nothing. There were three sisters and three brothers, the problem was there, it was no schools and my dad used to make us sit and study at home. I think I was about must be about eight or nine and I started to go to school on the train, the main train from Mombassa to Nairobi it used to stop there in the station, and I used to go on the train to Nairobi.

We had to wait till half past six to catch the next train and we used to sit at the station do our homework there and just wait for the train and sometimes fall asleep. Everybody knew my dad because, one he was in the same job he was in the railways and we used to get free passes to travel as well, anywhere we could go on the train and secondly he was a wrestler as well he used to do wrestling and everybody knew him. My dad, they never call him by his name, they always used to call him wrestler, and 'Whose daughter are you?' and then they'd say 'Oh the wrestler'. It was a good time, and that's how it went on and on and then my brothers started school, and by the time, my sister got married she was very young and she had to get married.

Was this your older sister?

Older sister, yes, she was a year and a half older than me. We knew the family, and well they thought she got married very young so they came with propose for me and I said no I still want to study I don't want to get married too young but one of those things happened, so I got married very young, I was only fourteen when I got married, and I moved to Nairobi then and stayed with my in-laws.

How did you meet your husband?

Well it was arranged, I knew them before because they were friends of my grandma, and his sister used to go to school with me and his sister, his older sister was our teacher in school.

You told me quite a bit about your father and his wrestling, was that in competitions?

Oh yes, in Nairobi he used to do and he was very, very popular you know.

Was he a very strong man?

He was physically very strong man, yes.

And tell me about your mum

My mum was a very simple lady you know very happy and go with the flow you know if somebody said anything she'd say 'Oh forget it, doesn't matter, leave it at that carry on, don't stop there,' she was a very easy going person and the opposition, my dad was very strong person and mum was very easy going and I think it was quite a balance in the house and Dad would do anything what we would say you know like she used to say 'Oh you've got your dad round your fingers' you know and I think all my grandparents they lived in Pakistan so he was the only one in Africa.

Tell me about when you went, when you were married and went to Nairobi, what was that like?

I got married, I got married in 1965, I was fourteen, went to Nairobi, moved there, lived with my in-laws and my sister in-law, Masooda, she was our teacher and meantime she wanted to go for pilgrims to Mecca and I think I was married only about twenty days, and she went for pilgrimage and from there she came to, came to England.

My husband, my father-in-law we were staying in Nairobi, the main thing was, is I didn't know how to cook, I didn't even know how to make a cup of tea, because we used to go to school on the train early morning, come home that evening, do the homework that evening, there was no time for cooking or learning how to cook and then dad had servants at home.

My mum told them that she can't cook, she can't do nothing so they said it's okay she'll learn herself and when they were gone the next day I had to cook, you know, my husband went to work in the morning and he says he'd be home for lunch and I thought, Oh my God! I said to my youngest sister in-law 'What shall I do?' She said 'It's your husband, you think about it, you know', I thought 'Oh no', I said 'I've got an idea what mum used to do, I'll just do that', so I put meat and onions and garlic everything in the Prestige Cooker, I didn't put no water in there, nothing and I put it on the steam. I just sat inside listening to the music, you know only fourteen years old. I could smell something and my father-in-law came and said, 'Something is burning.' So I went in the kitchen and I thought I'd better open and check, I went a bit nearer and I thought, it does smell, so I switch it off and checked it quickly, put it under the water to open it quick and the meat was black, it was all burnt, he says, 'What have you done?' I said 'I don't know, this is how they cook and this is what I did.' He just went off downstairs, he came back upstairs and said, 'I'd better go and get some more meat' and I said, 'Yes dad you have to because I don't know what to do,' I just sat there crying thinking Oh God you know I've burned the meat and I can't even cook, what shall I do?

So tell me about your journey to England then?

We just wrote to my sister in-law that, my father in-law did that oh they were thinking of coming and as soon as the baby, my daughter was about six weeks old in March '66 we came to England. They didn't have a car then so we travelled by bus from, I think from Heathrow to Cemetery Junction and I remember there were trolley busses then. We took another bus to Wokingham Road, we were living in Melrose Avenue. There were three rooms rented there and we came here, it was freezing.

What time of year was that?

Well it was in late March, it was freezing, I was so cold and you know when you are young you don't think it's cold, we wore open shoes and you know, no jumpers, you know sleeveless and all that, it was really cold, but I didn't mind because I thought you know we are here on holidays, make the most of it.

My mother-in-law said 'Oh try to find a job here and I don't want you to go back and your dad can come here as well.' My husband said 'No I don't like, it's too cold you know and I don't think I will be able to stay here I want to go back.' Then my sister-in-law explained him you know that is Kenya you know we don't know what the future is going to be there and it will be better for you to have your children here and they can go to better schools and you can have a better job and you try to find a job here.

So it was winter time and he couldn't get a job. He kept looking for one then he found a job in London somewhere and he went for the interview and he managed to go on the train and he got a job there and he had to stay there because he couldn't travel back every day, so he said 'Okay we'll find a room there and so we can move there.' He worked there for a week, he came home weekend and then he went back he did another week he left the job and came he didn't even give them a notice anything he didn't collect his wages he says 'I can't stay there I'm not staying there' he says, 'I'm going back,' he says 'Mum I'm packing and I'm going back I can't live here.'

What was the job?

The same this refrigeration and I said to him 'Try you know you might got a nice job,' so he got a job in Thames Ready Refrigeration in the Oxford Road and he loved that, they gave him a company car, a good job where he used to go to service the fridges. I said to my mother-in-law 'You know I think I should start working as well,' she said 'No you stay home look after your baby' so I said 'No you can look after it mum, I'll go to work you know I can help him and you know we can get a place quicker.'

So I started looking, you know for a job and there was a job in Frame Clothing and that was on Friar, no Station Road do you know where the Bus Depot is? You know the Top Rank and the Bus Depot it was there it used to be called Frame Clothing and it was a machinists job. There was no problem speaking English because we used to speak English in school and our dad used to speak a lot of English with us, he was more speaking English than Punjabi at home. The job was just keep stitching, doing the collars.

What year was it when you came here?

1966. Frame Clothing moved after a year to Basingstoke Road, Bennett Road so that got tough that's when the bus used to stop in Bayliss' then we had to catch another bus from there to the Butts Centre from there it was like running every morning.

Then I got pregnant again you know and I was expecting my son and you had to stop working, it was maternity leave and all that. I had my son and then I didn't go to work for a couple of months and then I said to my mother 'Is it alright if I go back to work?' She said 'Yeah if you want to' and then I thought I'm not going back to you know to sewing and I went to these agencies they have and I thought I will do this temp job. They said 'Oh there's a job in Racal Instruments in Bennett Road and as a clerk if you want to go' and so I said 'Okay, you know I don't mind you know' and I thought my English wasn't bad and I can read and write a little bit and as you do you know increase it so I went to Racal that was just for two weeks and I went there as a temp two weeks as a clerk and I stayed on there and they said 'Stay on' you know, so I stayed there till they moved to Bracknell.

I've finished that work and I went to was another Royal Guardian you know, Insurance in Caversham Bridge House I worked there for a couple of weeks and then that was like temping. I used to like doing that in that it's nice different places. It must be about three and a half years I was doing that temping job everywhere and my husband went to Kenya with his dad and after a year his dad and brother they all came to England. When he came back he couldn't get his job again, they said come in March or April because it's not the season and he thought he can't sit home and he joined the Post Office for a year about a year, two years until 1970. There was a big strike in Post Office and there was no work, everybody had to stop and he didn't know what to do and his friend, they just thought, why not drive a taxi.

He had a big car you know a Volvo Estate. He went and sold that and got two other cars and we just started doing taxi work. We got cards printed and we used to sit there a whole day and only one phone used to ring or there was days when there was no phone ringing at all. His older brother had a shop that was in Southampton Street and the front room we rented out from him. We made into a taxi office and I would sit and answer the phones and he would go and drive. Anybody passing you know we put the stickers in the window, and all that, one or two drunk people would come and he would take them home and he started building up like that and giving the cards out. It was very, very hard work. He used to sleep there at the office, he had a chair there he used to sleep in the chair and I used to go home and because I had two kids at home you know I had to go home.

So it started picking up, and then there was this really nice person and he used to pass from there every day, he had a room a rented room up the Southampton Street somewhere and he just came in one day and he says 'I'm a lorry driver' and his name was Geoff and he was a very nice person and he said 'I want a weekend job.' So he started working weekends with us. He was like a family he was like my brother he was so good and he was so nice. At weekend he used to tell my husband 'I'll sleep here at the office I'll stay here you go home get changed and dress up you know get ready wash up and then come back.'

Then slowly we had a few drivers coming in and slowly, slowly it took us a few months, six months even to pick up. The drivers were very nice but the public round, oh it was so tough, they would hit the stones on the windows and they would just scream 'Paki's just go back!' I said to my husband 'What's this behaviour we can't work here, close this office we can't do it' he says 'No I am going to do it, I'm not begging for the money I'm working for it so you don't want to come to the office you can stay home.' I thought he's just saying that in anger. I thought I have to do it with him so I said 'No, we carry on' and that used to be very often. We were for about twenty years, it kept on and on, scratching the cars, they would break the aerials of the cars and if they were passing they would just hit a stone on the window. One day we had this lady driver, they just called for a taxi she went, and she will remember, they hit such a big brick in the back window of the car broke and ambushed her.

Did you have many lady drivers?

No I was the first lady driver then we had another two lady drivers as well because there used to be a lot of people asking for lady drivers. It was in the seventies I remember the dates, there was Michelle Booth, she was thrown from the train. I used to take her to school and she would not go with anybody else except me. That poor girl she couldn't walk or nothing, she was scared of men, she didn't want no men coming near her. There was another lady she just wanted me to take her for lunch, you know, to the pub, sit with her, and if I said I didn't want any lunch she would get really upset she used to say 'No don't have any lunch, when you come have lunch with me' so sometimes you know I used to feel bad you know I'm charging her for the job and she is feeding me. She was very lonely person and there were a lot of people like this I used to carry.

These were regular customers?

Yeah they were my regular customers and they would just say 'Can you send Shabana' you know and I would take them.

You talked earlier about the racism that you suffered there with them throwing stones damaging the vehicles did you experience this in your life generally or was this just at the business where this happened?

It was just the business, I mean it wasn't like this happened this month and you forget about, it was all the time all the time we had that.

Did you know who this was? Was it certain people or was this kind of general? Did you know that somebody had a grudge in particular?

No I didn't know because we were, my husband was so good. At the Irish Club, my husband was the only person who would go in there and pick the drunk person up take him home and the manager of that club would give him the money 'Here is the money Sheik take him home' it was such a good relation with our customers.

And have you been back to Kenya recently?

Yes I went to Kenya seven years ago after about what was it thirty-four years, thirty years.

Why did you?

Because we still got our family house there and my youngest brother-in-law he was here in England he came for studies he lived here and he did his BSc then he went back and he's a teacher there now and he married a local girl there.

And what about going back to Pakistan have you ever been back there?

Pakistan I go like every year or every two years because all my relations my cousins are there. Only two weeks ago I took all my grandkids and my daughter-in-law and my son, we all went together because I wanted to know the roots mainly because of their behaviour and the attitude of children, they must know it is different, polite, how to be polite with your teachers with older people. You have to take them round and show them the world, look how people are living. We wanted to show kids, this it started, with my children and touch wood they are well behaved children never had any complaint from school and never had any complaint from the public. You feel proud you know when you know your children are good. I don't tell them but you know I know I'm very grateful to God and I want to do the same with my grandkids.

What do you feel? Do you feel you are Pakistani? What do you feel your nationality is how do you identify your … ?

If you ask me who you are I would say I'm just a human being right? And if you are Pakistani or you're English or you're European or Hindu or you're Sikh, any language, any caste, end of the day it's all one, it's all one God and the same manners for everyone, same attitude for everyone. We say, I am from Kenya, I don't know Pakistan because I was only three years old I'm brought up in Kenya and then left Kenya came to England. I've been in England more than anywhere. I've been forty years in England and I say am I English? No people don't say I'm English they say 'Oh you're a Paki' when they talk to you but I say I am a human being even if I'm Pakistani, but my parents are not Pakistanis they are from Kashmir, my grandparents are from Kashmir. So we are not from Pakistan, we are from Kashmir but it's all one. So to me I've never actually bothered me saying who I am, we just want to be good human beings and good people and teach good manners to the children and live in a good atmosphere, work hard work for your living I think. The attitude we always had but I don't know if I'm wrong or right but I have succeeded in that.

Michael Pollek

Born: 24th February 1954
Reading UK (of Ukranian background)
Date of Interview: 13th July 2006

Is it possible for you to tell us a little about your childhood?

I grew up in Newtown, road called 'Leopold Road' which was very much a working class area. There were lots of immigrants in that area, there were Irish in those days, Poles, Russians. There weren't any blacks when I grew up in 1954, although I remember seeing my first one when I was seven years old and I was quite surprised how curly the hair was. But my father, who was a painter, used to work down Oxford Road which is where a lot of the blacks in Reading settled, and he had friends within the black and Asian communities so that's how I got to meet with those.

What other early memories do you have of your childhood?

Well I learnt English at school, though I don't remember not being able to communicate with anybody in English, but I do know that I went to school at St. James' Primary School as it was known then, which is the school next to St. James Church by the Forbury Gardens. The Ukrainians predominantly that settled in Reading are of the Greek Catholic faith so that being the nearest, I was sent there. I remember going to school and not liking it and wanting to come home and I can only assume its because its I wasn't understood and couldn't make myself understood.

There was just my father, my mother and myself. We had two lodgers that lived in the house who were Ukrainian, single men and on a Friday night, there would be about four or five other single Ukrainian men would come round. My mother would do some sewing for them, or write letters, because a lot of these people couldn't write, she would write letters home for them. My father would play cards with them and I would sit under the table listening to their conversations and generally playing.

The Ukrainian community had a church service every two weeks where we would get together, I'd say there must've been about sixty adults living in Reading at that time of Ukrainian extraction and these people would've settled here after the war as displaced persons. There were camps just outside Oxford and one at Grazely Green for, as were known displaced persons, and of course there, there would be Russians, Poles, Ukrainians, Lithuanians, all the former Soviet Union people. They had to stay in the camp until their papers, if they had any papers, were processed. They were given menial work to do in the area, and I remember hearing talk that in the early days there would be groups going out walking up the canals, clearing the ditches of weeds and branches, clearing out the mud, digging and that, and of course a lot of farm work was done. Then as these people were trusted more, they were able to mix in the community but had to come back home to sleep at that camp.

Jobs   Self Sufficiency   Old Reading

Gradually they were allowed to leave and find jobs again within the area. Reading was quite a good place for people to work because at that time there was quite a lot of industry in Reading.

You had the brewery, you had Huntley & Palmers the biscuit factory, you had engineering works, so they'd find jobs, would have to commute back home to the camp, then would have to make an application for them to find digs.

I know of one family who, well a group of five men got together, made application, they saved money themselves to buy a house and they bought that house in cash, then, they carried on working, that house would be paid for, signed in the name of one individual, they would carry on working until all five of those men had finally bought themselves a house.

They would have to report to the police station initially on a weekly basis and then on a monthly basis to have their papers stamped and if they were wanting to travel out of the town, out of the area of that police station they had to inform the police station were they were going and then inform the other police station at that destination that they'd arrived.

My father worked at the brewery, he worked there for twenty four years before he was, took, well in truth redundancy before the new brewery was built. The house that we lived in was rented and I remember when we went through the papers that in fact he paid via the rent, 'cos there was no mortgages then and these people would've never been able to get a mortgage, he paid 650 pounds for the house which was quite a big house, three bed roomed house with a cellar in Leopold Road.

As a consequence of that and the work that happened in this area he had a compulsory purchase and he bought another house elsewhere but it was funny that the house that he sold that he bought for 500 had made these thousands of pounds which he could only thank, he was always grateful for this country for enabling him to actually a) live here and b) be able to work here.

Political Situation

That's generally the key thing with a lot of the Ukrainians of the community, is the ability of being able to work without the fear that you're gonna get a knock on the door and sent to a camp because one of the problems after the Yalta agreement when Churchill, Truman and Stalin signed the accord, a lot of Ukrainians who came from Eastern Ukraine were deemed to be of Soviet status and had to be repatriated. A lot of these people who were repatriated were killed. They were either sent to Siberia or shot as traitors out of hand

One of the discussions that used to happen at the camp, my father told me, when he was in Bicester camp was there'd be a long table with a white cloth and there'd be a, an English officer and a Russian officer and they would parade the people up and down and they would ask them the same question 'What's your name?' 'Where you from?' 'Why don't you want to go back to Ukraine, we've got a field there for you? We've got land there, your family's waiting for you?' In the early days it was a friendly gesture, later on it was threatening and the thing that was consistent about this was the English officer would never allow the Russian officer to be over-abusive.

My father, when Ukraine got its independence, I went to Ukraine for the first time and tried to arrange my father to come with us, he wouldn't, and I said, 'Well why? Why are you worried?' And he said 'No Hitler let me travel for nothing, I don't see why I should pay to travel back.' That was his sort of blasé way of dealing with it. I think he was frightened to go back 'cos he wasn't sure what was gonna happen when he went back home.

Family Values
Education & Training

You said that you couldn't speak English, what language did you speak-

We spoke nothing but Ukrainian at home. I remember when I was I think nine, again I was quite shocked 'cos I'd never heard my father have this kind of an outburst, because generally, both my father and mother and generally Ukrainians, and I know I'm generalising but Ukrainians have a respect for authority, and I think most foreigners do have this, in my opinion sometimes a little bit too much fear of the uniformed person, but if you get somebody with an identity card they give more respect, but this particular time my school inspector came round to say that there was problems with my English reading at school and they asked my father and mother what help did they give me with reading English and my father said 'I can't read Ukrainian, let alone English, why do you think I send him to school?' [laughing] And my mother was the only one that was literate, my father couldn't read or write. And I was shocked and horrified by his outburst but I must admit I absolutely agree with him. That's why he sent me to school.

Jobs

What was your mother's profession?

My mother, both my mother and father were born in 1922, they were born in the Carpathian mountains, they, of farming stock, my grandfather on my mother's side, my mother's father, he was a deacon in the church, so he would assist with the mass on Sundays. It wasn't an ordained position but it was somebody who would sing the chants, who would prepare the mass books, would prepare the documents, would be in charge of the writing process, and he taught my mother how to read and write. My mother only did two years of schooling because then she was sent out to work. She was the eldest girl of four girls and there was two older brothers but they died and we don't know what happened to them.

When she came to England she worked several jobs, all labouring. She was a cleaner, she worked at Crimpy Crisps, she worked at Ideal Casements on a packing line and then she became ill and had to give up work. My father, had a brother and a sister. He didn't go to school at all, he worked, my father's parents were butchers and therefore their knowledge was needed in meat and not in books.

Political Situation

My father left Ukraine 'cos there was, in, and I don't know the dates, the Germans had already invaded. They were looking for volunteers to work in Germany. There was hunger abound and when the Germans first came into Ukraine, they were greeted by the Ukrainians as liberators because what they were angry about, the Ukrainians this is, was the Russian oppression. So they were greeted as liberators and at first it was good, things did work out. And then of course the German position soon changed to what they always intended it to do, which was that the Ukrainians or the Slavs were only fit to be slaves or destroyed.

My father together with two others volunteered to work in Germany. His, the three of them were sent in cattle trucks, they were split up, luckily for my father he ended up in Austria, working in Austria for a very good family who

Political Situation

Self Sufficiency

Education & Training

Childhood

Education & Training

were just ordinary farmers but not Nazis. When liberation came he wanted to go to Canada and again get as far away as he could from the Communists. He had an opportunity of settling actually in that farm where he was working, the farmer was willing to let him to marry his daughter 'cos they were very close and so on. My father was just too concerned about the Russians and everybody in those days was just moving away from the Russians. So he wanted to get to Canada and got on the wrong boat and ended up in England. But he obviously thought when he got to England that this was Canada, how he would've thought that only a couple of hours on a boat meant he was in Canada.

My mother on the other hand unfortunately, because of money problems, she was sent into the equivalent, I suppose in English of service. She was working for another family, between five and seven miles away, as a house, general house help. She was taken by the Nazis when they came to Germany. That part of the war my mother never really talked about. Neither did my father actually, neither of them really talked about the war. I know that my mother became mentally ill as a result of what happened in the war. I don't know what camps she was in but I do know that she looked after German children as a nurse maid, she was very good at that and one of the things that I suppose saved her from others, was that she was very good at looking after kids, she had natural affinity.

You've related about your primary education, what about your secondary education?

I went to school, I remember one morning, and there was paper on the desk and a new pencil, and that was quite impressive 'cos I didn't think I had qualified for a new pencil yet. And on the board was written in big letters 'eleven plus', I didn't understand what that meant either, and the teacher started talking about not to turn the paper over, and I did, and he threw the duster at me which hit me round the side of the head and that was the beginning of my eleven plus, I failed that.

I suppose I should have sued the school for that duster hitting my head and therefore helping me fail my eleven plus [laughing] but in all seriousness, the Ukrainian community's quite a tight knit community and the priest, when I was twelve asked my father if I would be interested in becoming a priest. This said 'Well we'd like you to go to Rome to be a priest.' Well I didn't want to be a priest either but I looked at my father and my father said yes, I looked at my mother and my mother was crying. I couldn't understand why she was crying and I said well I don't particularly want to go. 'No that's ok we'll talk about it,' then my mother stopped crying she said yes you will go. And so I said ok I'll go. That would've been round about March, February time. Come July and the papers are all in and things have been signed up and there's a list, 'cos don't forget, as I said my parents, while my mother could read and write Ukrainian she could read a little bit of English but not a lot. My father had none, so I would do all the English stuff. I mean I used to fill in my father's tax returns when I was a young boy. All this paper work is now coming along both in

Ukrainian and a lot in Italian which meant absolutely nothing to anybody but there was an English translation to it and its giving us detailed instructions of what we were supposed to do about getting a passport for me etc, and a list of clothes they had to buy for me.

I seem to remember on that list apart from how many socks and shirts and stuff, I had to have a hat for the sun. Now I'd never worn a hat even when I was at school here I didn't wear a cap, that was a fiasco trying to find a hat for me. We didn't have much money and again in those days there wasn't, it wasn't as easy to borrow money as it is today. There was a new thing came up called the provident cheque which was were they would actually give you a cheque that you could only spend in certain shops and you paid it off, it was an early form of loan, but of course you were limited to what sort of shops you could go and therefore limited what you could buy.

They kitted me out and indeed I went to Rome, but before I went to Rome I said look if I don't like it can I come back home? And they said of course, give it till Christmas. Ukrainians celebrate Christmas according to the old calendar not the new calendar, so Ukrainian Christmas is January seventh, as opposed to December twenty fifth. I went to Rome, that particular morning it was an awful chilly morning, although it was summer, but a chilly morning, and the, my sister, I had a sister by then, this is in 1967, no six, 1966, so I would have been twelve. My sister, me, mother and my father walking to Reading station to get on a train to go to London, which was the second time I'd been to London, to go Victoria station to catch the boat train to go to Italy. And there were about 120, 130 other boys from England going to the seminary in Italy. The seminary in Italy had people from all over the world of Ukrainian parentage, the key thing was that you had to speak Ukrainian and you had to pass an entrance exam.

I'm not a priest, I could never be a priest. One thing that taught me, the training there taught me to lie, that's definitely one thing it taught me. It also taught me how unfair the world is and that, and in a way I suppose its thanks to that education I have, that I had that I do what I do now for a living.

How did it teach you how to lie?

Well because, for instance, if I, I was always upset about Judas. I don't mean to upset anyone's beliefs but I was always upset about Judas. If God is all knowing and therefore Jesus being part of the trinity was equally all knowing, he knew Judas was going to betray him in fact it was important for Judas to betray him because if he wasn't betrayed he couldn't have been crucified. But why? Why pick on this poor man? What had Judas done wrong? You knew from the beginning of time that this poor person would be picked on, would be victimised, would be, for the rest of humanity as long as Catholicism lives, would be treated as a inferior, even the term 'Judas' means betrayal now. Why pick on this one man? And I would ask these questions and the priest would say that's God's will, do you understand? If I said I didn't understand I'd be made to pray until I did understand.

Did you do your secondary education in Rome

I studied in Rome till I was fifteen, and then I came, when I came home, I finished my education here at secondary school. I started secondary school at Hugh Farringdon, when I came back I finished at Alfred Sutton because I really didn't want anything else to do with the church. I had my education that I had from Italy that bore no, at that time, no, had no bearing on my skills that I needed here. It certainly didn't teach me other than how to be devious and deceitful, how to do anything else. I worked in an engineering firm, I, for a time I was assistant manager of a shoe shop in Reading, I worked in a foundry in Langley. And then I met a girl and, kids I suppose 'cos that's all I was, I was just eighteen. We fell in love, we got married, and had a young son and I needed to have a proper job and I started working in Courage's in Reading, which is a brewery.

You said you didn't have a proper job before?

Well it was a proper job in as much as it was a job that paid me a proper wage, I didn't consider it a proper job because I would stay as long as I wanted to and if I didn't want to I'd leave. Like I said in those days it was easy to find a job, there were jobs everywhere. Now, I needed a job I could commit myself to and therefore to look to develop a career, because I had a family to raise and bring up.

So I got a job at Courage's and that was thirty two years ago. I worked for Courage for thirty years from the old brewery, and I'm sure you'll be talking to people who worked there, there are some other Ukrainians that I'm gonna try to persuade to talk to you who worked down at the old brewery, 'cos again it employed quite a lot of foreigners, and then at the new brewery here.

As a result of working at that brewery I got involved with the trade union movement. And then went through the, I was elected as a shop steward as a branch secretary, I was elected to sit on the constitutional bodies of the trade union, and really got about as far as I could go within the union movement and I, as a lay person, decided that I ought to put something back, both into the trade union movement that gave me the opportunity to do the things that I did and also to assist people that were not in the position to help themselves. So I applied for a job as a trade union official and that's what I do at the moment.

How was it that work, working amongst fellow Ukrainians?

Well it was funny because again, being white, we don't stand out and in those days people were very concerned about Asians and about blacks and really left us alone until we spoke. And then when people spoke in Ukrainian or you heard the Ukrainian accent being mentioned, everybody would be called 'Johnny the Pole' for a kick off, that's everybody's name 'Johnny the Pole'. People would sort of congregate on their own, I must admit in the early days I didn't like that, I didn't like that I was standing out in a crowd and I wouldn't mix with the Ukrainians. Made up for that since mind. I put that down to young stupidity, I just wanted to belong, I wanted to be normal, what I thought was normal. When I was a youngster growing up amongst the Ukrainians I used to pretend to friends of mine at school that I was Irish.

Children's Identity & Where Home Is

Racism

Again at St. James, a catholic school, you would have on St Patrick's day, the majority of the kids there were Irish, there were some English kids there, as I say there were no blacks, there were a few Poles, and there was me, a Ukrainian, I was the only Ukrainian there. St Patrick's day everyone would be wearing shamrocks except for a handful of us who didn't have shamrocks, and you stood out in a crowd and it was awful, it was awful, we'd be taunted, they'd take the piss out of us, they'd call us foreigners, I said I had a brother who was Irish, I clearly remember that that I had a brother.

My mother would come and see me at the gate to bring me some sandwiches and I'd hide 'cos I was embarrassed, I didn't want people to know she was my mother, much to my shame. As I say I, perhaps a little bit too far now seem to have tried to alter that position. But I can, this is again with the trade union movement, this is why I feel it's … when a group of people are joking about, whether it's a racist joke or whether its about somebody's appearance or somebody's look, the group will join in with that laughter. That doesn't necessarily mean that everybody's included in that laughter, and sometimes the butt of the joke of that laughter will laugh as well, and then will start to make those kind of jokes themselves about others, and that's the awful side of, but I mustn't paint the wrong picture.

Reading is a very tolerant town, always has been. Its greeted its migrant workers, its greeted its immigrant residents with open arms. I remember back in the early '70s, how the national front tried to campaign at the local elections in Whitley, 'cos they thought the Whitley area was a place where they could get friends. And they were ran out by the Whitley people. So no, Reading, but nevertheless you do feel that, not that, difference is too much to actually handle.

Jobs

You said when you worked at Courage's with the Ukrainians, did you feel you were part of the Ukrainians?

No, I, no I didn't. They were, although I was eighteen, nineteen, and they would have been in their forties, they seemed to have always been old, they were always old. And they would just get on with their work, do their work to the best of their ability, do some more, 'cos this was labouring work, this was menial work. They would do their work, they wouldn't muck about, they wouldn't joke, and then they'd go home. I would see my father, I was alright with him, but he was unique. I know every son says their father's unique but, he was unique. He was generally a cosmopolitan man. I remember him bringing home Asian sweets the Gelabi. I remember him bringing those home when you couldn't buy them in the shops and he was saying try it. My father respected everybody and said everybody's entitled to a chance and everybody's entitled to be respected, irrespective of colour, creed, in fact he said some of the worst people he knows are Ukrainian [laughing] just because you're Ukrainian doesn't make you a good person, its who you are that makes you a good person.

Family Values

But, getting back to the purpose of this, the Ukrainians were able to settle in Reading because there was the employment and then we set up a community home, which I must admit in the early days I wasn't part of, but later on I did get involved and I'm now the club secretary, and there's talk about me being

Community

Children's Identity & Where Home Is

head of the association here in Reading which, given the pressures of work I'm not sure I'll be able to do, however, unfortunately, our youngsters don't seem to be, they seem to become too cosmopolitan [laughing] they don't appear to be wanting to take as much interest in things Ukrainian, other than when Ukraine are playing football, or at Ukrainian Christmas. [laughing]

Wasn't it difficult for you that you didn't belong when you were at school and also when you were working?

Yeah, yeah that was a problem and its only just recently, funnily enough, or maybe that's why I'm member of a trade union because that's my desire to belong to something grand. Although as a young person, I certainly didn't like my own company, were now I quite enjoy my own company [laughing]. But the, no that's absolutely true, I've always been singled out even amongst the Ukrainian community here in Reading. We would get together, 'cos there are kids my age around and, there was a dance group, there was a choir, I haven't got a musical inclination but I can remember things so I used to recite poetry. So we would go on, we'd have festivals in Leicester De Monfort Hall there on an annual basis take part in like aconcert, and I would go up there and that was quite, 'cos I was the only one in Reading that did that although we had a dance group, we had a choir, I was the only one that declaimed vershes (ph), 'vershes' – that's a Ukrainian word, er, poems and that was deemed to be a high brow thing to do which was something that my mother said I was always born to do. {laughing}

You've also mentioned about meeting a lady and getting a steady job.

Part of the wanting to belong, and not really wanting to belong to the Ukrainian movement, I suppose, she was English, she was Irish actually, half Irish, half English. One of the things, there weren't many Ukrainian girls around and those Ukrainian girls that were around were obviously … monitored closely by their parents, and as when I was when I was a child growing up in Newtown, I couldn't do anything wrong, whether it be English parent or Ukrainian parent, you'd play out in the streets, you do something wrong, eventually it gets back to your father 'cos everybody knows who you are. It's the same in the Ukrainian community, you're a tight knit community, even though for instance we've got a big, big group in this country in Bradford, Manchester, all that area, I just wanted to get away from everything Ukrainian.

And that's, I think that's a sign of my immaturity and not yet coming to terms with who I was. So I married this girl, we lived at home for a while, till I was able to get a house. Unfortunately that didn't last, again we married too young, we had two children. But my two boys have taken on an interest in things Ukrainian, although they were born here. They knew my mum and dad, but other than that, but they've taken an interest in things Ukrainian so much that we went to Ukraine for Christmas, my eldest lad enjoyed himself very much over there [laughing].

Why do you think your relationship did not last?

I think we were just too young and shouldn't have got married. Its nothing more than that.

Ok. And what about your experiences while you were still working within the trade union itself, when you were still employed?

It was just a standard, nothing at all to do with my background as a Ukrainian, it was just me being an ordinary guy working in an ordinary environment defending people from a lay position, disciplinaries that sort of thing. Of course now, as a union official, I play a much bigger role in that and part of my duties now, my Ukrainian background is helping 'cos its not just about Ukrainians, I'm able to help Polish people, a lot because Polish and Ukrainian's very similar, the language, so we can communicate. So I'm helping Poles to try and integrate and actually helping them not become the new abused.

Do you feel that you've been accepted here-

Oh yes, oh yes, yes. One thing again in Reading, Reading didn't have a problem with me as a Ukrainian as I thought it did have, the problem was always me and mine, so I've been accepted everywhere I went and any perceived slights were my own. So the interesting thing now though is that the Ukrainians seem to have accepted me as a Ukrainian, this is the old Ukrainian hierarchy, they've forgiven me for not being their priest and they've, they seem to accept me more readily than what they did before [laughing] because when I first came back from Italy they were quite angry 'cos they had high expectations of me being their priest.

One thing they would say, and this is where I'm not sure if its specific to Ukrainians or generally [laughing] all people that live in a foreign land, they would call me English, they would say what do you know about Ukraine? You weren't born there, you were born here, you're English. Well of course that's true in that, not that I'm English, I'm British, but what do I know about Ukraine? No I've never been there, this was at the time when I was younger. But then when I'd go amongst my friends, they would call me the foreigner but now, I would be insulted by it but they wouldn't.

I mean my surname Pollek, my actual real name is Pull-yek. The trouble is that my father, 'cos he couldn't spell, when he was asked his surname, said Pollyek, the immigration official couldn't spell the sound that he was making so he spelt P-O double L E-K, not even a C in it, so all my life I had to try and teach people how to spell Pollek without an O on the end, without a C in it, and that it isn't a swear word. So I had as much trouble with my surname as an indicator to my difference from the ordinary people. But the Ukrainians said that you're not Ukrainian and my story would be that if a cow is born in a pig sty, does that make it a pig? No it doesn't, its still a cow and therefore were as I was born here, I'm still a Ukrainian.

You've spoken about your sons and your own background, that you spoke Ukrainian. Did you speak to your children in Ukrainian?

I did in the early days and fortunately when my youngest, my eldest son started speaking and he spoke in Ukrainian and his mother couldn't understand him, she got very angry, and said look, 'cos obviously he's growing up in the Ukrainian community and a Ukrainian home and she was saying that if he learns Ukrainian before he speaks English I'm not gonna be able to speak to him. Well I was stupid for listening to her because from then on I spoke to my lad in English and asked my parents not to speak to him in Ukrainian. Now he regrets that, he regrets that because, and funnily enough he's got a son who we're teaching Ukrainian so its skipped a generation but the youngster's learning Ukrainian.

Ok. How do you see your role within this society?

Well I ... I've got a sense of gratitude to England, specifically for allowing my mother and father to stay here, for allowing, and I know I suppose that sounds silly really but of course if they hadn't let my mother and father stay here I certainly wouldn't have been born here. So I have a multiple, lots of reasons of being grateful for that.

However that said, we have new Ukrainians coming into this country who are for what ever reason, finding it difficult getting work permits etc, there is a subculture appearing where they will become Poles, or they'll become, generally they'll become Poles in order to be able to work here and then send money back home because of the problems that are happening in Ukraine. Now I see my responsibility here to try and actively change that in what limited way I possibly can, certainly within the auspices of the Transport and General Workers Union, not just about Ukrainians, although that would be my specific thing I'd be looking at, but generally the principle of all workers being able to come over here and freely work and contribute to the society that they live in.

I'd like to be able to thank, by that way thank the English people for allowing my Ukrainian family to stay here, in turn get the Ukrainian people to understand their obligation to other Ukrainians and therefore develop that. Not to be in an insular, 'I'm alright Jack, I'm fine, I'm not worried about you.' So my, and that then would develop further on because I'm not a one-trick pony I'm not blinkered its not just the Ukrainians although that's my specific field of interest, that's an accident of my birth. But generally, and of course assist my family, to be able to take a bigger interest in all things Ukrainian.

Ukraine

Ukraine is a country in Eastern Europe. It shares borders with Belarus, Hungary, Moldova, Poland, Romania, Russia and Slovakia; it has coastlines on the Black sea and the Sea of Azov to the south. Its capital and largest city is Kiev which is in the north of the country and lies on the Dnieper River. Ukraine largely lies on the Pontic steppe and is characterized by fertile plains which are crossed by several rivers including the Dnieper, Seversky Donets, Dniester which flow into the Black Sea and the Sea of Azov. In the west of the country lie the Carpathian Mountains. The territory which forms present-day Ukraine was once the centre of the East Slavic civilization which formed the state of Kievan Rus. Over the centuries this territory was divided between various regional powers at the hands of the Cossacks and under Austro-Hungarian rule. It had a brief spell of independence between 1917 and 1921. After the Russian Revolution of 1917 Ukraine became one of the founding Soviet Republics in 1922. During World War II some of Ukrainian nationalist underground (who formed the Ukrainian Insurgent Army) felt that they had been ignored by all sides and so fought both the Nazis and the Soviets (although there were some who collaborated). In the western part of the country some viewed the Germans as liberators as they had only been recently occupied by the Soviets; however, this feeling was short lived as the Nazis committed genocide against the Jewish population and deported many Ukrainians to Germany to work. It has been estimated that between five and eight million Ukrainian citizens lost their lives during the war. At the end of World War II Ukraine's borders were extended to the west, taking on territory formerly held by Poland. Further expansion occurred in 1954 when the Crimea became part of Ukraine.

Pansang Tamang

Born: 1st August 1951

Nepal

Date of Interview: 29th August 2006

● Kathmandu, Nepal
○ Southall
● Reading, UK

I was born in a village close to the Himal which is the mountain ranges and its four hours journey from Kathmandu .

I'd like to ask, what are your earliest, from a very young child, what is your earliest memory of where you lived?

Ours a very picturesque village, they were they weren't any tourist here that travelled through the village because there was no path way there was another path way they took that sort of went all the way round the village so no there weren't many tourists where I was. Also the Tibetan, there was a lot of Tibetan tradesmen coming through that area.

And what can you describe when you say 'picturesque', can you describe the scenery?

It's a very, it's a village in the jungle, within the jungle, and all around the jungle you can see the mountain ranges.

Is this quite high up?

Its very high up, approximately 2,000 feet.

And thinking back as a young child, what sort of thing, can you remember?

At that time we women weren't taught, there were no schools in the area. The boys did go to school, some of the boys went to school but they had to go further away to learn.

What did you do as a young girl? If you weren't at school what would you do in a typical day?

At home doing the chores and housework. When I was seventeen I got married and then went to Kathmandu.

So going back to the village life, what about the family? How many brothers and sisters?

Seven big brothers, sorry, six older, one younger, and one older sister. Nine in total.

And what did your father do? And what did your mother do for a living?

Farming.

What sort of things would be farmed there?

Flour, corn on the cob, rice of course which they grow. All hand there's no machinery there.

Community

Childhood

Who would do the farming? Did the family, did the children help with the farming?

Everybody helped. Children, whatever they could do did. The ones that couldn't do the actual physical work would help with giving water, bringing food and so on to the ones that were working.

And you said 'a small village', how many people lived there?

There was one thousand homes at that time there, but when we talk about villages in Nepal, you've got one village there, you could have a river there and there'd be another, it'd be regarded as a village, it could only be sort of, you know, couple hundred yards or so but it would be regarded as another village.

How would you describe family life as a child?

They didn't have hospital facilities and so on, everyone was born at home. The eldest, whoever was the eldest would look after the younger ones until they got to an age where they could actually go and work for themselves. Mother made all the food, the eldest went, the ones that were old enough went to work and all the other smaller children would be looked after at home either by the mother or the next oldest adult/child.

Family Values

What's the main difference between family life there in those days and family life now?

It was a lot more hardship over there but food wise it was always fresh it was always plentiful because it was provided. Over here there's 'yours', 'mine', over there wasn't so much of, there was more sharing involved.

What would happen if somebody was ill?

If someone was ill they'd stay at home, they'd have certain knowledge about medicines which were available from the plants there, which they'd use and all the family would help to look after the ill member.

Education & Training

OK so when you were seventeen you said that you got married, how did that happen? Where did you meet your husband?

My husband was from a village two hours away walking distance but he'd moved to Kathmandu to study, learn, read, to go to school. And then I got married and went to Kathmandu. It was an arranged marriage.

So your parents arranged this marriage with his parents. What was his name?

Yeah the two parents had to arrange it.

So, you got married in your village and what happened next?

At that time, my husband was working seven until ten he went toschool, in the morning and then he worked at the king's palace ten till five. He used to arrange the, take the food to King Birendra.

How did he get that job?

It was advertised in the paper that whoever passed their SLC which is 'school leavers certificate' which is similar to the GCSE over here, then these jobs were available. And he applied for the job and he got it

So he was studying and working at the same time, and this was in Kathmandu, so you had to move to Kathmandu from your village, andhow did you find that move? What was it like for you?

It was nice because I'd never ridden cars or vehicles before, there weren't any in the village, you had them in Kathmandu. In the village they didn't actually speak Nepali, they spoke a dialect called Tamang which was my own clan's language as it were.

Was that a problem for you?

Yeah I didn't know it at first, but it was very difficult, but because everyone spoke it in Kathmandu, I picked it up.

You said it was four hours from your village to Kathmandu - how did you travel when you left home?

Four hours in a vehicle - it took about six days to walk. Now they've roads to the village and they've got electric aswell.

So for a six day journey on foot, what would you take with you?

You'd walk for five or six hours then stop. Tourists used to walk for six hours and stop, we used to walk for fifteen hours before we stopped. You'd stop, normally knock on someone's door and they'd have some food there and so on, someplace, someone would provide shelter. You'd carry your own blankets and stuff but you'd knock on the door and someone would provide you with shelter.

The first time I went from her village to Kathmandu, it took me thirteen days.

How old were ...

Thirteen years.

Thirteen days and thirteen years old.

[laughing]

Where did you live in Kathmandu when you got there?

We stayed in a place in Mukundo. We stayed there for four years. And then Shyam my son was born and my husband had to go with the king who was touring, round Nepal so I stayed with an aunt. Then after another son was born.

Was he still studying, your husband as well?

He graduated and then stayed with the king to work. And then when my husband came back, then they bought a house.

Working for the king, what was the pay?

270 a month although the position he was in was regarded as quite high up. I mean at that time before we were paying rent for fifteen Rupies per month.

Fifteen Rupies a month and being paid 270 Rupies a month, so that was very good.

At that time that was very, very good. Whenever people used to come from the village that they were from they used to send them their rice and vegetables as well so they were able to save money and buy a house. And then sometime in 1974 my husband came to the UK.

Basically he wanted to come over here to work, his friend organised a work permit for him to work in a restaurant in Southall.

After two years he brought me over. We stayed in Southall a year and a half, then Ealing Broadway for a year, and then my third son was born born at Hillingdon hospital.

So, going back a bit, your husband who was working for the king, a good highly paid job, what made him decide he wanted to come to the UK?

There was four of my husband's friends all worked at the palace at the same time, one of the friends became a lawyer, studied there, one became a doctor, the other two which was including my husband wasn't able to study. Because he wasn't able to study and had two children, he worked at a hotel at night so he worked the king in the daytime, nine till five for the king and six till twelve. Well, someone had reported that my husband was working there, I don't know why. It wasn't allowed, I assume it was, well it wasn't allowed anyway. And that's why he decided to not work for the king and do something else and that's when he got in touch with his friends who organised a work permit for him to work in the UK.

What did you think England would be like before you came?

Well when I moved from the village to Kathmandu it was much better, and then I thought the same thing would be when I came over.
[laughing]

And when you did come here, what was your first impression? What time of year did you arrive in the UK?

Very cold, it was snowing, I came over in December and then inFebruary, my third son was born.

So quite heavily pregnant, and you arrived and it was snowing in December, and what was your first impression of England?

When I came over it was snowing, it was very, very dark, very cold, and my husband came and picked us up, took us to a room in Southall. We had one room in one house, and then after hehad dropped me and everyone else off he went to work. And then he came back with a takeaway from the restaurant a little bit later. I didn't really like it that much because when I was in the village I had my family, food was plentiful, I understood everything, and when came over I couldn't understand Hindi either or English.

Jobs

Old Reading

Self Sufficiency

Tell me about coming to Reading

Five years were in Southall that's the limit of time on the work permit. After five years he told the boss of the restaurant he was working at that he'd like to go and do his own business and he went into partnership with the other three partners that already existed at the Ealing Tandoori.

Because my husband wasn't a smoker, drinker, card player, they had a fight, the partners had a fight and my husband got out of the partnership. They said 'you've got three children, where are you gonna go?'

So why Reading?

He'd been looking around for businesses at that time and one the businesses that was going for sale was the Star of India which was on the Caversham road actually, just opposite 'TG1's, there's new, obviously some new big office buildings there at the moment. They wouldn't sell the restaurant but they said they would give it on rent.

When the restaurant was ... when we took it over there was no business at all, and the rent was a hundred and fifty a week.

So this was your husband, he rented the Star of India-

So my husband went back five days later to the partnership he'd left and told them that he was leaving, he wanted his share of the profit, they owed him a thousand pounds which he'd put in at the very beginning, out of that they only paid him five hundred. When he went back he called upon- my brother was working in Southall as well so he brought him over to the Star of India to be his partner.

So with his five hundred pounds he rented the Star of India and started this, running this restaurant. It took about a year, we changed the menu. After one year when the business started picking up and so on, the landlord took the restaurant back. So at that time this was in a café, Joe's café. Machines, I think arcade game machines. So we started looking at this place.It would be one four three Caversham Road at that time. And we changed this café after a year to the Standard Tandoori.

Did you buy the English café?

At that time the café that was here they bought it for twenty five thousand. It was, can't remember exactly but it was somewhere around there.

Was that a lot at the time or ...

At that time that was a hell of a lot of money. At that time a vegetable curry was 60p. On the first day of the opening day from ten till twelve all the food was free. At that time there weren't any other restaurants, there was one – the Istanbul in town. When they opened this one the two restaurants that were in Reading closed.

Why was, why did you give the food free?

My husband, he knew a lot of people by that time in Reading and he'd invited them all as a promotional thing for the restaurant to get, just as an opening day thing.

Community

Jobs

Old Reading

Education & Training

Old Reading

Going back then, when you came to Reading and, your husband was working in the Star of India where were you living as a family?

There were four rooms above the Star of India, and after when we bought this there was rooms on top of this place. When I came over here I didn't know much English, so there was two people called Elaine and Chris who now works at the BBC I think, Elaine works in the library.

Elaine Bradshaw? Scottish ...

Yes, yeah. She came at nine o'clock, nine till ten she used to come over. But I didn't really have that much time because we had the restaurant and the kids and my husband was busy with the business. I had to take the children to school and I used to drop off the younger one in town at the nursery, and then I used to come here to work.

You worked in the restaurant as well?

And then because of the time schedule and so on Chris and Elaine changed it to the afternoon to come and teach me. Even though I didn't learn to speak English much I do understand a lot more. They did quite a lot for me and I learnt quite a lot of the basics.

So how did you find Reading? Was it different from Southall? In what way? And Ealing?

A lot of Indians in Southall is a bit like being in Deli. In Ealing there's a lot of English. When they came into Reading there was no big buildings none of these big buildings. It looked like a small village.

Where TGI Fridays used to be, there used to be a, I don't know if jungle's the right word but well, wild, it was a bit wild and we used to go and, it was a place for children to go and pick blackberries. There weren't all these houses round here. This road wasn't busy at all, and the road was a lot smaller than two cars could fit.

Was the IDR built then?

No it wasn't. Only old houses were there apart from, parks. There weren't any of those buildings by the station the big ones. It was like coming back from a village 'cos we'd moved back from London sort of thing to coming back to Reading which was more like a village.

Were there any other people from Nepal in Reading?

Nobody, first Nepalese here. And nobody would come and work in the restaurant 'cos Reading was very underdeveloped.

When you say nobody do you mean ...

There were no Nepalese, in a Nepalese restaurant the only people that are gonna be working in the restaurant at that time were either Nepalese or Indian, and because a lot of or the majority of the Indians that we knew were in Southall they weren't willing to come here.

How were you received by people in Reading?

When we came here we didn't know very many people at all but my because my husband knew a lot of people, the majority of them doctors, and they used to come here quite a lot. A lot of Indians he knew in Ealing who were doctors, they were based in Reading so he became friendly with them so they used to come to the restaurant as customers with friends and so on.

Did any English people come to the restaurant?

After the doctors, the Indian doctors used to come the English doctors used to come and so on. It was only the doctors that were there, Asian communities that came as customers, then it increasingly became more English people that were coming in, more of the public.

So you sent the boys to school, you paid for them because it was important the education. And tell me what's happened then, the restaurant we're sitting in now, its grown, how did this happen?

In this one section we managed to fit in sixty to seventy people, its actually, very obviously overcrowded. When we came over to Reading a lot of the doctors were already in Reading and because my husband knew them they all started coming here. At that time there were queues as well for the restaurant being only one section allowed only seventy seats but we used to have queues to get into the place. Because we were getting very busy with queues and so on we needed to extend the place so the building one four five there used to be a dog parlour. First of all we got that side on lease, and then we extended it to the two units. And on that side there used to be a laundramat. But the owner of laundramat was retiring he decided to sell it so we bought that and then after that they extended it to part of the restaurant.

So the restaurant now, the address is-

One four one to one four five Caversham Road. When we first started it used to be getting better and better and better all the time. After my husband passed away, in ninety five we lost a lot of customers 'cos my husband used to know them. Obviously when we came over there wasn't many restaurants, a couple of Chinese, one or two Indians. There's a Hong Kong restaurant in town which is a very old restaurant its been there a while. Now there's got to at least forty fifty Indian Nepalese restaurants. And obviously that's affected us because some people will try wherever that's open.

Thinking back over your time in Reading, you said originally you were going to go back to Nepal after five or six years. Would you go back now to live?

At first the idea was to earn a little bit of money and then go back to Nepal, after we had the children and started sending them to schools, giving them an education, the children that have studied over here have more or less become associated with the UK. If you said take all the family back to Nepal then the same feelings that I had when I came over from Nepal to over here would be the exact same that would happen to the people going back to Nepal now. If possible I probably will go back 'cos I can't work any more really, well I won't be able to work much longer. And in Nepal it will be good for me 'cos, I'm a practicing Buddhist so for Buddhist, Nepal would good karma. In '92 I think it was when we invited the Dalai Lama to come over we brought over twelve of our family members to come over at same time as well. Stayed for two three months.

Did he come here to Reading?
Yeah.

As a practicing Buddhist it must have been an honour to have the Dalai Lama come to stay. How did that come about?
Tibetan Foundation and another organisation were organising some talks in London and my husband was trying to organise something in Reading at that time. When he came over he stayed eight days at our house in Caversham. So the Dalai Lama was doing the talks in London and Wembley and he'd come back here and we'd be feeding him and looking after him.

So where do you regard home as being?
[laughing] Across the road.

How would you sum up your time here in Reading? What would you say about it?
At first when we were looking it didn't look like a very nice town, but we liked the people here and the business was going very well. There's a lot more people, a lot more businesses doing well but I think there's too many people here, its, I don't like that because there's a lot of negativity.

Has this been a change then?
I mean the town itself is developed, is very nice but you've too many people, not enough jobs and you've still got more and more people coming in- I don't like that simply because, you know. I'm always hearing all the negative in the news about this, that and-

Is there anything else that you'd like to add or say that you haven't said in the interview?
Shyam Lama [Pasang's son]:
I think my mum's played down the hardship side of things 'cos I mean I can remember sharing a room with about six people, this was in Reading.

When you first moved here or, in the early years?
Yeah when we first, in the early years. And obviously I can remember the amount of work, that my father and mother put in to provide for ourselves, even though I mean we went to private schools and such themoney that needed to be generated to keep that going was phenomenal. I mean it's a case now where I'm looking to put my children in private schools and to be quite honest I don't think I can afford it.

Self Sufficiency

So do you think that it was due to their hard work that this restaurant has been so successful? Its expanded originally from where you started hasn't it.

Yeah I mean I owe a lot to what they've done they've accomplished and achieved quite a lot in the short space of time I mean you're talking less than twenty odd years, twenty five years, and I know they've had problems throughout those years, and its absolutely awesome what they've managed to achieve.

Nepal

Nepal is a land locked country nestling at the foot of the Himalayas. It has a varied geography ranging from fertile plains to the inhospitable peaks of Everest. To the north it is bordered by Tibet in the People's Republic of China and by India to the south, east and west. Kathmandu is the capital and largest city, and as such it is also Nepal's most densely populated city. Kathmandu is home to most of the country's businesses and foreign embassies, as well as the King's Palace and many Buddhist and Hindu Temples. The dominant religion in Nepal in Hinduism, but there is a sizeable Buddhist community. Nepal is the birthplace of Buddhism; the Kathmandu Valley was home to Prince Siddharta Gautama (563-483 BCE) of the Shakya confederation who renounced his royalty to take up an ascetic life and eventually become known as the Buddha. An increased interest in Buddhism in the West during the 1960's saw the influx of any travellers and tourists to Nepal. Nepal's geographical position and the isolationist policies of the Rana administration (during the 1800s) meant that it had only a handful of friends on the world stage, including India, China and Great Britain. Nepal's relationship with Britain hasn't always been cordial – between 1814-16 the Anglo-Nepalese war raged over the annexation by Nepal of various minor states on the Nepal-India border. However, relations have since blossomed with the Nepalese assisting Britain during the Sepoy rebellion of 1857 and both World Wars (indeed, they continue to supply the British Army with Gurkha regiments). In 1923 Britain formally recognised the independence of Nepal and signed and agreement of friendship. During the late 1940s fledgling pro-democracy groups and political parties in Nepal were becoming critical of the Rana autocracy. In 1950 China annexed Tibet. So India, keen to promote stability in Nepal and thus avoid any possible future confrontation with a foreign ideology coming form China, sponsored a new king and a new government. King Tribhuvan took to the throne in 1951 and government was formed in 1959 with the Nepali Congress Party holding a large majority. The crowning of King Tribhuvan saw the Shah dynasty take back power after the Rana administration had severely curtailed the power of the monarchy and had made the post of Prime Minister powerful and hereditary in the mid-1800s. The experiment with democratic reform was short-lived and 18 months after parliament had been formed King Mahendra (Tribhuvan's son) had it dismissed. A new constitution was drawn up in 1962 establishing a system of panchayats (councils). King Mahendra considered this to be more in line with Nepalese tradition, as it was based on a pyramidal structure leading from village assemblies to the National Parliament (Rastiya Panchayat) with the King at the top of the pyramid. This enshrined the absolute power of the monarch, giving him power over both the Cabinet (Council of Ministers) and Parliament. King Mahendra was succeeded by his son King Birendra in 1972.

Alice Chigumira

Born: 15th May 1965
Harare, Zimbabwe
Date of Interview: 31st May 2006

Harare, Zimbabwe
Reading, UK

Childhood

My name is Alice Chigumira

Can you tell me where and when you were born?

I was born in Zimbabwe, but then it was called Rhodesia in a township called Mpopoma in Bulawayo on the 15th of May 1965 in a family of four boys and I am the only girl.

I have lived in Bolawao since childhood growing up where my father used to work for the national railways of Zimbabwe, it was called Rhodesia Railways, he was a messenger there. My mother was not a full housewife, who used to do most of the domestic work and make our clothes to sell and make extra money.

In our family we used to live in a place called Matshobane which was more or less a place for employees of the railways and that's where we grew up and I went to a school, called Campu Primary School from Grade 1 up to Grade 7.

My childhood was mainly dominated by male because I was the only female and my mum only and with four boys in there and I was the last born of the family. My father originally came from northern Rhodesia, what was then called Zambia and my mother originally comes from a place called Zvimba which most people might identify as where the President of Zimbabwe comes from and she speaks the language called Shona. Growing up we both learnt Ndebele and Shona together as our main language. We grew up with all the values of the Bula people and the Shona people and Bulawayo has an integrated society where it was dominated mainly by the Ndebele people.

I grew up in a family whereby I could not say we were very, very poor, we could sustain ourselves because mother used to do anything just to make sure that we could get a meal on our table and sell anything that was good to make extra money. Being a girl I was more or less daunted by everything that a girl could get from the family and I think it made me grow up with the spirit and a powerful kind of body and everything physically and mentally.

I became a Prefect at school in the primary school when I was in grade six and I used to do very well at school and I used to do long distance running, play netball and up til now I lost one of my teeth, which I don't have up to now playing netball all over the country when I was still in primary school. From there I passed my grade seven and went to what we call a high school here, that is called secondary school in Zimbabwe, called Mzilikazi High School which was one of the best schools in the locations in Zimbabwe.

By then my father retired from the railways he managed to buy a house where we lived for some time with my brothers, who had already finished their school, me and myself and my mum. It was quite a difficult time then because my dad was not working, so we probably relied mainly on my mum who was very, very clever. I think she has been a mentor in my life, who could

Education & Training

Self Sufficiency

Self Sufficiency

Political Situation

Childhood

Community

Jobs

Education & Training

go to Botswana, order clothes and come and sell and make sure that we went to good schools and had a uniform and everything, to make us sustaining everyway.

After going to High School for four years I kept on active with my running, I wasn't playing all that much netball, but I was very good in my English, like what they call composition and acting and drama and all that and I kept me going until I finished seeing hard times, whereby by that time the political up risings in Zimbabwe started. Also when I was in my form two in Zimbabwe there was the, a thing called the 'hit head', that most political people are aware about where many people were killed, and schools were stopped and the infrastructures in Zimbabwe were destroyed because it was more or less a civil war. It was really, really bad because there was so many people who died and I remember one time when I came from school, was sitting in our house and all of a sudden people came and started stoning the house and it was totally ruined and I don't know how we survived. With my mum, who was quite a big person, we managed to crawl out and go through the back yard and stay with neighbours. Later on we were called, by what they call the youths at that time to come and see a peasant being bashed to death by stoning. That's one of my first experience of seeing somebody killed by stone and we were supposed to look until the entire ordeal was done. It was quite traumatic for me because I think by that time I was almost about fourteen, fifteen years and looking at the ruins of our house, you couldn't know what was going to happen.

Because my father and mother were not politically active or in any way inclined to in group, so we had well wishes from the church and other people, who managed to re-build the place that we had and got somewhere to stay for the time being.

We were helped by a businessman called Vera, who used to own a lot of butcheries and shops in Zimbabwe, and they are a great family in Zimbabwe who managed to help us go through our school and build up the house, and I continued with my education.

I left High School and due to things of financial constraint, I couldn't go any further with my education and my mum all the same tried to sort of help me through and I managed to go to a private college to do what we call a Secretarial Diploma, which I did for three years. I did very well and from there I got my first job with the Government, with the National Archives of Zimbabwe where we store historic things and files and everything concerning codes, procedures and all the other things. I then left that job and went to join the Minister of Public Construction and Housing and also was a Secretary for some time and during all this period, now that I was managing to sort of get a little bit of my money, I managed to be doing a few other courses, extra courses to enhance myself and trying also to sustain my mum and dad because it was quite difficult for them to sustain in any way. The pension system, that was then in place wouldn't sustain them in anyway, they used to buy the house and pay for the fees for us.

I stayed with my parents for quite some time and then later on I found a job internally within the Government that they wanted people to work in the Diplomatic Services and they needed women to come and join, those they thought were single and were able to go out in the country and work and I thought it was quite a good challenge for me and applied for the job and I moved from Bulawayo

How old were you at that time?

I was twenty years by then, when I applied for the job to go in to the Minister of Foreign Affairs, so by the time I turned twenty one I was, I went to join the Minister of Foreign Affairs in Harare, it's the only chance I get. It was quite devastating to leave my parents but I went to stay with my brother, the one who was the policeman and his wife in Harare, as you know with our culture extended families are acceptable, we live as one and we love each other no matter what happens.

Staying there I went to train what they call diplomatic courses, mostly of the things were done by the British people and we were trained for six months by a teacher, who came from Britain. She was a fantastic woman who taught

Alica as a young child with mother and three brothers

us a lot about ethnic, different diversity in the world because we're going there alone, talked about us, about more or less what we call a finish school, about how you dress, how you eat, how you talk with certain people, and all the values of different cultures and how to persevere in a world where it is different from the norms of our own culture. It was a fantastic way of doing it and I was looking forward to that challenge, I was going out.

Then just before I left in 1989, my brother, the one I was very close to, the policeman just died in an accident in a, when he was coming from work. He was what we call by then a scuba diver who used to go in to different places and do different things and he had an accident and died on the spot, he left a three month old baby and a newly wed wife. This really devastated me because I'd only one month to leave, my father was approximately about seventy and almost blind and depended mostly on, they had children to sustain them and I left.

My first posting practically was to go to Yugoslavia, it was in December 1989 and due to the fact that I'd no experience about the cold weather and having had a system whereby in our country we always believe that because of our traditional values, which include British values, I was dressed more or less like in a suit way, in high heels and I had on my stockings and got on to the plane and came to Germany where I was met again by one of our officers from the Embassy. It was quite snowy, very cold and I didn't have anything to wear, which could keep me warm but they knew that I was coming and they brought some few things for me to keep myself warm.

It was a good experience to see the snow for the first time out of the country to such a far away place and I got on to the next plane, again to Yugoslavia, got in to the plane and I couldn't speak their language which was more or less like Serbia or Croatia, they're flight. We had a bit of mis-communication because when you wanted coffee, the one I'm used to is a bit lighter and they

Alice's home under construction, Harare, 1997

Political Situation

Racism

Community

Political Situation

Family Values

Jobs

have more or less like what you call the thick kind of coffee. When I got to the airport, again it was snowing, met by our Embassy officials who helped me and I checked in to a hotel where I stayed for a month without even knowing any single word. That was in Belgrade then, 1989, and it was quite difficult for me because during that time it was a time of transitional period, er the communist era and all that was happening in Yugoslavia and there was a bit of resentment looking at an African black woman coming in and single handedly staying in a hotel.

The language barrier were the other thing, staying in a hotel, you wouldn't know how to order the food, you wouldn't know how to ask for anything publicly or if you go to the shops how you could speak their language, so I was helped more or less by students, African students who were there, who could sometimes, if I wanted to go shopping they would help me, go with me and they'd speak the language and that's how I slowly learnt how to speak a little of Serbia or Croatia and I just started picking up on a few words.

I stayed in Yugoslavia for almost about a year, almost two years, but luckily I left Yugoslavia before the war that started, I was very, very lucky, I left in 1992 early, before the war started.

OK so you came to Britain?

My first experience of Britain was in 1990, we came as girls, one lady from the American Embassy, one from the Danish Embassy, one Ghanaian guy. We drove all the way across Europe from Yugoslavia to Austria and across Germany, Netherlands, Belgium, got in to the ship and came to London and we did what any other young girl could do, going around clubs and all that and seeing the views. I don't know what I could think about because by then it was more or less I had the money, I had everything so I was more or less living sort of you know what I could call a poshy life, living in a very expensive hotel and having all the fun as a young person, and that was my experience of, my first experience of Britain and we only came to London

When I went back to Zimbabwe after this in 1992, by then I was almost about twenty five years, most of my peer friends were married and had families, and all that, and you know our culture, twenty five years is quite out of the ordinary because you are not married and you don't have any children and my mum was worried whether I'd get married.

When I got back to the Foreign Ministry, I worked in a department which was called Protocol, which deals with the civilian, our people from different countries, helping out when the President is travelling or other officials of the Government and making sure that the diplomats, a new organisation or international organisation are credited properly, and had my first baby girl in January 1992, she was born on the 30th of January 1992 and she was a lovely baby.

Four months down the line my dad just woke up and he died of a stroke and he didn't know I was pregnant and it really obviously devastated me because looking at it, I really wanted to have done more for him, now that I was financially comfortable, but it so happened I couldn't and God had had his own way of doing things and he died like that and my mother was widowed

So your dad actually died, was that 1992?

'91, he died in '91, immediately when I came back from Yugoslavia so, well my mum was left alone now in the house and she still lived in that house that they bought in. I would have brought her back some things like colour tv and all that just to make sure that she's comfortable and give her most of the things to sustain her and I managed to sort of get somebody, as you know we have extended families to live with her so she doesn't become lonely. My mother is a very Christian person who has always gone to Methodist Church and was brought up in that and baptised as a Methodist, and up till now I still go to the local Methodist church in Kings Road and that's how we have been brought up

Is that Kings Road in Reading ?

Yes Kings Road in Reading, that's where I'm a member of the Methodist church. So, well we carried on after that and came back, I stayed in Harare continuously and I bought myself a house where I rented it out and still sub-letted the place, sub-let it so that it could give a legal income to my mum. In Harare I was also staying with a family sharing a house with a. who then became like my Godmother.

They looked after me very, very well because my mother never believed that I was not married and had a child, and I still continued having a relationship with the father of my child, but they thought that I, in our culture you can't live with a man without being married so you have to live with some elderly people to instil certain values and that, so I continued living with them for some time whilst still working in the Presidents' office, sorry in the Minister of Foreign Affairs.

By the end of I think it was just immediately when I get back, when I came back from maternity leave, I was told that I was going to be transferred to the Presidents' office for no apparent reason and this was something that really no-one could tell, even the higher offices. I wanted to find out why and they said it was something to do with the re-structure within the Minister of Foreign Affairs and I give my case because I still wanted to go on another posting and do all the other things that were there, but before then it was decided that I should get posted again and I was then told to go to Mozambique, that was in 19th September 1992.

That's when I went to Mozambique from 1992 up to '97 January, when I came back again.

During the time between the time '92 when I get back to my child and the end of '92 before I get posted, I had the privilege, well I did refuse in the first instance, but I think it was a privilege on my own way, to work with the Vice President of Zimbabwe, the late Simon Muzenda, worked in his office for almost less, than a year. By then Zimbabwe was in a devastating state because of the drought so I was more or less like a personal assistant, advisory on what to do about trying to find more food for the people, dealing with donors, going out in the villages to find out what people, accompanying him, finding out what people do, programmes about GMB, how food was distributed properly to every single person in the country. It was quite a very challenging post at

Family Values

Self Sufficiency

Family Values

Jobs

Economic Situation

that time and I really enjoyed it, I had the experience of meeting so many great people who did quite a lot to Zimbabwe at that time, during the drought period and really travelled quite a lot an he was a fatherly figure to me who made me see a lot of views.

Up to now I'm finding him as a person who was a fatherly figure, who never used to show that being a Vice President I have power to do certain things and instilled a lot of valuable things to younger children who would come thinking, because they are related to him and could get them jobs, he would tell them to go and get an education first and then go to the normal channels and apply and get jobs. I mean being a Vice President it's a simple phone call in my country just to say give him a job, but he never used to do that, he was a person who, during lunchtime he would sit in his office and make a cup of tea, he would eat 'umqutshu', what we call 'umqutshu' in my language nothing fancy, bread with some jam, that's all done, even if he's invited for dinner or lunch in anyway, he's not that kind of person who keep on eating all these other things. He used to love his village, he used to come from, so every Friday he would go to his village, be a village peasant or sometimes we would accompany him and see what he does and bred a lot of pigs, cows and everything, he was just a human person. I think I'd equate him to what we call Joshua Nkomo, people who had values for people, who would walk in the street and they never needed a bodyguard.

When I left for Mozambique in 1992, I went to Mozambique when it was the hardest part of it all. It was unfortunate for me also Yugoslavia was a hard posting, what we call a hardship posting and Mozambique again was a hardship posting, because it was the time when Romano went Frelimo heavy. The war that had gone on for almost over ten years, the country was devastated, buildings were all gone, running water was not there, there was absolutely nothing there. They were still negotiating to come to a peace agreement and the then President managed to do a peaceful agreement with Nkomo, which settled things a little bit, but to build up the infrastructure and make things work was not all that easy. We used to travel every Friday or Saturday to go shopping to Swaziland which is about fifty kilometres from Maputo to do our shopping because I still had, my daughter was about eight months and so ...

So your daughter was about eight months whilst you were in Mozambique?
Yes.

And so she was actually living with you in Mozambique?
Yes she was actually living with me, I still was single by then, I didn't get married to the father of my daughter and all of us at the Embassy, when I got to Mozambique we formed what we call the Young African Diplomatic Club, just to make sure we didn't feel out of place because it was quite difficult to more or less have a social life there.

So how long, altogether, did you spend in Mozambique?

I spent in Mozambique approximately about five years, up to January 1997.

And where did you go from there?

I went back home after 1997, I was married by then. I got married in 1993, my husband Kitson Chigumira, he used to be a metallurgist, originally was from a place called Mount Darwin, we had met at a party and it so happened from one thing led in to another. The devastating part is that eleven days before my wedding, when I was supposed to fly from Mozambique to come to my wedding, my mother just died of a stroke and it was quite, it was not a wedding any more. We just went to church because she had said that I should get married somehow and normally in our culture when we get married we always do things for our mothers so that they can be happy and be proud of us and it really, it really didn't go, up til now just didn't go well with me, it was quite a traumatic situation and I got married on the 4th of December 1993 in church in Bulawayo.

By then the situation was a bit stable in Mozambique and people could sort of come in and resourcefully do something. My climax of living in Mozambique was when I won an award. There was a time in 1995, where they did what they call a national competition for the whole of the country, which was sponsored by the South African, where they wanted to say people should write something about the Mozambique, because it had progressed from what it was in 1992 to this. I wrote my own sort of thesis about Mozambique and the things that I valued, how to communicate best and how I found my own way of making sure effective communication was done by learning certain things, especially the language and the culture and knowing how the people lived there, although we all come from Southern Africa, we've got different cultures. So I was one of the persons who was given an award by the President which was an honour, as you see with my picture there and I had the pleasure of having a dance with him, dining with him and winning that award which I still cherish up till now.

So you, you left Mozambique for the second time, in what year did you say?

So '97 that's when I was re-called back home, went back to the Minister of Foreign Affairs again and worked in the Protocol Section where I was working. During my time when I was working in Mozambique I met Geoffrey Nyarota from the Nordic/SADC [South African Development Corporation] training journalists and I had some talent in writing and we talked about setting things and he had plans of starting a newspaper which is called the Daily, Daily Newspaper, which is one of the newspapers which was private, started in Zimbabwe, the first private newspaper which was bombed by the present Government and destroyed totally.

Alice in Reading, 2003

Alice with President Chissana

Self Sufficiency

Jobs

When I came back home, I'd invested some money and bought some machines and all that and wanted to be part and parcel of all that and it was, it happened and the paper was started, but I was still working for the Minister of Foreign Affairs, I was married, I had my house in Emerald Hill in Harare and I had my child, Tadiwa, meaning you are so much loved, a girl born on the 17th of September 1997, and still went on ahead and became a shareholder of the Daily newspaper. It was quite a difficult time because working for Government and having shares with the Daily newspaper, which contradicts what most people would say, what Government believes in, which is a public view, which is an open minded newspaper was not okay at that very moment.

So working again in the Protocol Section I was really, I went through hell from 1997 up to the time I was supposed to resign to the year 2000, and it was quite traumatic for me, but I stood by what I wanted, I had my own principles. I wanted to do a lot of things, I had thought there was a lot of things which needed to be done, I'd worked within the system, I knew certain things were not being done and I think I was going to be a voice in everyway and I was forced to resign with no apparent reason.

2000 left Foreign Affairs and started my own company, although I still held on with my shares with the Daily newspaper, I used to write stories with them and mostly, they were not politically affiliated but they had some articles of them that had sort of a powerful voice to say how can, women especially, can stand on their own, even if you are a Government worker.

During the time '97 up to 2000 I was getting invited all over Southern Africa to go and be a speaker about what we call how to communicate in diverse community, because of my background of being a Diplomat and what I'd written in newspapers. I used to travel like to South Africa, Mozambique, Namibia, Botswana, Zambia and all the other places, in to Conferences and do a lot of things. So the year 2000, 2000 in September I resigned from Foreign Affairs, started my company.

Political Situation

OK Alice could you tell me about when you arrived in Britain, the year you arrive and your experiences?

I came to Britain, it wasn't really planned, it was because of the political pressure that was happening and I just came with just a few clothes and went to South Africa, just took a plane and landed in Britain. By then I'd called my friend, knowing they were on the phone when I was in South Africa and got her to wait for me at the airport at the Heathrow, came with the South African Airways. She waited for us and we got in to the First Great Western Buses, came to Reading. By that time she was living in Shinfield. My, when I first came to Heathrow, well experience of Britain was not that, all that new to me, but I was still in quite a traumatic situation when I came here and when I got to the airport it was more or less like you know the usual immigration things that got through, 'Why are you here?' 'Why have you come?' and all the other questions.

Community

Childhood

When you came was that the year 2000?

2002 in July. I arrived here 2002, July 28th . I got through the immigration and came and stayed in Shinfield with my friend and I stayed there for about two weeks. I was still in a traumatic situation. I'd left my kids there and I was just devastated about what had happened, my kids, my whole entire life had been left in Zimbabwe, I had a lot of properties that I'd bought, I'd had a very good house and was doing quite well ... to come here and sort of live from hand to mouth from my friend was devastating especially leaving my kids. By then Tadiwa was about two, three years and Michelle also born '92, was about ten years and I left them with their cousins.

Community

I stayed here for about two weeks in Reading and finding it very difficult to manage and most of the things that had to be done had to be done in London concerning my stay here. It was more or less like a political asylum and my friend, there was very little that she could do to help me going up and down by train to go to London and come back, the next day go again so I moved over and went to stay in Canning Town with another old friend of mine, we grew up in the same location. I stayed with her, she was very helpful, she was wonderful, people did help me a lot here and she introduced me to people, a lawyer who could help me through all of the whole system of political immigration and asylum system and I had all the evidence about my political asylum, I used paper cuttings, I had Diplomatic passports, more or less all that was needed and I was granted indefinite stay to live, to live in the UK.

Jobs

Self Sufficiency

I started working immediately, got a job as a carer, something very totally different and I was still in London then, because I moved from Reading in August just to go and make sure that all was done in London and it was quite a difficult time, there was absolutely nothing I could do except to become a carer and a cleaner. You imagine from somebody who used to have caviar and champagne becoming somebody looking after elderly people and not managing to even buy a handbag for yourself, do what they call long days. I could not take money from home to bring it here, I wasn't there to sign all those things and I've never gone through a period like that in my life, and all the time I could not sleep thinking about my children.

Where was your husband at this point?

My husband died in 19, my husband died in 1999, my husband just decided he didn't want to live anymore, he woke up the next day and committed suicide for no apparent reason.

What year was that?

1999 in January so I've gone through quite a lot in my life and I've generally I've lost all my brothers, they've all died, my mother is dead, I'm the only person alive in my family with my two children. It became so difficult I couldn't use any lawyer, it was difficult but I think sometimes experience of working within the Foreign Ministry helped me because I managed to write a letter myself to the Minister of what they call the Secretary for Foreign Affairs here in the Home Office about my children because they denied them Visas to come in the British Embassy. And they responded and I started, demanded to the British High Commission in Zimbabwe to do that and I wrote a letter to

Self Sufficiency

them also with the concern on humanitarian grounds and according to the EU Regulations about family being separated and all that, my children didn't have a living parent in Zimbabwe, I was the only living parent. So having an insight about the little regulations that I used when writing letters they managed to get a Visa. They came over in January, they came on their own from Harare accompanied by the, of course air hostess, clearance and all that, and arrived from Zimbabwe in January on the 27th and I met them at the Gatwick airport.

Were you still living with your friend then?

I was still living with my friend because she had said that I should until I managed on my own. She was willing to take me in, my friend had her own two children, daughters, a husband was staying in a council flat with two bedrooms, but as you know with our African culture you just have to sort of, it becomes an extended family.

As soon my children were coming she managed to sort of get a room for me to go and rent and she had helped me pay the deposit and all the other things, to go and stay with my children in that one room.

When they got to the airport, the air hostess who were escorting them out, I don't know, I just felt tearful, I couldn't believe that after six months I could see my children and they looked so thin and miserable and I was so, I'd lost a lot of weight, I was not the same person, I was never the Alice that they were used to, the vibrant Alice, the one who had the kind of diplomatic etiquette and everything, it had just gone. I took my children and went to the house, unbelievable for them, they were shocked when they got here, they couldn't, I mean I'm not, I'm not bragging about the way we lived in Zimbabwe, but we do live comfortably, they had a house which was massive, each child had had a bedroom, three bathrooms and all that and servants, garden, two cars, cars, everything used to happen to them. Coming from a mansion to come to live in a one bedroomed house, where there's no TV, where there's absolutely nothing, I think it was just devastating for them. My little daughter Tadiwa, when she started school, she could not even manage to speak and they had to bring in child psychologists to see what was happening because she was so traumatised in the aspect of what in the world is happening, why are we here, why are we in a one room and all that

Once your children arrived in the UK did you approach the council to see if they would help you with housing?

I didn't approach the council in, I didn't know that I had all those privileges, one way or the other and I think again also because of pride, being somebody who had always worked on my own and done things I never, I can never say like a refugee like what they say in the newspapers that refugees drain the benefit system and all that, I sustained myself with my two children with my carer's money, helped by my friend to baby-sit when I go to work and did everything on my own. I managed to save because my job was quite stressful, the one I was doing.

I say to myself I'd rather move in Reading there's vacancies of carers in Reading and decided that's the only thing I could do, I couldn't break the system in Foreign Affairs, one way or another through my experience, I knew that I would not get a job there, so I just went with the little that I could get at least to butter my bread, so that's how I moved to Reading

What year did you move back to Reading?

Because I'd arrived here in England in 2002 July and moved in to Reading in March 2003 and that's when I started working with the Reading Borough Council as a carer, in what they call a home carer. I was also helped by what I call, call my husband's relative, she found me a one bed flat which was a reasonably priced in Regal Street, my first address in Reading was 11A Regal Street, which is near the shops there.

Was that privately rented?

Yes privately rented and the rent was approximately about £600.

Well looking at it, I could manage to sort of, I shared a bedroom with my kids, it was furnished but I had to find two beds, I was helped by the Refugee Support Group here in Reading, to get extra beds. Things were really quite tight for me and came and stayed at that place and managed to register my children for school at New Christchurch School which is in Milman Road, where they started their school.

In the morning I'd take them to school and drop them, but my work was more or less flexible because I would finish approximately around one or two as a carer and then go and pick them again at three o'clock and be with them for the evening and all that. If I had to get an extra shift, I would ask my niece, to sort of baby-sit for me, because I really needed the money and I would work so hard.

I stayed in that place from March 2003 up to December 2003, when I saw that I could manage to sort of get a two bedroomed flat with my, the income that I had had and moved in to Highgrove Street, 33 Highgrove Street, where I got a two bedroomed house, when I moved in it's just behind Whitley Street, it's nearby so it was easy for me to walk with the children again, walk in to town.

One thing that I'd found with Reading again was it's quite accessible to any place that you want to go like going in to town it just takes you just five, ten minutes in town, it's very flexible and there's a lot of countryside, small town and all that where you can go and be with your kids and they feel much secure. You end up feeling the community helps you to look after your children in one way. There's one or two odd thugs but you rarely hear of incidents that are happening as great as other cities are and you know that one way or the other, things will be dealt properly if it's racial discrimination, it's done in a procedure where it's not over-ridden. Here there's different cultures here where you meet lots of black people, lots of Asian people, lots of different kind of people and you learn lots of things.

Do you meet lots of Zimbabweans in Reading?

There's a lot of Zimbabweans in Reading, I do a lot of things with Zimbabwe, what we call Zimbabwe network here, as you know with what I've said in my history. I'm also a member of Amnesty International, I'm a Vice Chairman of the Reading Refugee Support Group, I'm also currently formed a new

African Voices Forum which was launched sometime last year. I do a lot of things, I'm also a volunteer for the National Institute of African Studies and Zimbabwe community is involved, so I'm quite actively involved in so many things. I also do the Reading Festival when it happens, I participate in the WOMAD, political and doing other things concerning diversity, cultural wise and everything, I've been doing it for the past, since I've been here in Reading. I'm going to be in Reading for almost, now it's over three years I've been in Reading, so I've been quite active.

I write a lot of stories with the local media, Reading Evening Post. I've written several articles about my coming to Reading, why I love Reading, and I help them if they want to do stories about Africans and their diversity, to make sure the paper itself is not only oriented with the local people, but also with a lot of diversified communities. It gives me, it gives them a different perspective. I'm involved with RISC and we do a lot of things. Being the Vice Chairman of the Refugee Support Group I see a lot of different people, again from different parts of the world. I went through hell myself when I came here, and that's why I really had to do something, being part and parcel of the Refugee Support Group, because it's first hand information that I have. I know how the other person is suffering, it's not somebody who has been sitting in her house who will tell a refugee what it is to be a refugee, although it's just a name at the end of the day.

How have your children settled now?

My children have settled very, very well, as you see they are not here, they've gone to sleep at friend's places and those friend's places are not what we call Zimbabwe people, they are natural British people, my eight year old has gone somewhere, my fourteen year old has gone somewhere. My fourteen year old is in to dancing and all this, she has participated recently on Monday in the Reading Carnival, she did Welsh dance today. They've integrated in to society and I've made sure they do because one way or the other, if you go to China, do what they Chinese do. There was no way I would tell them let's stay in the house and be ourselves because we are here and we don't know how long we are going to be, the only way you can integrate in to the society is being part of it.

Do they miss Zimbabwe?

They do miss Zimbabwe, but the other thing is that we cook the food here, we play the music here, we go to parties where we have are own Zimbabwean parties, we still do the traditional parties which we do like our weddings, our you know ball and marriages, they feel the value, I speak my own language, I've instilled that on my children and they speak Shona very much and they try to learn that, and I think that's very important that everybody should remain with their own families

So what's your plans for the future?

Well my plans for the future are political, can I be a Mayor of Reading one day, I think so. I think I've coped, I'm not ambitious as such, but I've got a lot of empathy, I work for social services, adults in community, I've done a lot of

Education & Training
Self Sufficiency

Community

Jobs

Community

difference to several people. From a carer I've progressed and made sure that I got this job that I'm doing at the moment, not because of equal opportunities, because I could do something and I made sure that I got the job. I'm working as a Case Co-ordinator, planning to get trained and become a Social Worker. Contribute a lot to this community, make a difference to those that need it and do a lot with the community, continue lobbying with the Amnesty International about the rights of people, continue helping people with HIV in the community and also in Africa, making poverty history also, which are one of those things that I've done, going to Scotland. I want to make a difference in the world. It only takes a person to make a difference, it doesn't take a whole clan

If opportunity arises would you again get involved in politics in Reading?

I might say I'm very much involve in politics in certain ways because politics is not really about what you read at the university and become like a, you've got a political degree or whatever, it's what you believe in and the most important thing that I believe in is human rights. It has made me to be here in England because I thought there was lack of human rights in Zimbabwe and I spoke out about it and valued that and I think every person has a right to live a decent life. I'm sorry I didn't live a decent life when I came here, but I can't blame the system for that because, I mean in every aspect of life, everybody has to fight to get their way through and I did fight my way through four years down the line, I'm not complaining about anything, I've bought my house through the key worker scheme, I've got a stable life, I'm looking for a future with a career in the Reading Borough Council. I've had lots of haggles within the Reading Borough Council and I stand firm on what I believe in, never minding discrimination or prejudice against me, but I still stand on what I believe in and that's human rights.

Every person is a voice on their own. A voice does not necessarily mean speaking, a voice is practically what you do, it's a voice. Particularly how you cry, particularly how you look at people, how you dress, how you walk about, how you communicate with the rest of the world, how you persevere, that's what you call a voice. It's not about talking as being a politician talking, but what you do. The legal change that you make to one person who will tell the next person that she did make a lot of difference, I've done a lot of difference to many Zimbabweans, who believe I have political wise fought for their rights here, in the sense that now most Zimbabweans don't go home, they are not being sent home, but I had my own stay here, I used to go to London to make the protest, to say they should not be sent home, the judges revoked that and they're still not being sent home, so I made a difference in some aspects of my life. I've met signatories in Amnesty International concerning people who are imprisoned without charges and that is what we call a difference.

What are you saying then, that you're making Reading your home for the future?

I'm making Reading my home for the future unless something happens, but I still want to go home in the future, when I get old.

You miss Zimbabwe?

I do miss the sunshine, I do miss, I miss the food, I miss a lot of things, I miss the big houses, I miss all the other things that make in the values of a person. I miss just generally to be a Zimbabwean because since I was about twenty two years I have moved all over the world and travelled to different countries and really wanted to to make a difference in my country and stay and nurture my own family there, I miss a lot of it.

Is there anything else you want to tell us before we complete this interview?

Probably what I would like to say is that all to do with immigration and over emphasis, I've done something with the BBC South concerning statistics about refugees and my worry is still up to now about how people see refugees, their own perspective about refugees, asylum seekers, refugees, what are they? But unless you sit across me, when I'm walking down the street and coming to assess your mum and dad in their home, black as I am with my dreadlocks, you never see a refugee, you see somebody with empathy who wants to make a difference to somebody who is not from their own culture, but who values the other peoples culture, the diversity of people, diversity doesn't necessarily mean if you are British, everybody, it's Sunday roast dinner. Diversity means who you are as a person. African doesn't necessarily mean we eat salad and stew or we are loud, African means who you are, with your own perspective about life, your own voice, your own way that you carry yourself. You can't be categorised like people will say refugees and immigrants are the ones who make a lot of difference here in the UK, they've done a lot of difference in a lot of way. I am doing a great difference and I don't feel any bit ashamed of being a refugee.

But you love Reading?

The most important thing is I love Reading, I love Reading every time, I just walk out of here, I'm running to school, I don't have the pressure of going anyway. I've integrated so much that I've found good mothers here who are British who look after me like I am their own daughter. I've found families here who look after me as if I am their own child. I've found friends here from a diverse community, from the Asian community, from the White community, where I have felt comfortable with them. I've found that there are people who will listen here, the system here, Reading is, they listen to what you say, including Members of Parliament, the Council people, all those that are involved in service providing, the NHS wherever you are, the Education System, there's somebody who will listen to what you are saying, they will not take it as a file and put it aside, somebody will really listen and welcome you whoever you are and don't take it out of context.

Reading is just a place where you say, I can come here and stay here and retire and wont feel the hassles of being in a bustle and hustle town. It's just a place where you feel comfortable in every way.

Zimbabwe

The Republic of Zimbabwe is situated in the southern part of Africa. It is a land-locked country bordered by South Africa to the south, Mozambique to the east, Botswana to the west and Zambia to the northwest. It lies between the Limpopo and Zambesi rivers. Its capital and largest city is Harare. Zimbabwe was formally known as the Republic of Rhodesia owing to the British intervention in the area during the latter part of the 19th century under the auspices of Cecil Rhodes. In 1964 the white administration of Rhodesia demanded independence from Great Britain, but this was flatly rejected. A unilateral declaration of independence was made in 1965 and the Commonwealth imposed sanctions upon the country, within three years the UN followed suit. The rejection of independence was largely down to the fact that the then Prime Minister of Rhodesia, Ian Smith, held on to a largely segregated social system. Opposition to white rule grew, leading to civil war; by the end of the 1970s there was a black majority in Parliament. Between 1979 and 1980 Lord Soames was appointed governor and oversaw the transition to independence. A coalition government was formed with Joshua Nkomo of the Zimbabwe African People's Union (ZAPU). Robert Mugabe's Zimbabwe African National Union (ZANU) took power in the free elections of February 1980; the party has won every election since (although the legitimacy of subsequent elections has been questioned owing to the alleged intimidation of voters and harassment of members of opposition parties). In 1982 Nkomo was ousted from his cabinet and there followed clashes between ZAPU and ZANU supporters which spilled over into attacks on white farmers as well as the Shona peoples in some provinces. The Fifth Brigade were mobilized by the government to quell the insurgency and bloody conflict erupted across various parts of the country; multiple atrocities were committed against the Ndebele peoples (from southern Zimbabwe) and approximately 20,000 people were killed. Mugabe and Nkomo eventually held peace talks and the Patriotic Front was reunited and there was a return to calm. As part of the peace talks clemency was granted to those on both sides who had committed atrocities. The peace accord of 1987 also saw the merger of PF ZAPU and ZANU PF. In 1992 a national disaster was declared after southern Africa suffered its worst drought in over a century. This led to Mugabe's programme of Land Reforms and eventually the redistribution of farms owned by whites (in 1999) to supporters of Mugabe and his regime. These reforms had the unfortunate consequence of further destabilising the Zimbabwe economy as agricultural goods rocketed in prices. In 2002 Zimbabwe was suspended from the Commonwealth of Nations because of human rights abuses and election tampering, on 7th December 2003 it withdrew from the Commonwealth. Mugabe's regime has not only seen the departure of white farmers but also activists and supporters of opposition parties, with many of them seeking asylum in the United Kingdom and other sympathetic countries.

British interest in the land was mainly due to the abundance of natural resources including gold and other minerals. In 1922 a referendum amongst the white settlers of the area rejected the merger of the southern part of the country with the Union of South Africa, as such it became a British self-governing colony., although positions of power and influence were still very much under white control. In 1979 a conference was held in London to seek an end to the civil war similar to Apartheid.

Robert Browne

Born: 20th October 1938
Guyana, South America

Date of Interview: 16th July 2006

Guyana

● Guyana, S. America
● Reading, UK

Childhood

Self Sufficiency

Jobs

When did you come to England?
February 1958.

What was the journey like?
Very good, very exciting. I came in a boat SS Angeles. Took about eighteen days to get here. I had a good time on the boat. Stopped at a lot of countries. Different places.

So what made you decide to take that journey from Guyana?
I just thought well, I'll get a better life anyway. At least compared with what I was having out there and … well I was very young at the time anyway 'cos I was only just gone eighteen and I just thought, well I could do better. Came over here for five years. Well five years has turned out to be nearer fifty.

So tell me about your family. What did your parents think about you leaving home so young?
Oh, the only person there who was a bit worried was my mother really, but my father, he wasn't worried about it. He said 'He can look after himself' and I'll be alright, cos I left home two years previous to that to work away anyway.

Where was that?
Right in Guyana. A place called Mibikuri and I made good money there.

What were you doing then?
Plumbing. In the interior we were running pipelines and it was a British company out there and I made good money so when I came back home I said well, I didn't sit down there and just waste it I said I'll come over here and see what life could offer out there. Must be better.

Were you the only child?
Oh no, no. There were eight children. I was second to last. There was one sister who follows me.

So the others are there at home?
They're all dead now.

Oh just you?
Just me and the sister who was behind me, Mavis, only the two of us surviving. But my parents and all the others they're all dead.

Education & Training

So what was school like? You said you did plumbing, you went to work in plumbing, so did you do plumbing as a trade at school?

That was here. I came over here. I was working as a plumber here, 'cos I was doing it back home and then when I came over here I still went along to the Reading College for another four years. I used to go there in the evenings. To get more used to their system here.

Childhood

So what made you decide you want to be a plumber. What part of when you were a child did you decided that this is what you wanted to do?

Well, in a way because when I was at school I can remember that there was a headmaster, we had a nickname for him. His nickname was Monkey Jimmy and I never liked people giving too many orders and telling me what to do and he thinks well, there were the bench, we wanted to put a bench there. Getting all the bigger fellas to hold you down, pull the trousers off and started driving lashes at you. But he made a mistake with me.

Lashes, you mean to give you the strap, the belt?

Yeah and hold you down on the table. But he made a mistake with me because when they approached me, I just jumped over their head from off the stage and I went straight home and my old man, he was passing the school yard going home and all these children were waving to him to stop and started telling him 'Mr Browne, you son run out of school and he's gone home.' When he came home he asked me 'What are you going to do now?' I said 'Well I ain't going back to school anyway.'

How old were you then?

I was only fourteen. Course my father he was doing plumbing then. He was a contractor on the estate. So I said, I'll come in and work with you, so that's how I started out in plumbing.

Apart from that, did you enjoy school up to that point in time?

Oh … well on and off I would say. There's only one particular thing I liked at school and this is arithmetic. I wasn't brilliant in school in anything, other thing anyway.

Education & Training

So, when you came to England after that long journey what was it like leaving the hot South American country? What was the experience like for you?

What here? Well there were good times and bad times but the first thing I learnt when I get off the boat at Plymouth I was able to see right away that I had to go back to school to start training to be a plumber in England because the standard of work I see they were doing, I wouldn't be able to attempt it, straight away. So what I did was to get to a company and told them what I can do. That was cast iron and galvanised pipes, so I was doing the cast iron and galvanised and not to worry too much about the lead. So that's when I had to go into the college. Don't know about joints the way they do it. Gradually catch on to it. Different types of flashing. Step flashing, cold flashing and all that. Found it very exciting at college.

So when you came, what time of year did you arrive in England?

Oh in the winter. First morning I got up. Saturday morning there was snow out there and I was living then at 16 Lowndes Street, Coldharbour Lane, Camberwell Green and this friend of mine who was from Guyana as well, sent me over Marshall, and he used to work in the same place in the interior where we were working. He came over six months before. Then there was no heating in that room. I nearly died from pneumonia 'cos sleeping in that cold room. Course he never used to sleep there, he was a welder. The war had just no long finished and did pretty well. They were building a lot of aeroplanes so he was welding aeroplane parts. He left his job and just used to hang about in the Mambo Club in Brixton when the night come. So I used to be there on me own.

Course, myself and Ovid had soon fell out anyway 'cos when I came over here with a bank draft for £38 which was a lot of money at that time, and Ovid was supposed to take me to the Barclays Bank so I can open an account. He stayed outside and I went in the bank and when I came back out Ovid asked me where was the money? Oh I said, what money, I said I haven't got any money. I left the money there, I just got a bank book. He called me an idiot, 'cos I didn't draw the money and give him so he could go down the Mambo Club and start drinking. I got to look after what little I got till I got a job and get on my feet. He didn't like it, so I say 'Oh then I'll find somewhere to live,' so then I went and got a room with a Jamaican lady. He was a scaffolder. Mrs Jones. They were very nice people, treated me very well. No problems with them at all. Been there for quite a few, quite a while.

So when did you come to Reading? What year?

I came to Reading in 1960. I came to Reading in 1960, that's when I started living. But I visited Reading the Good Friday, no it was the Saturday, 1960 and there was a lot of people round Jackson's Corner, by the thousands. That's when I found they march from Aldermaston. They were going to London, so they needed to stop at Reading that night.

The thing was I was walking past and estate agent and this chap called me and asked me if I wanted to buy a house and I said I've got no money to buy a house. He said I never tell you anything about money. He said I was just tell you do you want to buy a house? I said no. I said I'm just a stranger, just come for a day to visit this place and he said take this leaflet about this house, go on since you're only walking around. Go along to Caversham, over the river.

Was this an Englishman?

A white man yeah. Mr Bryan and the house was being sold for £1,280. Nice two-bedroom house on three floors. Two living rooms. Living room downstairs and the kitchen in the basement. So went back to this agent and said yeah, nice place. He said 'Where you live?' 'I said in London. He said I want to write down your address. Write it down on a bit of paper.' They he started writing and writing like he was writing a letter. All the time he had me standing out there. When he finished writing he put this letter in an envelope and he said 'The way to go down the corner of station road there, go out from here, turn right into Friar Street. The first corner you come to you can see the

Cooperative Building Society. You go in there and ask for a man by the name of Mr King. He said, he's a very tall man and give him this letter. Don't give it to anyone else. So you can't make a mistake 'cos he's a very tall man.

I went in there and I asked for Mr King. I said, there's a bloke from the estate agents tell me to give you this. He read the letter and he start asking me if I had a job. I said yeah. By that time I was working in a school, a new school they was building. I was plumbing there. He said alright, you can go on in, you're going to hear from me. I didn't expect to hear from him but that was, as I said that was a Saturday. Went back to London. On the Wednesday morning I was going out to work and the postman said 'Is there a Browne living in this place?' I said that was me. 'I got a letter for you.' And when I opened the letter, was this Mr King from the Cooperative Building Society. So I got a mortgage. He gave me a mortgage. It was eighty pounds deposit for the house. Yeah. I came the next week and gave him the eighty pounds and took about six or eight weeks and I had the house. So I used to leave it locked up there. I only used to come down in the weekend and stay there. I used to go back and eventually by the June month I said 'Oh, I seen enough, I ain't going back. You stop here and find a job here.' That's when I got to stay in Reading. So I been in that house twenty-five years and then I moved.

So you moved from there to …

To Lower Earley.

So didn't you have any friends in Reading at all?

Oh I soon get some friends alright. I find one or two other Guyanese people who was living around here and one chap was Patrick Isaacs. He was living in Brunswick Hill or Brunswick Street and we became good friends. I know of a few other. There was another girl by the name of Beryl McLean. There was a few I get to know them.

Were there many black people in Reading at the time?

There were a few, mostly Barbadians in Reading, but I soon get to know a lot of them because there wasn't many in fact I was the only black fella around Reading who used to do plumbing. There was no other black plumbers around Reading.

Did you have difficulty getting jobs?

No. Jobs was pretty easy to get. Once there was no problem at all getting jobs because in them days most people belonged to a Trade Union, even if you lost a job today, you go to the Union Saturday morning you'd get another job, or the Labour Exchange. I never have much use for them anyway. I got only one job in my life from the Labour Exchange. I managed pretty well without, without all these people.

So you have moved to Reading since 1960? And we're now 2006 so you have seen a lot of changes. Can you explain some of those?

Changes I would say, for instance, Queens Road that only used to be one road, the car park didn't exist. Where you go the tax office now, Sapphire

Plaza, there was only a little hump backed bridge, goes over there and straight in front of that, going way back to where there's a Homebase that was all Huntley & Palmers biscuit factory. You come along there in the morning you would see West Indian women by their thousands going in there. That was one of the biggest employment places in Reading.

What year was that roughly?

From 1958, 1960 when I moved to Reading this was going on. More and more black people came to Reading. That's where all those women, the majority of women, that's where they worked. Huntley & Palmers.

You didn't know the Huntley & Palmers factory then?

Yes I have, yes I know it. 'Cos gradually they begin to run it down. But Sapphire Plaza, where the tax office is now, all of that place didn't exist. Even the underpass, the distribution road around the town, by West Street and all that. That didn't exist there. The big tall building in front of Reading railway station that used to, when that was built I was there as well. All that car park for Foster Wheeler occupied that building then. The car park and all of that was built by Bovis. Of course at that time I used to have a few plumbers used to work with me then.

Yes. I've seen quite a few changes in Reading. In Chatham Street, where all that car park, where they start building up again. You go all along the Kings Road, Reading University, Reading Technical College – it wasn't that large at the time. There used to be a lot of large houses on either side of Kings Road there, past the college. Big houses there used to be up there. The shops were a bit different then. Langstons. Langstons used to be a shop, used to be in the corner of West Street. It used to sell lots of working clothes for me, donkey jackets and that sort of a thing. Course, even Sainsburys place and that all of that didn't exist there at the time because that region of town, that used to be Drews. Drews, the builder's merchants used to be there. A big old house used to be there.

What did Drews sell?

Drews, there on Caversham Road now. They're an ironmongers. They sell copper tube now, fittings, any sort of thing like that. Drews Ironmongers and where that shopping precinct is, The Butts, that didn't exist. All them places they've been built since I've been here in Reading. I've seen them all go up.

So it's like a new town when you compare it to what it was then?

Oh yeah. Completely new place. The only, one of the best survivors I know now is Jackson's. Even, and a lot black people who bought houses first of all used to get their furniture from a man named Mr Gibbs. He used to be right near by Chatham Street. He had a furniture place there. Of course in houses in them days all that you could afford was that vinyl on your floor. You were lucky if you had a narrow strip of carpet or a piece of rug in your room because most people lived in one room then. That room was your bedroom, your dining room, and everything. Where you entertain people and everything, in one room, 'cos that's all you could afford in them days.

What was the rent in those days. You could rent a room for?

Oh you could rent a room for about, in old money, for about ten shillings a week. Yeah, ten shillings a week you rent a room. But Mr Gibbs, he supplied a lot of coloured people. As you buy a house, everybody used to go to him. To get their furniture.

So what was property selling for then in those times?

As I said, I paid £1280, but you could've buy, most expensive is probably, £2,000, two and a half thousand you could've had a good place …

And now so there's hardly any place, as you were saying, besides Jackson's, which remains the same?

Jackson is some very exciting people I deal with too. If I tell you. The store is a bit different inside now. They don't sell the sort of things they used to sell, years ago, 'cos Jackson's used to sell furniture at one time. Yeah. They used to sell very good furniture. Nice, good carpet, rugs and that sort of a thing. Jackson's used to make very, very good suits.

One Saturday after I was living in Reading I was going past there on a bicycle. The man said to me stand up off that bicycle. I was very lucky in Reading, that's why I remained here and this bloke said to me, he said 'Come.' He was standing right outside Jackson's. I said yes sir, 'cos people from the West Indies got a different attitude to elderly people. 'Yes sir, I said, what's the trouble?' He said, 'Man you look like you can do with a suit.' I said, 'Oh no I don't want no suit, I got no money for no suit.' Chap's said, 'Come with me.' Took me in upstairs, up top of Jackson's. When I went up there they had a room about twice the size of this, with different racks upon rack so suit lengths. They used to the tailoring up there. This chap, he started measuring and he said, 'Go on I'll be in touch with you.'

Two weeks later I got a card pushed through the door and I went down to what is it now about. This guy made me a three-piece suit. Wrapped it up in a bag and he said well you've come and you can pay us fifty pence a week or a pound a week. You got no card, nor nothing. They used to trust people then. The same thing happened that brought Mr Gibbs down with some black people. Just go. I used to go down there and just pay him fifty pence a week or if I got a pound, I give him a pound and that same old man, that man has made me eight suits and I've still got them on now. Because they're good quality cloth.

What were wages in those days for a plumber?

By that time. Oh, by that time you were probably on about twelve or fifteen pounds a week.

And for the people working a Huntley & Palmers? What sort of money?

Huntley & Palmers? Oh the women never got much, much wages, they never got much. They were only making biscuits or packing biscuits and that sort of a thing.

Must have been a good wage for a plumber then?

Oh yeah. That was good wages then. For a plumber, about £12 - £15. Lots of jobs then used to be you working on a price. So.

You were working on your own then, in your own business?

No. You work for a company. But the company used to say, well OK you get say, what we call first fixing, that's putting the pipes in the flooring, you might probably get so many pounds doing that, the first fixing and then you get so much for the second fixing and you get so much for the finals.

And you were happy with what you got?

Oh yeah. And I used to do a lot of weekend work, do anything. We used to do Ascot heaters for people. People I know, yeah.

So were you still biking then or did you learn to drive by then?

Driving. I started driving in … Mmm in '61. No, '62 I started driving. That was a funny thing as well because I used to go to Thanet School of Motoring, they used to be called. At the back of Heelas's, right on the corner there, there used to be a little driving school and at that time the lessons used to be about twelve shillings for a driving lesson.

I was going to driving lessons one day and right there, there used to be an estate agent and one day this bloke, he called me just the same way and he said 'You wanna buy a house?' I said, I only just bought a house, the other day, over in Caversham, 'cos that was early '62 and I only moved to Reading in '60. So this bloke said, 'Look man, you work on the buildings and from your clothes I see you wear on.' I said, yeah. He said, 'Well look, got this old house down at Cemetery Junction. Take this key, when you come back and go and have a look at it.'

When I come back from my driving lesson I went down to this place. When I stand on the outside, I looked at this house. I thought, my Christ, what does he think I'm going to do with that then? I went in inside. There was no electricity. All the windows were broken and rubbish in this place. So I went back and I said to this bloke, 'Oh you've got to be joking, ain't you.' He said 'No, not joking.' Well I say 'You work on the buildings, you got friends. Get them down there to fix it up, just like that. Yes. Get them to fix it up.' This was then in 1962. I said, 'Well how much is this house then?' The guy said '£800.' Yeah, £800. I said 'Well, even then that's a lot of money in them times and he said well you're gonna hear from me then. You will hear about it.' I was very lucky in Reading. Couple of weeks later I got a letter from Maidenhead Building Society in Kings Street saying yes I can have the house. £8 deposit. The Maidenhead Building Society repossessed the house. When I went and saw the people they say they are only interested in the money that is outstanding. That is £800. That's what we want for the house. We want our £800 and they said 'Well, we give you a mortgage for £800.' So I took it.

By that time I knew Mr Salmon. I told you about him the other day, he's dead now. I went to Mr Salmon and I said 'Well this place has got no electricity.' The electricity board wanted £35 to wire it and Mr Salmon said to me, he said, 'Browney that's a lot of money.' He said, 'Now look. I'll go down there and wirethe thing for you' and he went down there and wired the house. Didn't give him a penny. He said '£25' when he's finished. When he finished that's what he charged me. He said 'Well you can come and pay me fifty pence a week or a pound a week until you pay off that money or you get some people in there and start getting some rent.' Yeah.

Three times you've had people just pick you out.

Three times. Just like that. Just like that some guardian angel. That's what I always believe. There's somebody looking over me. Don't matter what. I had some wrong things done to me but I always seem to come back and I come back well, I get out of it. Oh yeah.

So you've got many properties now in Reading?

No I didn't want no more. Especially today they're too much trouble. I didn't want any more houses anyway. Looking after property is a full-time job really.

So to put it in a nutshell now. The changes that have come, you've observed into Reading, would you say that is positive or negative?

It is. It's a change for the better. Reading has changed for the better, there's no two ways about it.

What I don't understand, you just chose Reading out of the blue? To visit Reading when you came here?

Yeah. I can remember I came here a Saturday and a Friday, which was Good Friday, I want the other way. I went to Gravesend and that was a real Gravesend then because it was a, it was nothing around there! So then I said, I heard people talking about this 'Ban the Bomb' march that stop at Reading, so I said right! I gonna see these people, so when I came here that Saturday morning, it's cold and I see all these thousands and thousands of people sleeping at the side of the road. These people are cruel to themselves. Oh yeah.

So how did you deal with cold, coming from such a hot country and what month was it, you said it was snowing?

February, February. Very next morning I get up I see snow out there. I didn't know what it was and when I looked through the glass through the condensation, I see this thing out there. Of course, Ovid was there, and apparently there was a girl, Ovid's cousin and she had rented these two rooms from this young man. So she had Ovid in one and she and her husband were staying in the other one. So I went in and I asked her. What is this stuff you have out there, is that some sort of decoration for Easter. She say you must be joking, you go out there you're gonna find out. That's when I come to realise it was snow. I never seen snow in me life before.

The first couple of jobs that I had here I was going to work with me pyjamas on and two pairs of trousers and I can't take off them clothes. I went on a job in Cheapside in London there was a sixteen storey block of flats they were building and they were putting me up on the eighth floor, I'm surprised I didn't freeze to death. Oh yeah. I nearly freeze to death.

Jobs

You had a very varied experience.

You're telling me. Then I had to start finding myself down to Brixton where they used to sell surplus army clothes and those clothes are good for wintertime. I used to wear those, oh yeah. All those good clothes I bought from home I was able to keep them.

So Reading has done you well?

Oh yeah. Reading hasn't done me too bad at all. I got no regrets. All the time I've been in Reading I was alright. I haven't got rich, but at the same time, I'm not a beggar. I don't have to beg for anything. I survive. I survived pretty well.

Guyana

The Republic of Guyana lies just north of the Equator on the northern coast of South America. Guyana is bordered by Brazil to the south and southwest, Suriname to the east, and Venezuela to the west. Guyana is about the size of Great Britain and its official language is English. Its capital and largest city is Georgetown. Although it is physically part of South America culturally it is closer to the Caribbean and is often considered to be part of the West Indies. Guyana was first spotted by Christopher Columbus whilst on his 3rd voyage in 1498 – he didn't stop and it wasn't until 1616 that it was settled by Europeans with the Dutch setting up three colonies between 1616 and 1752. During the latter part of the 18th century Great Britain took control of these colonies and they eventually became known as British Guiana. In 1889 Venezuela claimed lands up to the Essequibo river, this led to a dispute which still rages on, even though in 1899 an international tribunal ruled that the lands belong to Guyana. In 1950 the People's Progressive Party (PPP) was formed with Forbes Burnham as chairman and Dr Cheddi Jagan as second vice chairman. The PPP went on to win eighteen of the twenty-four seats in the first popular elections allowed under colonial rule. Unhappy with the result (and under pressure from the USA who were concerned about the party's Marxist leanings) the British government sent in troops and suspended the constitution. These events led to a split in the PPP and Burnham went on to form the People's National Congress (PNC). At this time groups with colonial interests did their best to thwart the move toward independence. They instigated conflict between the Indo-Guyanese and Afro-Guyanese populations; the PPP was depicted as being pro Indo-Guyanese and the PNC was depicted as looking after the interests of the Afro-Guyanese. This ethnic divide caused the half Indo-Guyanese and half Afro-Guyanese Lionel Jeffries (Treasurer of the PPP and one of its founders) to flee to Great Britain with his family. In 1961 the British granted full autonomy to Guyana and Jagan became prime minister (although the British retained certain veto powers). The following year Venezuela revived its territorial claims and Jagan introduced an austerity programme which in turn sparked internal riots and a general strike. Once again British troops were sent in. This unrest lasted until 1964 with both the British and American governments joining forces to destabilize the Guyanese government. At this time leaders of the PPP like Jagan as well as Guyana's leading poet, Martin Carter, were regularly imprisoned and harassed by the British. The riots continued and there was much racial violence between the two ethnic groups, it is estimated that about 200 people died in the riots. In 1964 more elections were held, this time under the system of proportional representation – Forbes Burnham (of the PNC) was declared prime minister after receiving support from The United Force (a small conservative party).

Maya Malhotra

Born: 27th January 1937

Agra, India

Date of Interview: 7th June 2006

Childhood

Education & Training

I was born in Agra. I think, it's a famous city. It is known for Taj Mahal. And, I spent my early childhood in different cities, whereby my father was in a different job so he used to move around, three years mostly in every city so we travelled Punjab, widely travelled in India. But most of my education was done in Allahabad, that's another famous city in the religious point of view.

Can you tell me, thinking back to when you were a very young child, what's the earliest thing you can remember?

Oh I have a very good memory of my childhood. I remember my teachers in the first school where I went. I went to school at the age of four and then stayed in that school till seven, then change school again. And after the age of … nine I left school. I did my private study … I was a bit bright for my age so, so my father took me away from school where, I did my … what you say equivalent to O level, my matriculation at the age of twelve and then I did all the private education till my PhD.

What what was your father's job? Why, what did he do?

He was a bank manager. So because of his job, he was the manager so their jobs were transferable, every three years they had to move to different cities. So that's how we were moving about. And so, after the matriculation and then all was private study, my BA, MA, and then I did my PhD … at the age of twenty three I have my PhD. And that was done from Lucknow University, and then I became a lecturer. [laughs]

Can you tell me about your family? Did you have any brothers and sisters?

Oh, yeah, we come from a big family [laughs] because in our time the people liked it. My father was the only son so he have sisters but no brothers … and we were family of nine, six brothers and three sisters. And it's a nice big house and we all lived together mostly. My mother, she wasn't very highly educated but in, according to her time she have a good education so she helped us to … towards the education.

What was it like living in a big family in a large house?

I think it's very difficult for people to imagine here because the social set up in this country is very, very different. When I look back at my childhood now, I see the children in this country and I think we have a lot lot happier time when we were children, though we may not have as many things as the children of today wanted. I mean the materialistic things, the very expensive toys and all that. We may not have that but we were quite happy and contented playing with each other, looking after each other and you know there were … I won't say that we didn't quarrel, we did quarrel [laughs] but not any no trace of

Childhood

jealousy and, something like this. So we, I have a very happy childhood memories which I brought with me when I came here. And then, I … came to here, in this country. I was twenty nine year old when I came to this country.

Education & Training

You achieved your PhD at twenty-three.

I did my PhD from Lucknow University. By that time we were in Lucknow living in Lucknow. And Lucknow is the capital of … one state Uttar Pradesh, the state of India … biggest state, and that's the capital of that, Lucknow, University is a very old university, where I did my PhD.

Were you still living at home then?

Yeah. And well I didn't leave home till I get married [laughs] because in India it's not common for girls to leave home. Unless if they're working away from home then they do leave it. Otherwise they study and when they are marriageable age, they get married and then they leave home.

So what did you, what did you do your PhD in?

My PhD is a cultural study of a period of poetry in India. So it's a fourteenth fifteenth century poets, eight poets, so I did the cultural study of that time. And when I did the cultural study it was the pioneer work that nobody have done the cultural study before me. So I did the first time. And then I got an award for that because it was the pioneer work and … then my book was published and everything and I used to write at that time. Not any more.

What was the language you were using?

It is Hindi, Hindi our national language. And I studied, my PhD was in Hindi. I used to write books in Hindi. History books and some course books I have written because at that time we were trying to make Hindi popular in South India. There are so many languages that are spoken in India, so every area has a different language. So, and, by the time India got its independence, so we wanted to make Hindi the national language, so I was writing textbooks for these areas to make Hindi popular.

Political Situation

Family Values

How did you meet your husband?

Well it was arranged marriage. I never met him before and he was a lecturer in Bihar University and I was a lecturer in Lucknow University. But my parents have arranged the marriage, and I met him on the date of the marriage.

And how did that work?

It worked very well in my case and I won't regret anything. I think … people have some wrong idea about this arranged marriages … In my experience well, when you are at the age of eighteen nineteen, so often you don't know yourself very well. You don't know what you want, what is best for you and how to see other people. And when the parents look for you, they know you well and they will analyse your choice and more better than you. I remember a comment made by my father, I think just before I got married. And one day we were all talking and my two sisters who were older than me, they were married and

Maya, 2006

Maya's wedding day

Political Situation

my father made a comment about that and said 'If Maya don't get a nice mother-in-law this girl will suffer all her life.' Luckily I have a very nice mother-in-law. [laughs] So that one thing gave me this idea that how much your parents know about you ... and I think the upbringing is also different here. Many times parents don't know what their children want ... because they have been ... I can't say all the ... it's not a bad thing that they become too independent too quickly.

So ... your father was looking to choose a good mother-in-law as well as a good husband for you.

Yeah, yeah. He thinks and I think he was right there, that it's not only the person you marry, because in India the concept of marriage is totally different than here. So you don't marry just the man, you marry in the family, and because of our ... way of living, mostly it's a joint family, in my time, not any more now, but, so that you had to cope with other family members as well, apart from getting used to your husband, and I think the family background does make a lot of difference.

What was happening in India at the time? ... When you were a young person?

I think the ... apart from the family life we were quite happy but the most turmoil thing what happened when India got its independence nineteen forty seven, and I was just ten year old at that time. And ... you know though we were very excited at the idea of getting independence... weeks before we were making all the plans for the celebration. We were, we are going to fly the flag here, we are going to fly the flag there. That was the dream of ... all children and the young persons. But this Partition business have dampened all the happiness and the Partition was done, well, in ... at that time we didn't realise how it has been decided because we were too young to understand that ... It was just, like people were waiting anxiously on the radio news that which part is going to India, which part is going to Pakistan, and it was just divided like this.

And my husband's family, they become refugee overnight, because they were living in the, very nice area, it's near Lahore, Kasur, the name of the place is Kasur where they live, have a mansion there. But ... and nobody believed at the time that this very, this nice city will be given to Pakistan, but somebody decided that it goes to Pakistan. And when the news broke out that this is given to Pakistan, what I have been told by the family members, that they just leave home, whatever clothes they have on their body with that, because at that time the main important thing was to save your life ... and so lot of people's life had been turned upside down, with that.

Did people fear for their lives?

Yeah it was because ... though the, all the demands were met for the Muslims
to be given Pakistan to them. And India have never said, even at that time
India never said to any Muslim to go and leave India, but, the Pakistan, people
or the government or whatever they were encouraging them to do it. They say
it is our country. You have to leave it. And though in that area, because before
that it is all one country so people were living happily side by side. There might
be some areas where one area is mostly predominantly occupied by Muslims,
another by Hindu but they worked together, they lived together, they would
do business together, and all of a sudden they become enemy. So when they
became enemy they were thrown out like anybody who is uprooted from
their home, it's not a nice feeling. So that created a lot of chaos at that time.
So instead of all that happiness it was bloodshed everywhere. I have very bad
memory of that period as well because we were listening all those, on the radio
then in my time there were no televisions so mostly radio news but we were
listening that the people were fleeing here and there, you see them being made
refugees.

And then the next thing I remember of my early childhood was when ...
victory Mahatma Gandhi, when Mahatma Gandhi.

And I remember that procession when we went to see that ... although
I wasn't old enough to know much, but that crowd of people and so much
quietness I could not believe it. I used to read in the storybooks that this thing
happens but never believed it until we saw that and that memory is still very,
very fresh in my mind, even I'm so old now. [laughs] Seeing the crowd, because
there were thousands of people walking on the street behind that day there
were no traffic, no transport was allowed at all on the road. And so people
walked miles and miles on feet without any complaint.

How old were you?

At that time I was just ... fifty, nineteen fifty, I was twelve years old ... He died
in 1948. [pause, then speaks quietly] Mahatma Gandhi was assassinated then,
yeah ... soon after the Independence.

You said you then came to England shortly after you were married. Why?

When my husband wanted to study here, though he was a lecturer in India, he
did his MSc. Then he wanted to do his PhD in this country and he have a ...
scholarship to do the PhD, then he came here and so I have to follow him.

How did you feel, about coming ... to Britain, at that time?

To tell you the truth I was never ever keen to come to England. I never, well in
my time, everybody was very keen to go to foreign countries and I was quite
happy in India so I never wanted to go anywhere ... once I got married and
my husband was coming to England so, that was accepted that I will follow
him and I did follow him. Not straight away I didn't come. We didn't come
together because he said 'I didn't want to take you to a strange country. I have
no money there. I don't want you to get you into problem. So let me go there,
find my feet, then I will call you.' So, and he did that.

It took him nine months but once he found his place and, you know he had enough money with him then he called me. So I came and joined him. And first year he was a student as I said but ... things have changed. There was two things for the family circumstances. The year I came, within a month my husband lost his father, he died, and then after three months I lost my father so we both had family tragedies and we couldn't go back home, we had no money to go back home. Then the same year they increased fees for the, to foreign students and because his scholarship was not extended the following year, it was done for one year and ... they didn't have the money to extend it and ... he couldn't finish his PhD in one year so they gave him a diploma for that, and we couldn't carry on.

Where was it?

That was in Cornwall, you know. We were doing a mining degree ... we thought all I, we will work and get enough money to start back the study, that was the intention ... but as things have worked out ...

How did you travel to Britain?

By air, yeah we both came by air, did my husband came by Japan Airlines and I came by Air India. But we both travelled by air. Well we stayed in at his friend's place in London and spend the day there. And then in the night we took the train and went to Cornwall, and we reached early morning to Cornwall there. He had a flat there in Cornwall. We went there.

And my experience of Cornwall was very very different. I think that there ... although it was a mining area, because of the mining college there were not many foreigners in that. And in that whole town there were two Indian families there. I was the second one. One student was there senior to my husband. His family, his wife and two children were there and then we reached there, so wherever I go everybody say 'Oh I know you.' And I was thinking 'Oh what a thing to say.' [laughs] And first I was very puzzled why people say 'I know you' or do I look so different. And then I realised afterwards when we found there are only two Indian families in the whole town so everybody recognised me and because I always wore my sari so it's easy for them to recognise me.

There was a post advertised in Reading so he came to give the interview and he find out ... well in those days it wasn't that hours, weeks waiting, they said yes he had been selected and we have a vacancy. You can start from Monday. So then he wrote a letter to me, the phone wasn't that easily available that 'I got the job so you can pack up your, things and come back and meet me in Reading' because we were very, very short of money at that time so he couldn't come and pick me up and all that.

So I made my way to Reading. But ... in the meantime we find out, that in those days nobody was giving flat to ... Indians. There is the flat advertised when you ring them ... and, if they ... don't recognise you from your voice, when you go there then they say the flat is gone. So you don't get a flat in, in Reading at that time. And I remember there were only two Indian, well two landlords of ethnic minority. One was a Pakistani man, one was an Indian man, the only two people who have houses at that time, but they were more keen to rent room than to rent a flat. So ... in the end my husband said 'You

Self Sufficiency

Jobs

Racism

Self Sufficiency

Jobs

Family Values

Old Reading

have to stay in a room now, you can't have a flat any more.' We stayed in a room. And I was expecting my first child at that time … it was … we moved to Reading in December and I had my first child in February.

So where was your husband's job?
At Ministry of Agriculture … He was working as a scientist there.

What was it like, what was it like for you arriving in … in Reading in the winter, in a room, expecting your first child?
Well it was very hard for … first of all … any first time mother it is a difficult time. Second thing we have all this worry about, the money problem, then the family tragedy because we both lost our parents, so I was emotionally upset, financially … burdened, but then only one thing we kept on doing and … we have to … we decided we've got to face it together, face it as better as we can because this is, all the time we had said 'No this is not permanent, this is just temporary, phase in our life. We will get through it,' that kept us going.

And soon after the baby is born though we couldn't get a flat, so we, I think I stayed in that one bedroom for three months. Then I find out the place, though it wasn't a flat as such, so I said 'Can I have two rooms on the same floor?' So that landlady allowed me to have two rooms on the same floor so at least we have some privacy with the baby. So we have two rooms and there I stay and I … could have … bought a house at that time because by then we had the saving to buy a house and in those days houses were not that expensive. You can buy a house for 800 pound 1,000 pound in Reading. But … I don't want to do it. I keep telling my husband we want to go home. I don't want to settle here.

And initially he was on a study leave for three years so the second year was passing so I said 'We will finish the third year and then we'll leave home. So I don't want you to buy the house, we will buy a property, we will be stuck here.' And, so this was another reason that kept us going, that I, knowing that I could do it but I still not doing it. After the second year when my daughter was two year old, then I realised it doesn't look like I'm going now. So then we bought our first house. We thought we had to get our house and my husband keep telling. He said 'Nobody here making our life difficult. And we can buy it so why don't we buy it.' Well I never worked when I came and, so he was the only person who is working. And then I said 'All right if you want to.' After … my daughter was five years old then I started work.

Let me just take you back to when you first came to Reading, you said, there that you had the real experience of being an immigrant. What did you mean?
Well I think when I was in Cornwall we were treated like guest because they all knew there are students here, they are here for a year or six months or twelve months or maybe two years and they go back. And because people treat you like you are doing something for their economy because the students were the main source of income in that area so, there were not much prejudice there, they were very friendly, very, very co-operative people. And here when I came to Reading, though I personally have been very lucky, I've never been abused by anybody. I have good friends, good English neighbours and all that, only a

small incident, one or two where you can see that it was not right.

Well I remember when my daughter was … small, she went to school, she was going to nursery and one day she come home and says to me, and she was only four years old at that time, 'Mummy, are you going to arrange my marriage.' I said 'Of course I will arrange your marriage' [laughing as she speaks] I thought, she must have, heard somewhere arranged marriage, so … 'No way!' I said 'Why?' 'No way. I'm not going to marry a Paki.' And I said 'What do you mean by Paki?' But I have to explain to her at that time what is a Paki means and what is Indian means and I said 'Look. They can call Pakis but you are not going to call anybody Pakis from today.'

So I've told her now, and so this was the small things like when … I remember when I bought my first house. We went to see the house and the next door neighbour, they were all eager who is coming to see the house and we were … we went in the evening to see the house and so she just come out. And, out of curiosity I just said 'Hello' to her and say 'This is nice area and is a quiet area too much noise?' She said 'No it's a nice area.' And after that we left it, and I didn't see her any more. When we bought the house, when we moved into the house, then she didn't like it, that I … that was the English lady and she didn't like it that we've been Indian buying this house. And she stopped telling even, I say whenever I see her I say 'Hello, good morning' and she will not respond to me at all. After a few days I stopped telling her, I say if she don't want to respond to me let her do it whatever she wants. Well my daughter she will stand in the back garden [laughter in her voice] on the steps and, and she keep on saying 'Hello' until she reply to her. [laughs heartily] And she was thinking, why don't she reply to me [laughs] so, that's one thing. Then I think I … after that, after a few months of resentment they become friendly, and then I find out one day that they were evicted, when I come home I was told they were evicted they were the tenant they hadn't paid their rent and so.

So what was Reading like as a town in 1970?

It was … it was quite nice and friendly, don't … the real … I think now I have seen all the changes in Reading since then and some areas you can't even recognise it now. Because that even the Howard Street area where I got my house and is all this Castle Hill area, they have quite a bit changes there.

And you know, I was booked into Dellwood Hospital, that was Dellwood Maternity Home when I came first. [pause] The first impression of that hospital … in the hospital there. It was a maternity home not a hospital and I went to visit there, the very first time, when I moved to this town because my doctor in Cornwall said 'Whatever you do when you go to Reading the main, first thing you find a doctor for yourself. First thing you book yourself in a new … place because Reading I know it will be crowded you won't get a place there and you are very late stage of pregnancy so you must do that as soon as you reach to Reading.' So they book, I find a doctor where I was, I was living at that time, and then he booked me to maternity home, the first … So when I went my first visit that was very, very [pause, takes a deep breath] I should say at that time, I felt very bad the way the nurses have talked to me.

Self Sufficiency

Well my husband have started a new job as I told you so he couldn't take time off to go with me and anyway, from the very beginning he left me very independent, he said 'You can do it. You can never go anywhere with me, you know even to go to' ... When I came, in this country when we were in Cornwall he gave me his first cheque of his scholarship and he said 'Look this is my money I get and ... now it's up to you how you manage it, you go and open account wherever you want and this is the, you know this is my income, is all right.' I asked him 'Will you come with me to your bank to open account?' 'No you can do it yourself.' I went and opened the account and he never bothered me after that. 'Cause what you get what you haven't got, you know what I get, all right.'

So, going to visit the hospital first time, I went on my own. I didn't have ... a car at that time so where I went, find out where which bus goes there and I went, I clearly remember it was winter evenings when I be there, the snow was everywhere and I would get down from the bus walking to the maternity home. And when I reached there greeted by a nurse to give her my card that I had, 'It is my appointment I came for that.' And the very first thing she said

Racism

'Can you speak English [crossly]?' I say 'Yes.' 'All right, that's all right then' she says and she took me inside and show another nurse. And she says to her 'This woman says she speak English.' And I felt so bad about it. I said 'What does this mean, this woman says she speaks English.' [laughs] And the nurse asked me 'Where do you learn to speak English? [laughs] I said 'No don't you worry I just come here for check-up, you just check up, I'm not going to talk to you after, where I learned from.' I'm not a person like that but that day I felt like it.

When you had the baby ... were you?

Em ... the baby having the baby and that was another experience because ... baby first child, I did not know about all this labour pain though my doctor was very, very nice, he explain to me all this and how the labour pain will start. I spent all night at home you know turning tossing and in the morning my husband asked me 'You haven't slept all night, shall I go to work or shall not I go to work?' I said 'No you go to work.' And because a week before when my doctors checked me, only a week before he test me, 'Don't bother if you don't have your baby on the date we are telling you.' I said 'Why not?' He said 'Because your baby is not developed enough.' So he went ... so I packed up my bag and everything the week before. And then my husband left home, gone to work, if I ... his office wasn't too far so he was just walking to work.

Community

And as I recall I went, very few minutes I went to the loo and I can see some ... blood coming out. I thought 'Oh my God, now I have to go.' And I remember in those days we used to use old sixpence for the phone so I have two sixpence piles and told the lady who was in the same house, living in the same house. I say 'Can you Margaret do a favour to me?' She said 'What?' I say 'Can you ring my husband please.' So I gave her two sixpences, I said 'One you can use to ring my husband and another for the ambulance.' She said 'All right.' She took it, and went to make a phone call, because he was already on the way so she couldn't, she couldn't get hold of him at the work, but she used the second sixpence to call the ambulance, and come back and tell me that 'I

Community

call the ambulance, they will be here in a few minutes but I can't talk to your husband.' I said 'Please' and gave her another sixpence, said 'Will you please ring my husband.' She said 'I will do it now when I take my children to school' … it was early in the morning, so 'Fine.'

And the ambulance people came here in no time … so, we, I … ask me 'How are you?' I said 'Fine.' 'So are … can you walk down?' I said 'Yes I can walk down.' So when the ambulance man was there, he was very cheerful man, he said 'Isn't anybody coming with you?' I said 'No, there is nobody to come with me. [laughs] At that time I really wanted to cry, for I come from a big family like this and nobody to go with me, so … Then he said 'Don't worry, we are with you.'

So I went in the ambulance. So they took me to Dellwood Hospital, and I was greeted by a very very stern nurse and who tell me off that she said 'Why do you spend all that time at home?' And I couldn't tell her why I spend all that time I was at home … She should have understand that's my first child, I don't understand. And she said 'You spend all that time at home, you will have … baby in no time.' And in my mind I was glad that I have baby in no time, what's the problem? And she says to me 'Now you go and have a bath' and she send me to bath and at that time I don't want to take a bath, and she made me go in the bath. I say 'All right.'

Family Values

Self Sufficiency

The baby was born in hospital … So that was a different … that is I think the first time I really sorely missed my home because … though I want to be brave and not to say anything to anybody, but I can come from a family like this, and here at this time nobody's with me. I'm all by myself, nobody's going to do anything for me. And that was a difficult time … But after the baby is born I found everybody was very helpful, the nurses and … once they knew that I could speak English their attitude have changed.

You said you'd gone to work when your first daughter …

Yeah when she was five year old then because of the circumstances we bought the house and we need to, support ourselves a bit more and then because he, my husband lost his father so he have to support his mother as well back home. So we need to help them at home. So we both worked so then he could help his family and then I can bring my earning, we can manage to live.

Jobs

Where did you work?

I worked with Department of Transport. I have financial knowledge so I have got in the finance department.

Old Reading

Where, where was that?

Well that office is closed now, in that place is The Oracle built now. That's where the office was, behind Debenham's in Minster Street, that's where our office used to be. It was a big office, Department of Transport where they do all the car tax and licensing and all that.

How did you find out about that job?

It was advertised in the paper you know and … good job. You asked this thing because I, in those days we were not getting clerical jobs. Mostly our womans

Old Reading

Self Sufficiency

Jobs

were working in the factories, so any clerical job you are applying, you don't get it. I got so fed up with it, because my husband said to me 'You are not going to work in a factory with your qualification and all that. I won't allow you to work in a factory.' 'I don't mind doing it,' I say 'Well it's work is work. If I work in a factory, does it matter?' But he said 'No. If you find a reasonable job like in a, a school or anything, you go to work.' So I a-, I apply and every time I was getting regrets. Sometimes they say you are too qualified, sometimes they say you are not fit person so different departments ... the work ... I've keep applying.

And when this post came so you know in those days Chronicle, we used to look in the Chronicle for the, jobs. And my husband said 'There's a job advertised in the Chronicle, you apply for that.' I said 'Which one is that?' He says 'PSA they are advertising for it's Property Services Agency.' So all right. I did not even bother, I was so fed up with getting the rejections that I did not even look at the paper, I just applied for it. I shown him the application that I'm sending this, he said 'Why you are applying for the clerical assistant job, there's a clerical officer job there' so I said 'Is it?', he says 'Yes' so I crossed the assistant and put officer on it. I was so desp- ... I knew I won't get it but I just sent the same application.

And they called me for interview, I went for the interview, and this time ... I'm, as it happened quite a few times the same people were interviewing me so the faces were familiar. And they, in the form they asked have you applied before. So last time I tell a lie, I said 'No I haven't applied before' [laughs] because I thought 'What they will think of me, that she is not even getting a clerical job.' To my mind it was a small job, so why, I was thinking 'Why I can't even get this job?' The policy was different, they don't want to give the job to us. He asked me 'Have I seen you before somewhere?' And I ... just did not answer that neither yes or no. I just smiled. [Laughs] And then he said 'All right' and so he asked different questions and then he said 'Do you know what the job entails?' and I said 'No I have no idea.' I was honest. So what do they do? I say that the property, PSA stands for the Property Service Agency but I don't know what you do. And ... then he asked me about questions whether I can speak other language. I said 'Yes, apart from English I speak Hindi, Punjabi.' Then he said 'If I, do you do get a job then it won't be in this office. Do you mind?' I said 'No it doesn't matter. I have to start anywhere so if you give me a job wherever you like.' Well then I knew I might have got the job. So then they gave me the job in Department of Transport because there they used to get quite a few Indians who were not well spoken in English. So he thought I might be useful there. [laughs] So I think that's how I got the job. So ... But that's the only job I did in this country. And then I retired from there.

So you, how long were you working there then?
I think after that I worked twenty two years.

What ... changes did you see in Reading in this time?
I think lot of ... roads have been different, all this IDR and all that was built here in my time. And, the main change I think is the ... mix-up ethnic groups. For when I moved to Reading the first ... at that time there were not that

many. But you see other ethnic groups were less as well and apart from Indians and Pakistanis there were not that many. But gradually I can see the build-up. Because in seventy- ... eight or seventy-six when the influx from Kenya, and Ugandan people came, so that have increased the numbers of, Asians there. And after that now is a lot of, from African countries. I know certain areas of Reading where there were only ... I remember the second house we bought. I was, I was one of the first house of any Asian in that area. Now you will see the whole row of those Asian houses there. So that have changed the ... build-up of Reading, and certain areas are becoming really, really ethnic area now.

Was it, did it become better as more ... Asian people came, for you or ... ?

I have been lucky neither at work, well apart from one or two incidents that ... now I can laugh about it, but at that time they were hurtful but then I thought if I am going to make it a issue, then I am the one who will pay the price for it. If I ignore this issue and then carry on working then I won't ... I will manage it and I think I was right.

When I got my first job in the Civil Service ... in that office at that time there were two offices together. One was run by the Berkshire County Council and the other was run by Civil Service and I was employed by Civil Service. So I was not a Berkshire County Council person but there were two managers in that building. My manager greeted me at the door on the day I have to start work, so as he come in ... he took me out. 'Hello Mrs Malhotra' and all that. I went in and then ... as we were passing he was going to show me my, desk and all that. He met the another manager who was the manager of Council office, Mr S so he introduced me and what greeting I got from Mr S was 'There, there's no room for her to hang her coat downstairs.' I thought 'That's a good welcome!' [laughs] On the first day I am in this office and he's telling me this! And I knew the make-up of that office there was not any Asian person in that office. I was the only one person in that office and I remained one for so many years. Then they haven't had any other Asian there. I say 'All right.' So that was the first experience of his prejudice.

And then there were two ladies in that office who will not respond to my good morning, though they are good friends now but at that time they would not respond to my good morning. And I thought 'What's the matter with these two people? Why they are not even ... ?' I've been a polite person. Every morning when I go to office I will say 'Good morning J,' I will say 'Good morning B.' No answer. After few weeks I say 'All right, I have given them enough chance. If they don't want to respond to me, all right, I will pass them by.' And I did.

But after a few years working with them, when both offices became one and those people, they were employed by Berkshire County Council, when they become in Civil Servant and because, by then, I have more experience of my job so, one day this lady was stuck, she couldn't balance it. So, she went to my manager, she don't want to ask me. So my manager said 'Go and ask Maya she will help you to sort it out.' It was against her then to ask me any questions. She came and dump everything on my desk and says [angrily] 'Can you help me?' I said 'All right.' So I thought I wouldn't be like her, if I want to degrade myself to her standard. I will say 'You ask me nicely,' and I didn't do it, I said

Jobs
Racism

Self Sufficiency

Jobs

Racism

Family Values

'You leave it, I will sort it out.' So soon I sorted out. There was a mistake which was why she can't balance. So I sort out the mistake and I, in doing that I was so annoyed with her. I just took it back to her. I said 'Look, there is the mistake. If you correct this one you will balance.' Otherwise I should have done the balancing for her but I was so annoyed with her behaviour that I'm not doing it. [laughs] You do it. [laughs] That I regretted afterwards, I say, 'I've become mean with her.' And I know. If she, she doesn't deserve to be, nice so I don't want to do it. And I think that day she changed her mind. Then she start to talking to me nicely.

And now she's a good friend to me, after we retired. ... I, I took this attitude if you don't want me, so I am not going to bother with you. I will fit in if you want me to do it but, you know, I, the very first Christmas they say 'You want to join us?' I said 'Why not? I will join you.' I am here and I, I know that I had to ... and my own religion is my own part but it is here I take it as a social function. And they ask me, there was one lady asked me 'What are you going to do? Do you drink?' I said 'No, I don't drink.' 'Do you go to dance?' I said 'No I don't go to dance.' 'You smoke?' I 'No I don't smoke.' And she say 'What do you do then with your life?' And I said 'That's your point of view with your life. You think drinking and smoking and dancing is the life? It's not to me. My social getup is different. To your, the life may be just that. I have my life, I enjoy my life, do I look miserable to you? I'm not.' [pause] It's a different social ... makeup I think.

And I think one thing I find now, whether it is, I don't know whether it is due to television or due to ... papers or what. The people are a bit more knowledgeable about it now, than they were when I came to it, because that time people had no idea what is the life in India is about. People used to ask silly questions, 'Do you live in a hut?' ... And one lady asked me, is a long time, I don't know where I met her. She said 'Why, did you work in India?' I said 'Yes, I did work in India.' 'So what was your job, was it a tea-leaf picking?' And I thought ... I wanted to tell her, no that's not the only job in India the women do. And I said 'No there's too many other jobs to do it.' And I couldn't turn round and tell her I was a lecturer but I thought how ignorant it is, you should know a bit more about it. And I said to her 'Look, not everybody lives in a hut in India and not everybody just do tea-picking and there so many other' ... and by then I think the ... few years after, they had the first woman prime minister.

You talked about your religion, the little bit back you were talking about, you know you're invited to Christmas. Have you been able to practise your religion here?

Yeah, I have done it because, when ... well when we came here there was no facility. There were no temple in Cornwall, no temple in Reading but ... and ... the first ... few months I was very very lost, that there is nothing to do here. And then I thought All right. If it is not there we can always ... do that religious part in our own home, so I started doing all the prayers whatever I used to do it in my own home, and ... we started, because ... it was very important for children to understand where they come from and what is our background so I did that at home. We used to do all morning prayers, evening prayers with children at home whether I have a ... shrine or not.

We started this ... campaign to build a temple in Reading, that was quite late but not at the early stage. And then in eighty-, nineteen-eighty-three they thought we should have a place, so we, a group of women, we get together and we started that thing. So it took us nearly eighteen years to build a temple in the end. It did build it one. So that's the temple in Reading now. And it took us nearly eighteen years hard work.

Was it mainly ... you and some friends, or ...

Well, we started four five ladies together and just like a general discussion that we need a place and we haven't got any place, the Sikhs have gurdwara, the Muslims have mosque, why can't we have a temple of our own? So we said 'All right, we will start something.' So we started weekly prayers and finding places where to do it and that ... And then ... gradually we got more people involved in it. Then after retirement we took, both of us took early retirement then we put our whole and full force in it. We thought now it is time. We got no commitment of the job, we will put our force.

Luckily God help us, so we find this place and ... bought it. That was bought without any help from, without any grant from anywhere. It was just our own fundraising. And, the, well we had to take a mortgage out, to have it from the bank and then from the public. And we managed to do it. So ... that is a very important place for any, any group of people, to have their own place. Like ... community centres serve a different purpose, but the places of worship serve a different purpose. And that is a place where people can meet together and work together and ... It's a two-fold thing, religious and cultural thing. It's not all the time prayer.

I am not believer on those people who want segregation, I've never wanted that. Wherever you are living you must accept the host community and you must adjust and adopt the way. Only thing I always said from the beginning that we must integrate but not at the 'cost of identity. We should keep our identity. That is what ... from the day one, my ... aim being that I cannot lose my identity. I am Indian and I will remain Indian all my life. But I would like to integrate and I think I have done it quite well in this society where I'm living. And no society is perfect. I won't say that all the Indians are perfect, all the Hindus are perfect. We all have our drawbacks, we all have our shortcomings. But if we take the ... what is best for all the society and try to accept it then we will have a wonderful society.

Where is the temple?

Temple is in Whitley ... Street, 112 Whitley Street. It used to be Methodist church and when that came on the market we had short talk to the trustees of that ... church and we told them 'If you sell the place to us we will, yours is a place of worship, we will keep it as a place of worship. But if ... we may not be able to, we won't demolish it, put it that way. But it's up to you.' And in the end I think they were bit impressed by that. Since we have that place, we have done a lot of work in that place and still using it as a prayer hall as they were using it, and enhance the value of it more. It's a great achievement I think. [laughs quietly]

Do you ... have you been back to India, and what is it like when you go?

Well the first [pause] time, the longest time, when I came to this country, the very first time I went back to India it took seven years to go back to India because it ... there were personal circumstances, we didn't have money, we had family tragedy and all that. And another thing was, most difficult was, we came separate, me and my husband came separate so I wanted to go back first time together. I don't want to go alone and then we didn't have enough finance to go back together so that took us seven years in the end. After the seven years we had enough money and I being a person of my very own, I don't want to take any help from anywhere, my family at home offered me so many times that we send you a ticket, you come home and I said 'No. I don't want to take ticket from anybody. I will come, we will come, not I will come, we will come together whenever I can afford the whole tickets.

Well India had been changing since then. People's attitude towards finance, people's aspirations and the achievements and the whole sort of social ... brought up into society, is totally different. The achievement is OK but they are leaving their culture behind too quick, and that, I think they have to pay the price for it. I ... I may be wrong but to me, they are going a little bit too fast and without thinking these consequences of this cultural change

How do your own daughters ... see their culture, having been brought up here?

It's ... again, as I said before I never insisted on a very strict ... upbringing. I knew they are born here, they are living in this society, they are living in this culture. So I don't want to impose any values which are not relevant in this society. I always tease them, what is our values, what is it we would like to do, what we don't like to do it. But I never enforce even the question of ... say very ordinary thing about food, all about your etiquette, all about your social beliefs. I never forced it down to their throat. I said 'This is, I would like you to do it and this is how we do it at home' but never force it.

It was, again was my older daughter Neera was in the nursery, and I never said to school that she shouldn't have something food. One day in those days there were dinner ladies to help children ... to cut their food. And the dinner lady said 'Neera, shall I cut your beef?' And Neera said 'I'm not supposed to eat beef.' 'Why not?' 'I am Hindu, I don't eat beef.' And the dinner lady took the beef away from her and she ... I don't know whether they may not have anything else to give her, so the dinner lady have informed the teacher and the teacher informed the head teacher, so by the time I went to pick her up, I had a message through the teacher that head teacher want to see you. And I thought, when I went there she said 'Mrs Malhotra head teacher want to see you before you take Neera home.' And she said to me 'I can look after Neera, you go and talk to her.' I say 'Fine.' And I thought what on earth this girl had done today? Has she been naughty? And when I went there and she announced 'Mrs Malhotra you never told me that I, that we shouldn't give Neera beef.' I said 'What happened?' She told me the whole story. I said 'Look.' And again, in that whole school she was the only Hindu child so I thought it's too much for the school to ask, just for cater for one child. And I said 'If she don't eat meat in one day does it make any difference? I am not a ... meat-eater any ... so she doesn't get meat at home. Is only vegetarian meals she gets.' So then I said to her 'Oh, don't worry about that.' She said 'At least she should have told me.'

And then a few days later she called me again 'And do you have any objection if she attend the assembly?' because in those days assembly was totally Christian assemblies. And I said 'Miss J, I don't, I'm not that religious person. Let her attend the assembly, for I'm sure no religion will teach you wrong thing. So if she go in and listen the assembly or she sing the hymns, doesn't matter, let her sing it.' So she take part in the school nativity play and all that. And I said later on when they were a little bit older, I said 'Look, you can study, you can go to assembly, if you want to go to Sunday School I have no objection, go to Sunday School. When you are old enough to decide which religion you want to follow, then you follow it.' I'm glad to say that my children say 'No, they are proud to be Hindu, they are born a Hindu, and they are proud to remain a Hindu, that's it.' So I never force anything.

Is there anything else that you wanted to say, that I haven't asked you about?

Yeah, I think for any immigrants whichever background they come from, when they come, to my mind, if they decided to come and stay in this country, so then they should have an open mind as well. You read a lot in the paper about the host community but they, if the host community have a obligation then the immigrants should have to fulfil their duties towards the host community. You can't have everything one-sided. It have to be both sides make effort. I do believe that you can keep your culture, you can keep your identity, you can keep it but still there is so many common grounds where you can integrate better and I don't believe in seclusion. One thing I will, I don't agree with these faith schools. I have never liked them. Whether it is a Roman Catholic school or a Shi'ite school or a Sikh school or whatever school, I don't believe in it. I think children are better off … being taught together. And they, when they are in school they should learn how to live, how to be educated.

I remember there was a … when I went to my daughter's graduation, a very nice thing the speaker have said in the welcome speech that the university is not a place just to get a degree. University is a place, university education gets them prepared how to live a normal life, how to be sensible in our life. It's not just to get a piece of paper in your hand. And that is what education is all about. So if you segregate children, like make a special school for the Shi'a, for Muslim children, a special school for the Hindu children, Sikh children and then just try to teach them the Sikh values or the Hindu values or the Muslim values. What that will do? But the value of every religion should be the common ground, the humanity. Human values are more important. All right your culture, your traditions can be still kept within a limit. There is no harm in it. But you cannot overlook the basic faces of humanity. So that is where they should be taught tolerance.' Cause nowadays everybody knows their right but nobody knows their duties. [pause]

So that is a thing I, I'm all for these temples, all for these, you know, places of worship because there's the best place where you can meet, you can meet in your own society, you can mingle. And I find it now, I see people coming from India when they come and meet there they have a nice place to meet people.

And then I look back that when I came to this town there were no such place where I can go and meet people, I can talk to people. I remember because we miss it so much, we have had no common place. We start an association of the young people, Indian Association, and that time we don't have a place. We used to meet in our ... well, houses. They were, we were living in homes, even and then once a month we will get together in one room, all the friends. We bring our own things and we get together and eat it there because they don't have enough facilities to cook for so many people. And then we say already, everybody will bring one dish. At least we share and we started celebrating our, you know, special days, Diwali and festivals and all that, our Independence Day [unclear] you know democratic day. All this ... we started doing that because there was a need to get together, need to know each other and that's how this thing developed. Nowadays there are so many community centres. When I came to Reading there was not any. So there were ... nice development in the right direction.

And now all these places of worship are there. I see now every week there's somebody new comes from India and I know there a lot of IT people coming in this country now. So where they come, when they will come, they stay with their work they say 'Oh there is a temple over there. You go and you meet people there. And they all come running there and they feel so homely, that they can see so many faces there. So that is the place, that is the central focal point for the society, but that should not be a point where they separate, [quietly] no I don't agree with it.

I think this is the main thing, if we had made this country our home because as I said to you in the beginning, the day I came I always thinking 'Oh after two years, after three years, I'm going back home.' And now I'm ... sixty-six years old and I can't see now when I'm going. Now only last two years I accepted it that I'm not going to go back home and this is my home now and I will die in this country. [laughs] Only last two years I have accepted it.

India: Independence and Partition

On the stroke of midnight 15 August 1947 the British Commonwealth saw two self-governing nations come into being. India had been the jewel in the crown of the British Empire, but after long campaigns for independence India finally achieved its goal of self-governance. Independence was celebrated in Karachi (then capital of Pakistan) on 14 August so as Lord Mountbatten (the last Viceroy of India) could attend the ceremonies there and in Delhi on the following day. The Indian National Congress had long been petitioning for independence, but these pleas had fallen on the deaf ears of successive British Tory governments. At the end of the Second World War the Labour party swept to power and the India question was looked at afresh by Clement Atlee's government. Independence didn't have to mean partition but the seeds had been sown long before 1947. During both World Wars India supplied many soldiers who fought for Britain, and the end of the conflicts some of these became the first Indian immigrants to settle in Britain. The British Colonial Administration took the first steps towards Indian self-government in the late 19th century, appointing Indian councillors to give advice to the British Viceroy. In the 1920s Subhas Chandra Bose and other Indian leaders (including Mahatma Gandhi and Abu Kalam Azad) drove the Indian National Congress toward a campaign against British colonial rule. Independence was finally achieved through a mix of non-violent resistance, non-cooperation and parliamentary action. The All India Muslim League (AIML) was formed in 1906 by Muslims disaffected by what they saw as a Hindu bias in the India National Congress. In 1930 Allama Iqbal made an address to the AIML which foresaw the birth of Pakistan as a separate nation for Muslims. In 1935 the Sindh Assembly made the creation of a separate Muslim nation a stated demand. Up until this point the AIML leader Mohammad Ali Jannah had canvassed for Hindu-Muslim unity, but he too eventually joined the cause. Under the terms of the 3rd June Plan (or Mountbatten Plan) the country was eventually divided according to the report commissioned by the British Government from Sir Cyril Radcliffe. Pakistan came into being as two enclaves separated geographically by India, viz. East Pakistan (now Bangladesh) and West Pakistan. The Princely States of India were given the choice of which country to join – this decision was mostly based on the religious make-up of the state. The partitioning of India was a rushed process and little provision was made for the huge migration of people that was to follow (a total of twelve million people moved between these new borders). There was much rioting at the time of partitioning between Hindus and Muslims that left many dead (estimates range from 200,000 to one million). Partitioning had been seen as a way to end the violence between Muslim and Hindu communities, but this was not to be with conflicts still flaring between them as well as between their nation states. The repercussions of the partitioning of India are still felt today, with disputes still raging over certain territories (eg Kashmir) as well as a more general emnity between India and Pakistan.

Grace Browne

Born: 31st October 1932
Barbados

Date of Interview: 11th July 2006

Barbados

● St. Thomas, Barbados
○ Reading, UK

Childhood

... Let me see ... some years ago back, ah 74 years back, let me see ... my mum used to do sewing and I did like doing bits of making doll dresses, yes and looking after the chickens, because they used to keep lots of chicks ... I had three other elder sisters, and we used to just play together, yeah.

Did you have any brothers?
No brothers, had one brother and he died when he was two years old. And she never had no more boys. That was her second child.

Well, you said your mum, you remember her when you were a young child doing sewing?
Yes.

Did she make your clothes?
Oh yes that was her job, her living.

So who else did she sew for?
Oh she sew for the district, lots of brides, yes, baby christening dresses, school clothes. We have a lady here in Reading now that she used to make her clothes when she was small but she's blind.

So as a small child you can remember, did your mother, how did she do the sewing did she have a machine or?
Yes, in those days it was the hand, hand machine yeah.

And what would people do, come to the house to ask?
Yes, bring, sometimes they bring material and she cut it out, if not they give her the money and she go into the town and she do the shopping, and if it's a bride she goes into town with my mum and choose her material and then my mum makes her dress, and makes the bride's dresses, and the bridesmaids dresses, and the guests.'

Where did she, how did she learn to sew?
When she was a child her mother sent her to learn it because that was when you leave school that was a profession like, the boys go and do tailoring, and the girls go and do sewing or if not the boys do joining work. Making chairs and tables, that type of work. Yep.

So how did the people, where was this in Barbados? A certain area or district that you lived in?

At first it was in Saint Thomas, Pourer Springs, St Thomas, yes. She used to live there first and then we moved from that area and been into the city which was in Black Rock, St Michael's.

Why did you move?

Well, my father was working at the biscuit factory and save him getting bus backward and forward … and moving on, you know.

Who owned that factory, what was it called?

Well to be truthful all I knew was the biscuit factory, it was the only biscuit factory that was in the country and it made all the biscuits and then import them to different countries. So I would just say it was Barbados West Indian biscuit factory yeah and he worked there for many years as management.

So when did you, where did you go to school?

I started school in Saint Thomas … I leave there when I was about … seven and I went to school in Black Rock at St Stephens' School it was a parish school … I been there until I finish school.

How did you get there?

I walk it. Oh, we had to walk more than bus, unless it was very far you get the bus but we do a lot of walking.

And what was school like there, in Barbados in those days?

Yes, it was very good, very strict, yes, be in school in time, do your work, if not you get a smack, or misbehave you stand on the bench, or you stand in the corner yeah. And you couldn't be rude to the teachers. No, it was very, it was very strict. You used to get lashed in the palm of your hand [lashing noise] with a ruler, yes.

How long were you at school for then?

I finish school when I was fifteen and sixteen that age.

When you came home from school what would you do?

First thing come home, you had to say good evening whatever you call your parents, take those school clothes off and if it's, have something to eat if you have homework you do your homework. Most people they keep goat, sheep, cattle, chicken, pigs, you go and do that and water the garden. We have coops that the chicken used to live in and you had those to clean out, see they have clean water.

You see in our country it's a sanitary inspector, he comes around to the house, at least twice a month and see if there's any water, dirty water around the house and he have a ladle and dips it into it and see if there's any little creepers into it and he will warn you and if he come back again and its not there you have a fine. So round the place must be kept clean and you keep pigs and the pig pen must be kept clean or you can have a fine.

Family Values | Childhood

How much would the fine be?

Well to be truthful I was a child, we didn't know what fine would be all we was interested to know was that is been kept clean yes and if it don't keep clean well you know what you going get. Because each child have their little jobs to do yeah. On Saturdays you had to clean the house, see everything in the house is nice and clean that was definitely a Saturday job, all kids have to look around and make sure that sweep around the house, the houses are not like these, but they have to go out and clean around the house and put the garbage out and see that everything has been kept clean.

What did you do on Sundays?

Sunday was church. Wake in the morning, if you live near to the beach you go and have your sea bath, you come back have your breakfast, and you go to church, come back and then you got to Sunday school. And then in the evenings, depends on what your parents like you might have to go back to church. So definitely Sunday was the time of worship, yes, if parents don't even go to church they make sure that the kids go to church until they get fifteen, sixteen.

Was this typical of the whole neighbourhood?

Most people would tell you that, yeah, that they had to go to Sunday school, yeah.

Jobs

So you left school when you were fifteen or sixteen, what, tell me what you did next?

Well … first I used to go to a music lesson, but I didn't keep that up and then I started work as a nanny. Yes, I used to look after the kids yeah … and I done that then until I got married at twenty.

How did you meet your husband?

Ah when I met my husband at a funeral, I been a friend of mine had died, and I been to this funeral and that's where I met my husband. Yeah.

And what did he do?

He a joiner, used to make chairs, yes well, we say a cabinet maker here.

You were doing the nanny job until you got married?

Yes I done it until I got married after I got married then I start getting babies so then I didn't work anymore and I came here when I was, in fifty-three, yeah I came in fifty-three time I had three kids.

And tell me about coming here then what, why did you come?

Well, then there were emigrating people from the west here, so my husband came over here and then I came, he came in the August and I came in the December. I should have travelled before but we had a storm by the name of Jeanette and it was a very bad storm so I couldn't, I couldn't travel than and I travelled by boat.

Grace, second to left
with husband

And he did he come straight to Reading?
Yes, to Reading.

Why did he come?
Well, he had a friend that receive him when he come so he came to Reading
and he lived in Reading until he went back to Barbados … I came straight to
Reading. I land here Christmas Eve night. Yep, and I been in Reading from
then on, until now.

So tell me about that journey?
It was … it was sad leaving my mother to be truthful, it was sad leaving my
mother and the two kids, but I came here and I haven't have much complaints.
I really did miss my mother.

How did you travel here?
By boat, yeah, I came on a ship. I think it was the Erika? There were two I
can't remember the other name, but there were two that always used to travel
backward and forward bringing passengers.

This was your very first passport?
Yeah.

So did the ship call at other places? can you remember what is was like?
It, I know on this ship we had people from Jamaica, from other places and
then we stop in Genoa … and then we came across the channel by boat.

What was it like?
Well that experience it wasn't bad you know because you met a lot of people
that you never met before and then travelling on water for so many days, when
we got to Genoa we got off the boat and then you walk around then we got on
there, back on to the boat and then come over then by another place and then
we get the ferry and come over.
    When we come it was cold, I said to my husband, I wanted to go back to my

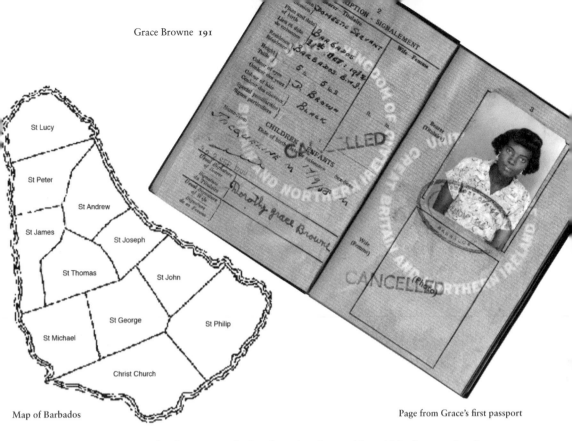

Map of Barbados

Page from Grace's first passport

mother because see in the place then it so cold, and I had to stay in where we were living then … it was just the one room and everything had to be like done in that one room, and never used the fire. The lady she had a fire in the sitting room and we had to use these paraffin heaters and those things used to be so smelly.

Where was this in Reading, Grace?

Edges Street, 17 Edges Street. Yeah and then I lived there but I wasn't very happy to be truthful. She never used to bother me but changing my way of living in Barbados and coming here I wasn't very happy and then work at Huntley, Bourne and Stevens.

A lady, probably must have heard about her Mother Walker? She took me in and she thought I had come to do nursing and I leave the hospital and come to live with this man which was my husband. My husband and her was speaking and he talk about his wife, and she said to her husband 'That girl I see she's a married woman and she have three kids,' and they took me in and I live with her then for about two years, but she was like a mother to me then because she was from Jamaica I was from Barbados. I lived with her and she make sure that we got a house and then we had 27 Harts Road.

So, I'm, I just take you back, did you have your children come with you?

No … no, because I didn't know what is was going to be like, so I leave the children with my mother and then afterwards I sent for the kids, and the kids went to school here.

Children's Identity & Where Home Is

Jobs

Community

Family Values

Mrs Walker, from Jamaica, she had a house, a house herself?

Yes she had her own house, and it was an open house I would call it, and when people come they don't have nowhere to live she would take them in and then they move on. Several people in Reading would tell that they live at Mrs Walkers or Mr Piet, those were the two homes that used to care for people when they come here.

So that was a help to you?

Yes, that made me feel then more comfortable. Before we got our house we were walking out one evening, and I can remember the place was off the Oxford Road because when I come out back into the main road I was under the bridge. I been to a house and I knock and the lady never wait to find out what I want but she came to the door and said 'Sorry, no rooms to let.' So I was just going to ask this other lady if she had any rooms, she didn't know what I want, nothing she just go up and draw her curtains and that really upset me I said to my husband 'No. I'm going back to my mother,' and I often remember that bit. And as I walk and come up, I find myself just under the bridge, near the Oxford Road, yes because it was a bright evening just walking around to know the place.

You said you were working at Huntley, Bourne and Stevens? Tell me what you did on that job?

Oh all bits of things, used to cut the, there were machines and you used to put these sheets of tin and you stamp it and it shape the tin, you can either make the lid, you make the bottom, or you make the side, whichever part the machine you go on to work.

What sort of hours did you work there?

I used to work, we start at half past seven, until one for lunch and then you finish at five. Sometime I work from Monday to Friday, sometimes I go in Saturday mornings and I stayed there for a year and then I been to Battle Hospital. I worked at Battle Hospital on maternity for five years.

What did you do there?

I was an assistant nurse in those days called orderly or auxiliary nurse. I work on the admission ward and then from the admission ward I went into the prem unit and the labour ward. In between that time I had a baby and after the baby, I went back to work and I worked in the prem unit.

Did they give you training? ... While you were working there?

You used to go to Henley to do your training but at the same time when that batch was going off to Henley I was pregnant, so I didn't go then. But then I done a part of my training in Wokingham. I work at Wokingham hospital. And then I leave Wokingham hospital and I went to St Marks hospital in geriatric and I stayed there for twenty-two years. That's where I retire from there.

Old Reading

Racism

Jobs   Old Reading

Where was St Marks hospital?

Maidenhead, yeah, travel from here to Maidenhead every night, like I said from the time I was there I done all nights.

So what, what time did you start then on the night shift?

The, nights they start at eight, until eight in the morning but what I used to do I wouldn't have a night break, I would finish at half past seven in the morning, that I can get a bus, or transport to bring me to Reading to take over from the kids.

And where was your husband working was he working as?

No, he in those days then he had went back to Barbados, so I was live alone with the kids.

At that time did you want to go back?

I was missing my mother and my kids, but then after my kids came here I settle in so I didn't bother then any more about that.

When did the kids, when did your children come?

Well when my kids come it were, let me see, I think one was about twelve years then think I leave them for five year with my mother between five, six years with my mother yes.

How did you keep in touch with your mother and the children?

By writing letters, because there wasn't no telephone in those days like that so I was writing letters until telephone, was extended then I could phone her about the kids.

How often would you write?

To be truthful I would write nearly every two week because by the time one letter get there and she send it back and send it back to me, the letter is going there.

How long did it take for a letter to arrive?

Well it depend sometime it might take four days, a week, depends of the travelling time.

So, you ... tell me you were doing this night shift for all these years, did that mean that you had to sleep in the day then?

Yes ... I come in in the morning, depends of how tired I am, I will go to bed for, well not to bed, I had a chair there and it was my bed, because it was more comfy than going up to my bed. I will get a sleep and then I will get up and I will do the housework and do what have to be done and get dinner for the kids, and as soon as kids comes in I'm off again yes. So see more than any time I had an extra job at the weekend as well ... I used to work at a nursing home.

What was it like doing nights all that, all that time?

It was fun, not that every night would be the same but we used to work in the team, so you have someone you working with for a long while you come as one, so I know what you I like, and you know what I like, so we gets along together.

Were there lots of other black nurses working there?

All about, I had, well really my team, she was from Ireland and one was Grenada. And three of us worked together for many years, yeah.

In the meantime your bringing up your family, your children, so how many, just remind me how many children you have, is it six did you say?

Six girls and one boy.

How did your daughter, you had one that was twelve, when she came here, how did she find it?

Well it was a bit tough for her first at school, but then she got used, then she just move on … she been and she done her nursing and she's living in London.

What sort of changes have you seen in Reading over the years?

Plenty, plenty, yeah there plenty changes in Reading … when I came here it was trolleybus, know what I mean, yes the electric buses, those finish. Then it was the red buses with the one door at the side, that's finish and now you got great big lovely buses. In those days I had to push my pram along the way, you don't have do that now the bus, load up and you push your pram in it, easy going now.

Where did the trolley buses go, did you use the trolley buses?

They used the seventeen, from Tilehurst to Wokingham Road. Remember the chap going out and pulling the same and turning it back round yes, were you in Reading all your days? no answer It was from up where the fire station in the Wokingham Road. Well there was the junction and to the top of Tilehurst and then it get there, turn round and go back.

Where did, what did you do for entertainment?

Oh, well, we used to gather together and you get some what your country, provides, what how you cook, and I done mine and everybody do theirs and we get together or you have a large family get together and have a time of it. In those days it was the big old radiograms and they play the tapes and that were your entertainment, well then, then they start having different places having dances and excursions and all like that.

You told me earlier about these women saying no room and closing the curtains, were there any other times when you felt you were being discriminated against?

Yes I have met some patients, that wasn't very good, and definitely I met some patients that, they get on very good, yes … I met some that was have prejudice in them but they couldn't really show it because they were sickly in bed but

Old Reading

Food

Racism

you could see for yourself and some again was very pleasant. I did have some pleasant people, old people to work with. I couldn't complain.

How do you see the future now?

Well, I don't think there's as much prejudice now as there was when I first came here. It don't make sense being prejudice, you will find a few but they don't show it if you know what I mean, they have it down inside but they don't show it, we all mix together now not like before.

Grace, you've got a picture there, of Barbados, tell me about it?

Now this is the picture of Barbados and it have, a shapes like a leg of mutton. It has eleven parishes the, one to the top is St Lucy, St Peters, St Andrews, St James, St Joseph, St John, St Philips and Christchurch, St Michaels, now there are two in the middle which is St Thomas and St George, those don't have no sea, the other have sea but those two don't have no sea. And the main, our main fish is the flying fish. And the flying fish is the people goes out in the boat, they sleep out in the ketch, flying fish, they coming in the evening, and they comes back in and they puts them on a string and they sells them.

How do they put them on, on a string?

They have a string and push it up the gizzard and it come through the mouth and they put so many on the string and then they sell it for different prices, yes, some people weighs them and sell them by the pound, yes.

When you were a child, did you go down to the beach to buy this fish?

Yes, you go on the beach and buy the flying fish or people walks along the street and they say 'Flying fish, flying fish, six for the bit?'

You were telling me about the crabs?

Yes, there're two types of crabs, is the land crab and it's the sea crab. The sea crab, we eats the sea crab, but the land crab is not very wholesome to eat, because they on the land and they lives around different places, dig holes and they get down into that hole they do. And lobsters is a very nice fish they puts pots into the sea like net and the lobsters goes into them and then they can't get back out.

When you were a child you, what would be the main meal you would eat?

It's fish, yes, it's fish. And it's fruit by the name of breadfruit you have breadfruit. Potato, yam, pumpkin, yes. And it's so … meal that is Barbados people generally have they call it Cuckoo. Which is corn, the corn they grows on the cob is dried, and then it goes to the mill, and grind and it make flour, what some people calls it, some country calls is maize, we calls it cornmeal and you cook that with okra and, you make the gravy with fish, could be flying fish or other fish. And its another fish that is imported, in those days a lot used to use, but it very expensive now, salt fish, it's like a cod fish and it is been, dried in salt, it been cured in salt, but you have to soak it to get all that salt out. Because there was no freezer in my days they used to clean the fish and they used to hang them out like you hang out clothes on the line. They used to hang the flying fish out and dry them. And that's you curing them like, that the sun would dry them out and then you would store them, store them away and then when you want them to cook you just get them to cook like that.

What did you store them in? Jar or a box?

Yes, yeah, you can put them into a box, or can put them into a jar. And in those days, even with meat there were no fridge, so when you have meat, like pork, you put plenty of salt on it and you know pottery. There used to be big pottery jars with covers, lids we say and you would take your pork and you would wash it nice, clean it and put plenty of salt on it, and put it into that jar and cover it, and when you want it you just go and take it out, you soak it in water to take away that salt. Thats how they used to cure meat ... but I would not say for today because there lots of fridge and different things that are going but we used to save meat, meat like that.

What were you saying about the sharks?

Yeah, and sharks, in the month of May. Baby sharks used to come in on the seaside and people, and people, would get nets and they would go down at night and they would catch the baby sharks and they used to eat baby sharks in those days, yes the baby ones.

 And turtles used to come in on the beach, and dig a hole and lay their eggs, and you would keep an eye, what you do, you go on the beach early in the morning and if you see like the sand move away you will come back next night and you will watch it. Well then we know how many days it would take for a turtle to hatch its eggs and because the turtle comes out the sea, digs a hole in the sand and lay the eggs and cover it over and then it go back into the sea. And then so many days it come back, it open up and got all the baby turtles and people would get nets and catch them.

When you came to Britain, how did you find the food?

It was very hard with the food. The meat was alright because in those days Union Street had lots of butchers. Them only have one there now, but some three or four was there and there were lots of different butchers around, so the meat was alright. But different things that we get from our country like sweet potato, yam and pumpkin and those things you didn't used to get them as you would like. It was a place not far from Jacksons, think it was a big butchers shop now, just there past Jackson, they have just in front of the bus stop it was, we used to call it the continental den. We used to go in there and you would get, different little things that was the only place that you could get things, foreign food and it was always packed with people because, from every country, you would get something in that shop, yeah. So that's where you used to get it but otherwise you couldn't get no food around. We use brown rice and it was not brown rice it was only just the, like the pudding rice in those days.

Leo Jones

Born: 16th November 1933
Barbados
Date of Interview: 5th June 2006

St. Davids, Barbados
Reading, UK

And what ... going back, right back, can you tell me what your earliest childhood memory is?
Well my childhood memory if I can remember right is I was always an ambitious boy. I had always wants to travel, and I would call myself ... a god-given, cricketer from my young days.

How old were you when you first played cricket then? Were you a very young boy? Or first watched it?
From the time I start school, I was playing cricket we used to play cricket in the road as youngsters. From the time you could actually walk, it was the only sports that we had in them days in Barbados. Used to be a bit of football at school but cricket was the most number one sport or you used to have athletics running and thing like that at school.

So out, tell me what it was like out there in the street playing cricket then?
[laughing] I tell you had to be very good because, you play cricket in the road you got the traffic coming up and down you have to be on the alert, as soon as they is passing you had to be running out the road 'cos the traffic pretty fast.

Whereabouts was this?
In Barbados in the little village that I came from. So I was from St David's, Cox Road area.

St David's?
That's right.

And how big was that place, what was it like there?
Well, I was schooled at St David's, I was churched at St David's, 'cos there's the school and the church is right opposite side of the road from one another, so my childhood schooldays was at the St David's school and my confirmation classes and thing like that was at the St David's church. Still a member of the St David's church and still what you call an old scholar that any time I go back I will visit those places.

So who else was there in your family?
Well just my sister and I ... my mum only had two kids ... but the other family, like my uncles and aunties they had more children, so it was actually a big group that could have been playing and thing together.

And did you all play, did you all live in that St David's area your family?
Yeah between St David's and Cox Road yeah from the area.

And your father, what did he do?
My father? He was a they call a book keeper … at one of plantation.

Was the plantation nearby?
Yes yes St David's we call … call the name of the plantation I'm [laughing] … I will have to come back to that. Can't remember the name of the plantation.

Do you know what he did with the book keeping? W as it records of what was grown there?
Well he was actually the book keeper of the plantation and he used to look after the workers, to pay the workers and thing like that.

Was that close by to where to where you lived then?
Yes it's in same area … Staplegrove plantation.

And your mother did she work?
She work on the plantation.

What did she do?
She was a labourer.

So you would go off to school, tell me about a typical day, when you were a young boy?
The typical day was that, in those days you would have to bring water to, put in the house before you leave for school. You have to make sure you get to school early, and after school, three o'clock in the evening then you come home.

What did you do at school?
What did I do at school? I just learned … the best thing I was at at school in those days you used call it arithmetic, but more or less these days now you call it mathematician. That was my best subject at school. I was proud of that 'cos I teach my children a lot about that now and I got a daughter that she's more or less an accountant now … But figures, figures to me and adding up figures was just as normal [snaps fingers] as snapping your fingers, I could just see a couple of figures then I could give you answer that's why I love … this programme here with Carol Vorderman. I'm not good at the words but I gets the Countdown.

I get the, yes, I get all those figures out [snaps fingers] by the snap of a fingers, I'm pretty good at that.

So how long, when did what age were you when you started school there then?
I started school … I started school in Barbados at five years old. So I startedschool in 1938.

This was the plantation school?
No it was a church school.

Leo in the Purley Cricket team, 1988

Who organised the school?

It's a government school ... You call it, in those days you call it elementary schools in Barbados ...

So you used to get the water you were telling me, where would you get that from before you went off to school?

Well in those days you used have a place called a stand-pipe, because the government would run the pipes right through the village and they would have a pipe in every village. Each village would have one pipe so you have to go to the pipe. But things have changed so far now you won't see those things in Barbados because the majority of people now got, everyone they got their own water in their house and things like that now as well.

How would you describe life then?

What, life? I was lucky that, as a young boy when I start I was pretty good at cricket after I leave school. And I got called up to represent the BCL against the BCA ... And lucky for me that, the great Sir Garfield Sobers and his brother Gerald was selected in the same team that I was selected, and that's how we became friends.

Leo Jones, Rothman Tour, 1970

Leo Jones today

What does BCL stand for?

Barbados Cricket League.

And you said against?

BCA is the Barbados Cricket Association. The BCA is the top boys, the BCA's the local boys and they improve your cricket, like through the years, through the year. They would check you the progress that you make playing for your home team and the runs that you make and luckily that you your performance is to the standard that there what you get called up. And that would improve you from the local cricket to the BCA cricket from BCA to Barbados cricket from Barbados cricket to test cricket ...

So how old were you when you left school?

I left school I was about ... between fourteen and fifteen, I think it was about that time.

And what did you do then?

I didn't do anything I was just playing cricket.

Did these, where were these games, where were they played?

There was a lot of cricket grounds in Barbados, because cricket was the number one sport ... So you would move from a certain grade up a grade until you met the test grade. I think after I ... represented BCL in 1952-5 ... There was a time when they was emigrating people to work in America in the fruits and veg and sugar, in the sugarcane, to work over there. I remember, some of the boys and I leave Cox Road and St David's excited that we was going down … to join the police force. I was too old for the police band, too young for the police force and the only place that I could get fixed up was in the fire brigade.

In the in the what?

In the fire brigade, that was a police department as well … the fire service. And, I decided well while I was in town to go and list you name in the park to go to America. So the older boys that I was with they go and list their name so I sat down and worked out that you have to be twenty-one. I was about nineteen at the time. And I went in and I list my name, I remember this police woman, she was the first police woman in Barbados … and she started to laugh. Said 'What are you laughing at?' She said 'I'm sure that you're not twenty-one.' I said 'Well I taking the chance.' So she put down my name and everything. And you know two weeks afterwards I get a slip to go to register myself to go to America … And lucky for me I did get a chance to go to America so I went to America in 1954. And I spent a year and a half down there, and I came back in 1955, '53, '54 yeah, I came back in 1955. And I leave a couple of weeks after that and came to England, hoping to improve my cricket. I had a friend in Reading … we was in America together and he get this place for me and my first address was 49 Zinzan Street.

Was he, he was already here your friend was he?

Yeah. He came, he came up in December and we came up in August the year, the year afterwards.

How did you travel when you came?

I travel by boat I came up on the SS Orbita, take 12 days from … Barbados to England we land at Plymouth.

What was that journey like?

It was pretty good. It was only the very beginning the channel that it was a bit rough but it was pretty good … of course there was a lot of Jamaicans in … But but put it this way, there was a whole heap of West Indian people that came up on that ship. From all round the islands that we could think about … But the majority of them was Jamaicans that came up. And I think we travelled by train, I don't know what train that was … But we got in the Sunday day time, got off the boat get up on train and we never got in to Reading till about three or four o'clock the Monday morning. For I tell you how long a train would take to get from Plymouth to here now things change innit? That must be was a slow train.

Can you remember how much the fare was from Barbados on that ship?

365 dollars, I remember … 365 dollars [laughter] … That's what I paid 365 dollars to travel here.

Jobs

How did you get the money?

Well I earned it in America.

Was that your sort of plan or did it just happen?

It just happened. It was a plan like that 'cos … What they was saying in those days 'If you come to England you improve your cricket' and that was … something that I was looking at as well. I only come here to spend about five years to study accounts how to play cricket, and … it's fifty-one, going on fifty-one years now, amazing innit? But as I said before and will always say I still think England is the best place in the world to live, and that's the God's truth. I had my time in America I went to Rome I went to Germany on a cricket tour and things like that. Around the continent. And well America and England is about the only two place that people think is to live or anything like that but, I wouldn't even want a pass to America … But England, I always call England my second home. Well it's my first home now anyhow. And the Barbados you will know as well is called little England. From the time we grew up all our history based on England … When I was at school. I didn't know about the river Thames before I even come up here. I remember it was supposed to be the longest river in England. [laughter] Luckily for me I come next door to River Thames in Reading.

So you felt you knew, did you feel you knew Britain before you came here then?

Well I can show you my passport and you will understand that it's what you call British Barbados passport. We were born British. But, the passport I came here on I still have it, to this day. I will never get rid of that, it got on it British Barbados passport. Now you have British passport and Barbados passport. I mean I've got dual nationality … but I haven't used the Barbados passport, I've got Barbados ID card.

Let's go back then you you came over to stay with your friend and you lived in Zinzan Street.

Yeah my first address.

And what time of year, what date was it that you arrived can you remember?

The date? That I arrive? Let's see, I leave Barbados on the 8th I think it was, two weeks, twelve I would say about the 20th or 21st August. 'Cos it took two weeks to get from Barbados by boat.

And what was your impression when you arrived in Reading?

When I first looked in and … When we was coming into England I see all those houses with the chimneys and the smoke coming out and here. I was saying to myself 'Wait, they've got a very lot of factories in England' … And they was houses. My mate took me the Monday over here to get registered and then I went to the Ideal Casement. 'cos all the majority of the black fellas that was working up here before me, they was more or less working at Ideal Casement Windows.

Whereabouts was that?

That was just up up London Road here, at the back. I think that closed down now. And the other part, the other couple of fellas that was about was working at Huntley & Palmers on the biscuits. Or Huntley, Bourne & Stevens. They was the tin, just up here in used to make the tin to put the biscuits in.

Huntley, Bourne & Stevens? Southampton Street?

Yeah. All that buildings and things there? That used to be a big factory there that was called Huntley, Bourne & Stevens. That went right up to the back, up to about nearly back to back to London street, or London Road. which is which? London Street is here and London Road is near the hospital innit? London Road is the hospital. It will be London Street then. Huntley, Bourne & Stevens went right back up to that. It was a big factory. But both of these belong to Huntley & Palmers ... I work at Huntley, Bourne & Stevens as well ... So that I could play cricket for Huntley & Palmers, in Kensington Road. They have one of the most beautiful grounds in Kensington Road.

So your friends took you along, you were telling me to Ideal Casement Windows was it?

Yeah.

And did, what happened then?

I got a job there. I worked there for about eight months I think.

What were you doing?

I was putting the handles on the windows. Little screw handles that you open the windows and close the widows and that was my job.

What did you do next? You said you were there for eight months.

I leaved there and I went to work at the bakery. The Court Bakery that was in Grovelands Road. All that knocked down now and there's bare flats in there. You ever hear about the Court Bakery? It was the only bakery we had in Reading at the time it used to make all the bread for the whole of Reading, Berkshire ... I worked there for ... a good, I can't remember how many years I worked there ... But then I leave there about, in the, and teach myself to become a metal polisher ... and I stick to that for until I retire.

What did you do in the bakery then? What was your job?

In the bakery? I for what you call a handyman. I used to do the shift, I used to relief, go around relieving all the workers for they to have their breaks. So I actually work on every machinery in there.

Tell, just describe what the working day was like?

If you do you have to do eight hours a day in those days ... plus overtime if you want overtime, but in those days the ... your hours were four, I think it was forty-four it is forty-four hours a week in those working days ...

What kind of thing did you do? How did you, how did they make the bread then, was it bread cakes?

Yeah it was all type, there was all types ... I was in the bread department then but the cakes department was, the cakes department was at the top of the factory, the bread department was at the bottom of the factory. But I used to work in the bread department. And I used to I more or less used to put out all the bread for the delivery fellas when they come in the morning. And so they had the racks the thing that you would, and the numbers on the racks that the vans will come in to go to their rack to take up their bread that they want. So when I'm on nights I used to do that job, put out all the breads to the, to the amount for every driver to collect in the morning when he come in early.

So you went from there you were saying about being a metal polisher.

Yeah.

Tell me about that?

I went over to Caversham, Caversham Road. I can't remember the name of the company now I remember that. And I worked there to teach myself, they used to do ... chroming, and silver different things like that. So I went in that department and I worked there for some years as well. And then I leaved there then went to CF Taylor. I walk in there they ask me to work on the aircraft. And I work there for about twenty odd years before I to retire. So I move up a grade then work in the aircraft department. I was lucky to work on the first jumbo that ever built, and the first Concorde that ever built. I had to go up to London in the hangar and fix up the galleys and the luxurious part of the plane ... So I had a good time with my life.

What was the name of the company?

CF Taylor ... Molly Millars Lane Wokingham.

Are they still there or?

Nah nah, I think they all closed down now. But the old man used to live in Reading just up there on the, old man Taylor ... Just going up the Wokingham Road as you pass the school, Alfred Sutton school on the left hand and go round the bend he was on one of the big houses there on the left hand side. I don't know if he's still there or if he's still living or what, old man Taylor.

That was your kind of employment what else was going on in your life?

I was still playing cricket within all those days! And as I said to you ... I realise, looking back at my life that I actually bring the black and white community together. And it's so simple, it's just through sports ... Back in the fifties there was a chap he start up a cricket team. He used to get the teams to play some teams in Prospect Park ... I remember my first season, I had just come up from Barbados and the fellas heard about me just representing BCL and playing with Gary Sobers and those boys. And, I can pick the line of the ball because the ball doesn't divert ... And they used to laugh me and say 'You's all this cricketer and you can't make a run in this thing.' And the next year, the next year, every time I picked my bat up I used to score a hundred.

But how this thing happen, some the fellas decide that they were going to improve the they were going to put ten pence each of the member used to ten pence in the kitty and … All who make their first fifty will get the money. And I used to win the money every week. And then they said look they will improve it to twenty pence and you have to score a hundred. And that encouraged me more 'cos a pound in those days was a lot of money. 'Cos I remember we used to a pound for rent and half a crown for the electric and gas in those day. So a pound was a lot of money in them day. And I remember my first pay pack, was five pound nineteen and six in those days … So when you pay a pound for rent out of that as I say. But you see you could get, a pint of beer for about three pence or a pack of cigarettes for about something like that.

I remember people used to put up signs and said room for rent and soon as they see your black face they would say 'Sorry … it's already gone.' And that encouraged me and encouraged the other fellas that you have to look for your own place. My first house I bought in England I paid £600 for … And that was number 23 Mason Street. And there was another chap that owned all those houses down there and he had liked me through my cricket ability and he give me the house at £2 a week … With no interest or nothing on top of that … I can't remember his name but, he used to have his office here in, the street the street just here where the Citizens Advice Bureau is.

Gun Street?

Gun Street. He was right in Gun Street his office was right opposite there in Gun Street. And when he heard the name Leo Jones, for every week my name used to be in the Evening Post or the Chronicle. They haven't got another cricketer of my calibre. I can tell you that I scored a hundred for every ground they have in Berkshire, every park. I'm the only batsman to score double century … in the innings, the only batsman to score three consecutive hundreds at the weekend; Saturday, Sunday and Monday Bank Holiday. I done that twice. And I think that if they had a man called Charlie I think he used to keep the records but, looking back on my life I must admit to me I must admit over a hundred hundreds. In my life.

But as I saying to you we go back to that part way to bring the communities together … I start then the team called Reading West Indies Cricket team. The teams that I know I play with before, I used to get matches with them and teams like Kidmore End and Eversley and Wokingham. And you were surprised that the people that used to turn up to see us play, for the other white teams … And we became so friendly that then people was begging you to come and live at their place … So you see where the sport come into the community and make the black and white community become one … 'Cos you read about it every weekend, and people from round the countrysides and thing that have to on cricket ground they used to look forward, and then they used to say well look let's make a day of it which you call a family day. You would call it an all day cricket match. Start at ten or eleven o'clock in the morning. You would have tea, you would have dinner, you would have this and then it would become a family occasion.

Do you still play cricket now?

No ... 'cos the boys now that is playing cricket ... And football and everything, they're not sportsmen ... You have to love something, to be good at it.

Cricket is a game that I ... I get a bit proud to say this - cricket caused my wife to divorce me. 'Cos she find out that I had love something more than I love her and my children.

So you mentioned your wife there, take me back to, when did you meet her?

[laughter] I was in town one day, I was working at the bakery at the time, I was in town one day and I saw these girls, she came up here I think in 1956 or '57 to study nursing, that time they bring nurses from Barbados then. And she was at Heatherwood hospital in Ascot, so they came to Reading to do a bit of shopping. I saw these four girls in town. I said 'Oh my God.' She was the most beautiful black woman I ever see in my life.' So I walked around behind them, and I went to talk to one of the other girls, you know. And she was from somewhere and she said to me 'Oh those other girls they're from Barbados.' So we start to talk and things like that you know, and I was saying 'I same from Barbados when you come up?' Said 'I came up in 1955.' 'Oh we only came up this year we at Heatherwood hospital and everybody.' So we exchange addresses and eventually I did get get her, I marry her. Yeah, we got married in 1958 or '59 ... if I remember ...

Around that time were there many black people in Reading?

No no there wasn't a lot, and, people used to look at you ... like they never see a black person before. It was really amazing you know ...

Well you see as I said I was in America and when you over there on contract you have to always walk with your ID card. And the things that we could get away with in America the black Americans couldn't get away with. So if you link the two together ... I mean you have to respect white people in when I was in Barbados you had to call them master the white people, the master this and if you working for them and thing like that. But being born as a half caste and I grew up within that area I had the best of both worlds, my mother was black and the old man was a white man. You know? 'Cos he died he died I didn't even know him he died when when I was a little boy or something like that ... I was well capable of getting around ... And sometimes when some of the white fellas look at you and tell you 'I can't understand you.' I say 'Well look the same way I try to understand you you should try to understand me.' ... You know? And the other thing if you get in a fight with them, they beat you or you beat them, they would get up brush their pants off, the gentleman said 'You the better man, shake hand?' and go along and forget about it ...

The other thing that, people must realise as well, that Barbados have got the highest population in Reading in the whole country.

Why is that?

That is a good question. Why is that? If you go back in the early days that, as I said to you ... They had a couple more before me. In the early days some of the Barbadian boys come to Reading. And when the others was coming they more or less coming to Reading, some break away went to London, or went to other parts. But Reading in those days then was the number one stop for spot for Barbadians to come to. 'Cos you know people, they had some clever fellas from St Andrews that used to work at some of the factories in Maidenhead. And those people had wanted people to work and they used to give them a slip or pass as you call them in them days, that you used to send back to the West Indies and they would pay the money and bring them up then they pay back the money and thing like that. Like Brylcreem. The popular one in Maidenhead I will try to remember the name, in those days, that. It was not emigration something like that, it was nothing like that, it was you know. If you as you was a good worker at this place they would tell you tell you about to bring some of the fellas to work at their factory. It was a fiddle somewhere along the line, you know. They was sending money for them and they would come work there and they would take back the money and that's why there so many Barbadians.

So you think it might have been to do with employment?
Yes, yes, yes. Don't let no one fool you.

And tell me about your family.
Well I, my family we had there's … There's three girls, and two boys.

How many grandchildren do you have?
[laughter] There's three … Two is five … Three is eight … Three is eleven … Eleven that I can remember so far. But luckily no great-grands yet [laughter] … Let me count on the back of me hand now: Debbie she got three, let me start from the first. Geoffrey he got two. My big son Geoff. Judy got, two. That's four. Debbie got three that's the three of them there. Seven. Suzanne got three she's the last girl. And Junior got three, he the last boy.

It would be thirteen then.
That's thirteen? Thirteen.

OK you were talking about how people have come together more, since, you came. Just tell me a little bit about that.
Yeah what I was say trying to explain … Back in the '50s, like when the fellas go out for the night, which you will understand that in those days in the '50s they had the the American service people living in Newbury they used to come to Reading town every weekend. And we all used to mix up together and in those days, the early days if any white girl or woman was to come into that pub where the black people was they had a reputation saying that they was prostitutes … And that went on for such a long time that, even if a decent person was to pass round here to come and have a drink they still would mention the word 'Oh, them's prostitutes.' But the fact was, that after the cricket teams and their wives and children everybody used to get together with the black community and the white community was concerned, and they had mixed together then you didn't hear nobody saying that she is a prostitute or that is a prostitute or not. 'Cos that's where the cricket association bring the family and thing together.

So they all realised then that we were all one people. So this word 'prostitute' had disappear, after the black community and the white community become an item. So, where people is concerned now people realise that we all human beings we don't look at white we don't look at black, 'cos black and white is together, black marry a white and white marry a black ... And, it's more or less now the word gone from prostitute to love ...

Forget about the half-caste children, they are children. You don't hear half-caste this nor that do you? All you hearing now is the community, the children, the father and mother and I'm so glad that I'm part of that because people is not looking at colour these days. They are looking at what they should be looking at; human beings ...

Barbados

Barbados is located in the western Atlantic Ocean, just to the east of the Caribbean Sea. It is an independent island nation and along with Saint Lucia, Saint Vincent, or the Grenadines is considered a part of the Caribbean's Lesser Antilles. Barbados' land mass is generally low lying although there are some higher regions toward the interior of the island. The island has been relatively lucky when it comes to tropical storms owing to the fact that its eastern location in the Atlantic Ocean keeps it out of the path of most tropical storms. However, in 1955 Hurricane Janet (the 10th most intense Atlantic hurricane in recorded history) hit its shores causing much damage to the island and 681 deaths in the region as a whole. Barbados' relationship with Great Britain stretches back to 1620 when British sailors landed on the largely uninhabited island (the locals having either fled or been enslaved by the Portuguese some 70 years earlier). From the British colonization of the island in 1627-1628 and independence in 1966 the island was under British control, although it did enjoy a degree of local autonomy (its House of Assembly first met in 1639). During the 17th century many slaves were brought to Barbados from Africa; as well as these African slaves a large number of Celtic people (mainly from Scotland and Ireland) were taken to the island to act as a buffer between the Anglo-Saxon plantation owners and the African population. With the growth of the sugar industry Barbados moved from the small holdings of the early settlers toward a system of large plantation estates. These estates form the current administrative parishes of the island – Christ Church, Saint Andrew, Saint George, Saint James, Saint John, Saint, Joseph, Saint Lucy, Saint Michael, Saint Peter, Saint Philip and Saint Thomas. The abolition of slavery in the British Empire took place in 1834 but the majority of the population had no say in the democratic process until the reforms of the 1930s and 1940s. A key figure in this drive toward democracy was Sir Grantley Adams (who formed the Barbados Labour Party) who was eventually elected as the first Premier of Barbados in 1958. In 1951 universal adult suffrage was introduced on the island the move toward self-government was well under way, by 1961 it had achieved internal autonomy. Between 1958 and 1962 it was a member of the West Indies Federation. Upon the break-up of the federation Barbados went back to being a self-governing colony of Great Britain. It tried to form another federation with the Leeward and Windward Islands, but these attempts were ultimately fruitless and at a constitutional conference in Great Britain in June 1966 it negotiated its own independence. Barbados formally became an independent state within the Commonwealth of Nations on 30 November 1966.

Janet Collyer

Born: 14th August 1958
Uganda (Born in UK)
Date of Interview: 12th September 2006

● Kampala, Uganda
○ Cambridge
● Reading, UK

And where and when were you born?

I was born in Hampstead in London in August 1958.

And where were you brought up?

When I was about two, my parents went back to Uganda, and I was brought up there.

And can you remember what your very first memory ever, as a child is?

My very first memory was getting a rash, all round my face. It just came and went, and, they thought it was because I'd been sitting round the back of the house, thought I'd been bitten, it turned out it was just too much sun.

And how old were you?

I must have been about three or four. It was quite a scary rash, 'cause it made my face all grey and ashen.

So, what happened about this rash?

They said it was the direct sun which was very strange, 'cause I'm from Africa so the sun is there all the time. And they just put camomile lotion on it. And it, when I was older they gave me what I now know to be steroids, and that seemed to clear it up … so it just kept coming back whenever it felt like it, until I had my second child and then it stopped … never to be seen again.

So your parents were both Ugandan, so what were they doing in London that you were born here?

My dad was a mature student, not very mature, maybe in his mid twenties, and he had come to do an engineering degree at Imperial College … and a year into that degree my mum came, and she was going to do a teacher training diploma and then she fell pregnant and, so I became the hobby. So once he finished his degree and did a bit of work experience we went back.

And were you the oldest, have you got brothers and sisters?

Yes I've got four sisters and a brother, I'm not the oldest, my other sister's three years older than me, big sister, and she stayed with my grandmother … and then I've got a brother who was born a year after me also … and then a sister who is seven years younger than me and twins who are ten years younger than me.

And where did you live in Uganda?

Quite a few places … First we lived in a … school. My mother was teaching. And I'm not quite sure what my dad was doing, it was a boarding school. And

Childhood

Community

Political Situation

Self Sufficiency

Education & Training

then we … and that was about eighty miles from the capital. And then … we moved to the capital, and my dad was working in the Ministry of Works. And moved around there really for the rest of our, the rest of the time.

And was your mother still teaching … or?

No she, she stopped and did … she used to do voluntary work, so with Save the Children Fund and the polio clinic and things like that, still in the area of teaching but maybe she'd do three hours at the polio school, I used to, it was a school where children with polio went and they would have intensive therapy you know water therapy, physiotherapy, and they'd give them three hours of education a day and so she'd do that, and sometimes and various other things like Girl Guides and … so she was always at home, when I was at home.

How did your, do you know how your parents met?

No I don't, actually I'll have to ask them. I [inaudible] my mother saying that if my father used to move in very high circles cause his father was the Prime Minister and then he was murdered … and the family had to sort of fend for themselves and so she said that she wouldn't have met my dad otherwise because he'd have been moving in circles way above her, but I never thought to ask her how they met so I'll have to ask her that.

[speaking at the same time] So this was your grandfather who was murdered, so what was that about?

He believed in … he used to, he himself wasn't educated, so he couldn't, he could barely read or write, but he believed in education of … boys and girls, so he donated land to what now is the main university in the capital. And people felt that educating the masses was not a good thing and so it wasn't very popular. So that's what I was told, I think there were possibly some other things, but someone just … stepped up to him as he was going to church and shot him.

And was your grandmother alive?

Yes, yes she was.

And do you remember her?

Oh yes she lived 'till she was about … at least ninety. Yes.

And tell me a bit about Uganda, the geography of it.

It's landlocked, it's got a very big lake in the South, called Lake Victoria, which is the source of the Nile, so it's … the explorers, I think it was Stanley or Speak[sp] or someone like that or Livingstone, one of those, sort of trekked up the Nile from Egypt and trekked all the way up and when they got to Lake Victoria they sent a letter which arrived I think three months later saying 'I've found the source of the Nile.' So it's very green it's got lots of water … not very big only a population of about fifteen to twenty million … so, and that's doubled in the last fifty years.

And are there many large cities, or is it mostly … rural?

It's mostly rural, there, you know I mean it's probably the size of … Wales maybe, North to South, it's maybe about two hundred miles East to West, maybe three hundred so it's not very big.

And coming back to your childhood, what's your next sort of memory that you recollect as a child?

… Next memory is going to a nursery school … called Aunty Claire's nursery and they would give us books that were maybe half, about the size of the palm of your hand, maybe a third of an A4. You have these books and she'd have written all the numbers and all the letters in them, just traced it … and then, what I remember is that you'd write AAAAA, and then BBBBB, and then you'd close the book and then do the next … the next day. I used to think I wish I could just keep going writing all these letters and numbers. And now I think about it, the, the owner of the nursery and her staff had sat down and written, in all these books for all these children, and yet I felt that they were really excited about what they were doing, so that was, that's a memory I had.

How old were you when you went to nursery … was it nursery school?

Nursery school it was like kindergarten. Yes I must have been, maybe three, it was very soon, when we moved from the boarding school back into town was when I went and I maybe did about two years before school.

What, what language were you speaking at the time?

English at the nursery school … yes all the education was in English. At that school, it wasn't the case in all the schools, even today, especially the rural schools they teach them in the vernacular language, change to English when they're about six.

So what would the vernacular language be?

Depending on where you are in the country there's, I mean there are probably six or seven languages, main languages and then maybe five or six …

[speaking at the same time] It's quite surprising for the size of the size of the country.

Yes, yes and maybe five dialects of each one. So my mother can speak, both, lots of languages, she can speak, she can be understood in the East of the country and in the West, she's had an ear for languages so she'll pick it up.

And did, did you speak English at home?

Yes, we spoke both.

Janet at 14 years with sister and twins

And what, do you have an, a Ugandan name.

Yes, yes I do.

And wha, what is it?

Its, I'll say it and then spell it it's Nkabidwa.

And what was your maiden name?

Kiwana, which is K-I-W-A-N-A.

And that would have been your father's name, would it?

Yes, yes.

So, after nursery, was this a paid nursery school, did you have to pay to go there?

[speaking at same time] Yes, yes it was paid.

And then you went onto primary school?

Yes, went onto primary school and that was paid but it was subsidised by the government so, you pay, you were paid, it was fairly cheap.

Is that the system is it typi … you have to pay for education do you?

Yes, yes - now you don't now it's free up to the age of eleven or twelve. And then you pay. But you can still pay. There's still a private system.

And what did you, was this a mixed school?

Yeah mixed boys and girls.

Education & Training

Childhood

Baby Janet with
parents, 1959

So what was home life like?

We used to play quite a lot, in fact we weren't allowed in our bedrooms during the day. I'd go to visit friends and they were allowed in their bedrooms during the day, which, so you'd either read or play in the garden.

Why was that then?

I don't know, don't know why. It was just a house rule that you don't, sit in your bedrooms, 'cause it was socialising or whatever, I don't know or knowing where we were or what we were up to.

Why did you move about so much?

It was my father's job, so … it was only about twenty miles away but it was far enough away that it was a different school … I think we were … I don't have much memory of it except the house that we lived in then had two stories, well the other houses I'd been in were bungalows and this was two stories, so I remember that, a lot.

Was that … unusual?

Two storeys. Not really, I think we'd just, had different, maybe the houses we'd lived in were government houses and they tended to be … bungalows.

[speaking at the same time] These were houses owned by your father's, well the government he was working with the government, so came with the job?

Yeah, yeah so his civil servants got, they did, they got housing.

Did everybody in the family get on well then?

My father's family did, very much. My mother's family didn't figure as highly. I think they were, she's one of the older ones in her family, so and in fact all my, almost all my cousins are either, on her side are either my age or a lot younger. And also I think my father's family was just much more dominant in our lives.

So as you were growing up and becoming a teenager, where were you living then?

We, still in the capital we moved … my father was getting, he got quite a lot of promotions and he ended up being the Head of what was called the National Housing Corporation so it was within the Ministry of Works but, it was what they called a sort of half … not quite a quango but you know half state, half private. This job was to build housing that wasn't government housing so the town planners would come up with plans and then the National Housing Corporation would build them, as part of building houses, houses for workers. So he was Head of that. And when he came out of that we moved, moved house … to a much much bigger house again within the capital.

I remember he, he had a secretary and she did shorthand really really quickly I remember that. And she used to be able to sit in meetings and she'd record everything that was said and then she'd type it all up, so she taught me how to type. And she was also the Sunday school teacher so we'd meet her on a Sunday, so I remember that quite a lot. I used to wonder why my father didn't do his own letters, as he could type, everything that he did would be typed, so

I hardly ever saw him write anything, and I saw [inaudible] what I remember of him was his signature ...

Did you visit him at work then?
Yes.

And this was in ...
School used to finish at four, and the system there was that he, he had a driver so sometimes we'd be picked up from school, he wouldn't be quite ready so we'd be taken to the office to wait for him and then get home maybe for five thirty six o'clock. And sometimes if he was going to go out visiting sites we'd go with him to the building site and then get home but it was always before dark and it gets dark around seven, so I remember we it never felt like we'd be home late ...

What did you think about those visits to his place of work?
I thought it was quite fun, actually. It was right up at the top of a, maybe twenty storey building so they had balconies so we'd go up and look at the balcony and that's when the secretary showed us how she typed and changed ribbons and all that sort of thing.

What sort of relationship did you have with your parents?
I was much ... very close to my mum. She was always there ... which was good and she seemed more gentle. 'Cause my dad was more autocratic and ... would just say 'No' or 'Yes' and wouldn't necessarily explain the reasons whereas Mum would explain ... everything, and she was always, like the one time, there was one time when she went off on a Girl Guide trip to Japan. And that was really strange, to wake up and she wasn't there, and to go to bed and she wasn't there.

How old was your father when his father was murdered?
He was about ... he wasn't quite ... I think he was in his late teens. In fact that's why he ended up being a mature student because then he, it was late teens or early twenties and ... yeah I think it was early twenties and he was at the university. And so he left school to, because he was one of the older ones of the family who left school to, basically look after his mum and ... siblings. And I think that's why they ended up being very close. Because they'd always had to get together. [pause] A lot of people who were friends would have just disappeared at that time because they weren't really friends they were ... what happens when you're a certain status you get people surrounding you that ... really only round you for ... the status rather than friends. And he had ... he dropped out of school at that point so that he could work and put his younger siblings through school, and that's why he, when he came to do the degree he was really finishing off ... something that he'd started, maybe [pause] ten years earlier. So that was in the mid '50s.

Janet, 2006

So at that time he had, was able then to finish?

Yeah.

And, it sounds like quite a privileged life, in terms of, the country. Did you feel that, at the time?

No, no, no that was really, I think a lot of that's down to my mother. We certainly didn't feel privileged … at all I thought there were lots of people that were a lot more privileged, who don't have to wake up in the mornings who don't have to wash up and do kitchen rotas and all that sort of thing so, but looking back yes, yes it was. [pause] It was.

And how did you, what happened in schooling then as a teenager?

So after primary school finished in year seven, then the options for school were, for secondary school were, the best schools were boarding schools. It was just the way it, the system was because many of the school were set up by, at least in where we were were set up by missionaries and they tended to be boarding schools because … no they weren't just for education it was for the whole person. Including Sunday chapel and things like that. So … And we, there's a girls school that one of my aunts had gone to, so my sister and I went there. And my brother went to the school my father went to which was, it was a boy's school but by then it was mixed. As a boarding school and that was quite a shock. That's probably when I started to realise that have … we do have, we are privileged. But until then I hadn't really, really felt it. That's what you'd get, because you still had to pay but then it was, I don't know what it was but it wasn't a lot of money. But it was a government school so pretty much you were just paying for your food.

And how did you feel going, and how far away was this from … ?

Not too far maybe about fifteen miles.

Janet at school in Kampala (Second row first right)

But you were there throughout the term?

Yes.

So how did you feel about leaving this ... quite close knit family and your mum who you were close to?

I didn't like it at all and I never really enjoyed it, and that's ... I never really felt that I wanted to put our children through boarding school because, it's very exposed especially I think an all girls school. It's very very insular.

And were all the students were they black ... Ugandans?

Yes almost, almost entirely. Yeah. And most of the non Ugandans would leave. So up to the top of primary school it was very international, depending where you went but for secondary school it ... most of them would go, if they were not Ugandans they'd go abroad to school. So it was almost from all parts of Uganda as well so I met a lot of people from, who were, there's me coming fifteen miles and they'd come two hundred miles. On a bus, so they'd say goodbye to their family and jump on a bus. So they'd be luck to get one visit a term.

So when did you finish secondary school, the boarding school?

That was six years of that, so, 1976.

And what did you do next?

I then came to university here, and we finished in because the calendar year's the academic year. So I finished my A Levels in November and then had seven months of just dossing around really. And then came in July to start university in September.

And where did you come to?

So I went to Girton College Cambridge. I think they, I came early because they were running a summer school for people who were doing engineering and sciences because they said they had worked out that the maths teaching was very variable, and so they offered a, must have been, wasn't very long maybe two or three week summer school where they'd bring you up to speed on maths. Or bring you up to the same level, really. So I came for that and there wasn't, it was a bit expensive to travel, so I stayed on and started university in October.

So did you, what how did you come to this decision to do a degree to do a degree here, in the UK?

It's kind of one of those things that happened to me. I wasn't really sure and my sister did her degree in Uganda, my elder sister. So I thought you know that's what I would do. But by then the situation was really quite dire, so the time I was at secondary school the situation in Uganda was getting worse and worse and worse, and security was ...

Do you mean the political situation?

[speaking at same time] The political situation. And it meant, you weren't secure at night ... and there were a, it was just, there was a lot of, there was guerilla warfare going on, in the rural areas, and so, my mother who was on her own by then, felt that the safest thing to do was to or the most stable thing was to educate us out of the country so that there wouldn't be disruption.

And did you you chose to do engineering. Why was that?

Because I hated writing essays. And I just found, and I still do find words very, very difficult. I write an e-mail now and it takes me nearly ten minutes to formulate ... maybe twenty sentences ... to do it and it's just ... it's writing blindness, you know it's almost like some people read and they can't see what they're reading I find the writing is, is really painful so I ... and I could do it but it really was ... effort. And so I ... thought engineering I could get away from writing much, it's maybe not quite, the place ...

Was it anything to do with your father's career?

Maybe a little bit but not much, not much. In fact my other sister, Maria she had ... there was a big fuss I remember when she chose her A Level subjects it was Physics, Chemistry and Maths. He was not at all happy with that cause he thought, he thought she'd be much better off as a Doctor. And at one point there was a very heated discussion and one of my uncles was trying to mediate. And ... and it's typical of my father's family they just all support ... the other without asking too many questions and at one point the, the uncle said 'By the way what's the combination that she wants to do that you don't want her to do?' And he said 'oh some stupid combination' which happens to be the one he did. And he said 'OK so the stupid combination' and there's my sister thinking 'it's what you did!' [laughs] and ... so he wasn't keen and I think it, I was, I was though, I was fascinated by it, 'cause having visited his sites and seeing buildings go up and all the scaffolding and how they decided where to put the windows and so on and so I did find just engineering in general quite interesting and not writing essays was a big bonus.

And ... it's and even now, not very common for women to take up engineering. it was regarded as a men's, a man's career. Did that occur to you or anybody else, was it part of the objection that your father made of your sister?

Possibly. He never really explained it. Never, think he just felt that, I think by then things were starting to get you know very dangerous and he felt that medicine was a career you could pick up and take anywhere, whereas engineering, he felt wasn't, even though he had picked it up and taken it everywhere. But it wasn't a male thing in fact he used to, he was very, he as almost stricter with us than he was with my brothers, saying you've got to be able to not rely on men to support you, so it wasn't that he didn't want to educate, in fact he was, he wanted her to be highly independent and not have to worry about ... men.

So it was quite a pragmatic approach really wasn't it?

Mmm ...

And how old were you when your father died?

About fourteen.

Was that a sudden thing or ...

It's one of those things we never really got to the bottom of it, but it looked like just a car accident. But it seems that there was a bit more to it than that. And ... so, his car was sort of in, taken away very quickly by the police, and he was delivered to the mortuary and ... fully clothed. And it used to be that especially if you had an accident in the rural areas that the local people would come and you know maybe take your watch and take your shoes or anything of value. He was completely ... intact in that sense. So it does appear that it was, it wasn't a real accident. It's something that we, as a family just don't talk about ... very much.

And my mother's, one of the things was at least we got a body to bury because many people didn't. One of my uncles he just disappeared one evening, and was maybe twenty years later that someone showed my aunt where they'd dumped his body, it was in a big reservoir, was about a hundred miles from the capital ... and so he never ever had a grave so in some ways we were lucky that we did. And that was quite ... quite a shock he'd just brought my sister back to school she'd had 'cause she was doing these...[laughs] wretched A Levels, wrong A Levels, and so they used to get allowed out a lot more, so she'd gone out on a Saturday you could leave at dawn, and you had to be back by dusk. So he'd just brought her back, about, just in time between six thirty and seven, I remember talking to him at the school gate because the gate closed at seven so it was oooh you know how are you and so on and then off he went. And that was, that was the last time I saw him and he um ... I've lost my thread now, what I was saying there.

Well we were talking about, that you were about fourteen at the time, so your older sister was seventeen.

She was seventeen, yes so she was doing her A Levels.

And this must have been a terrible shock to the whole family.

Mmm ... [pause]

And how, was this to do with the partly to do with the political unrest you were talking about?

Yes. 'Cause he'd been ... he'd been doing through a lot of change 'cause he'd been effectively sacked from his job. And not for an underperformance it's just they wanted to give the job to someone else. There was a lot of procurement in the job, you know you're building, huge estates it's like building something the size of Lower Earley, so there's a lot of ... lot of payments to be paid and a lot of, and you know, someone else wanted that job. So he said 'fine you know, I'll leave it' but they had actually gone through the process of sacking him rather than letting him leave it. He'd just started up his own engineering consultancy so he was just building that up ... and you know even then there were the odd phone calls that used to come to the house so ... people ... just at the house and for no real reason.

Was this a change in government at the time?

No. It was still, you know the same government. Well there was a change in government every four years before. There was a military coup. Well not four years before no I … Yeah I guess it was four years before there'd been a change of government. So the overthrown the military government had come in and they'd gradually started to dismantle the things that they didn't like. It was a time that the Asian community was being sort of forced to leave the country. He was just part of that. He had a lot of friends from the Asian community 'cause that was the business community. And so the people he dealt, many of the people he dealt with in business were from there. And my aunt, my uncle who died he was a minister in the previous government. So when it was overthrown he'd fled, and then my aunt and her five children I think she had then had all come to live with us. It's just something my family my father used to do … just open their house and we'd all double up in bunk beds so that they, until he came back, he came back about a year later. 'Cause he was going on assurances. But then a year after that he had, he had died. So um … it was quite a turbulent time.

And did the, the young people at the time, did you feel afraid?

Again, not as afraid as we could have been, I think my parents both of them did a really good job of just shielding us from a lot of it. Being at school, you'd hear it 'cause you'd hear 'Oh so and so's father's disappeared', so you, 'Where's so and so oh their father's disappeared so they can't afford the fees anymore' so they'd be gone. And so you'd see some of that, but no at home we didn't really, didn't really feel it. And when my aunt came to stay with us, with the family, again, we were probably more exposed because effectively we were harbouring someone the government had an interest in, not a positive interest in, and my father was saying 'Oh we just need to stick together and it'll all work out and we'll find a way.'

Did it cause financial problems for you when he died?

Again, not that I noticed, and I don't know why unless he really, provided. He must have just really provided for us. Because we didn't notice he had a lot of insurance policies. And he'd put a lot of effort into making sure that things were … OK. And so we didn't really notice as children we didn't notice a difference … in our standard of life at all. In fact my mother was here recently I meant to ask her how did she do it because she wasn't working. And for at least a year after he died she didn't do anything. She just sat at home and wore black. And … didn't drive, didn't go out visiting, and she came to my confirmation service, and left as soon as it finished and didn't go to the reception and went back home but otherwise she just stayed at home. I remember 'cause she'd buy, her clothes would wear out her black clothes and she'd buy more black clothes. I think she started driving two years after … afterwards.

And then she started to go out more did she?

And she started to go out. And, we stayed on for two more years, nearly two years, and then she bought a house from a family friend who was leaving the country. And we came back from school and she said, 'Right, we've got a new house.' And then she changed, she sort of got out of herself and started doing things. I don't really know how we survived financially for those two years but we did. And I didn't feel I was getting anything less … for it.

So you came, what were you thinking England, UK, Cambridge would be like, before you actually arrived? What were your sort of … thoughts on what it would be like?

I was fairly open minded actually I knew it would be cold, but I was quite looking forward to not being at my boarding school, 'cause I just really didn't like it at all, and so it was just exciting.

And did you fly, to the UK?

Yes.

So where did you take off from and where did you land?

I took off from Entebe which is the international airport, the main international airport and then I arrived in London, and a family friend … of my father's, picked me up from the airport and took me to his family house, where his wife was Ugandan the children were Ugandan. And my memory was, oh television all day. It must have been in about a few days, we were just sat, ate scrambled eggs and watched television. And then I went off to this summer school. And afterwards I stayed with family again, friends, who had been in Uganda, friends of my parents.

So apart from scrambled eggs and television, what were your other early impressions of the UK?

Calculators. We had this introduction to maths and we had calculators. I'd never seen [inaudible] my slide rule. So that was an impression, I think the other impression was the early dinners. So at home we used to have dinners quite late, and it was partly because when my father was alive we'd used to wait 'till he got home to eat so it'd be eight nine o'clock. And here people eat at six so the first time I had something at six, I thought I'd maybe get something else … and I realised no that's it that's the end of … food. You might get a slice of toast if you're really lucky at ten o'clock, but otherwise that's it. That was the other thing. And I think the third thing was … how young people were when they left home. Had sixteen year olds living away from home. And that surprised me.

Do you mean setting up home, for themselves?

[overlapping with interviewer] Setting up home, yes.

This wasn't, something you'd … ?

No. In Uganda people just couldn't afford, it was very rarely could they afford at sixteen, seventeen, eighteen to set up home. And live away from home.

So what about social life at university?

Socially it was very nice I made some really good friends, that I still keep in touch with. I found the work really hard. And I think it's probably the first time in my learning career that I felt I was struggling to keep my head above water. So that wasn't fun. [pause] And I felt … it was quite hard work just getting, 'cause I was a long way, about four miles from the college to the faculty. And that was quite a chore every morning, getting up and cycling four miles in the snow and the rain. And we used to get real snow then. And I remember trudging back one day and had to go to a building on the ground for some reason, and the snow was up to my thighs, so I was trudging through this orchard, to get to, think my lecturer lived in that building and I had to get there for a tutoring session, trudging through this white field, and it just felt like really hard work.

And how did you find the cold?

Quite difficult at first. Quite difficult. But living in college accommodation, once you were inside you were very warm. So it wasn't too bad it's just whenever you ventured out you got cold.

What did you bring with you when you came?

A few jumpers and an anorak. So I had to buy, one of the things I had to do when I was here was buy a winter coat. Which was, I thought I'm not having a duffle coat which actually would have been the wisest thing to have. And I got introduced to jumble sales where you could get some perfectly good winter clothing for not very much.

Were they, your fellow students doing engineering were they a male-female mix?

Not too bad because I was in a girls college I was tutored, there were three other engineers two of three of the engineers were there, so Girton was half the engineering contingent in my year, or women, so we were tutored together so we didn't feel … different. Our tutor group I mean we had more tutoring in the male colleges than in our college because Girton just didn't have enough of the right engineering fellows they just tended to be men. And in the classes we weren't treated any differently at all. The only one that was treated differently was a girl who used to change her hair colour all the time. And so she got a lot of ribbing and we didn't have any real trouble at all

Were you considered as equals in … ?

Yeah, very much so. In we worked, in fact one of the things we had to do was work in industry to find ourselves summer jobs in the industry, and so my first summer I went to Rolls Royce in Derby, and I can't remember how I got that, 'cause I don't remember being interviewed.

What about racially?

Very … hardly any at Cambridge, um …

Were there many other black people at university?

No, almost as many as there were women engineers, about forty, women engin-, women, maybe in the black communities maybe about forty, forty or fifty, it's not very many, I know that because they did a count. It's one of the things the university did was to count how many sort of African students it had. And it came up with forty. And ... but no there really wasn't any.

The first time I really did experience racism was when I went to work. I was looking for accommodation in Bristol, in a shared house, and I encountered prejudice there, but I didn't in Cambridge.

So it, you graduated, and you were just talking about your first job.
Yes.

So where was that then?
In Bristol, so I ...

For a company?
For a company, an American company. And the reason I I applied for ... I got most of the jobs I applied for so I had about four or five job offers, all in engineering, and all except this one were in sort of G, C Marconi pleasant type places which were very good places to go then, not so good now I think I'd have been out of a job if I'd have gone there. And this one was because, I went to speak to them because they had offices in Singapore, it wasn't even electronics I'd applied to I'd applied to Schlumberger which was oil, and the person who interviewed me, said he was the [inaudible] director and he'd come up to the university to interview so they were running interviews in, one of the hotels, and he said 'I'm terribly sorry, we shouldn't really be interviewing you for this job.' So I said 'Oh, why not' and he said, 'Well, we don't send women into Singapore. Its just, it's not, you know single women aren't welcomed by the government. So we shouldn't have really been into, but since you were on the list I thought I'd better see you.' He said 'But I've got another company a small electronics company and they've got an office in Bristol would you like to go and work for them?' So I said 'Ohhhh, I don't know.' So he said, 'You could get to America that way' because I was thinking maybe I'd go and end up working from Singapore to America so I said, 'OK I'll go and have a look at them. And that's how I ended up in, in Bristol.' And it's ironic that, this HR Director, I still keep in touch with him, then he phones me and says, 'Do you know anyone who could do this job?' 'Cause he's a headhunter now, he says 'Oh I've got to find someone the person I hired for them disappeared, you know decided he didn't like it and then he walked off so I've got to fill this place really quickly can you get someone?' So we still keep in touch but our first meeting was really not ... not auspiscious at all. [laughs]

In the meantime, what, you'd been back to visit Uganda, and, what was happening with the political situation? You'd left it being quite in turmoil ...
Yeah ... So one of the reasons I was struggled in university is that there was even more fighting, and when I went back, just after I'd finished my degree, that was ... 1980, they'd just had a new government that appeared to be better than the old one, again it was still military. And it was peaceful but it was still very dangerous, and you'd had people over a decade who'd been living in lawlessness, so you know the ten year olds had become twenty year olds, and

Political Situation
Self Sufficiency
Family Values
Old Reading

so it was still turbulent and it had another six years before it really started to settle.

But thorughout it, my mother had almost got second wind because she had the three of us, my sister and brother as a big group, and then the baby group which was my younger sister and the twins, and she just threw herself into getting them through school and sorted out, and so though it, things were tough, she was finding ways round, making it happen and so they all, got them all through school, educated them in Kenya which is the country next door and which was more stable. And so in terms of what I remember is how my mother was coping, because she decided, when she came out of mourning, she thought right I, she tried farming, and investing in farm, but the distances were too far, and she wouldn't be back in time, and she was late getting the children from school, she thought I can't do that, so she decided to go into property. And has been doing that ever since. And so she each time I got back you could see she was more and more settled in what she was doing.

So your plans were, you would have been happy to have gone to America, or anywhere else in the world?
Yes.

What, why did you stay in England?
Well I did get to America [laughs] after about a year, year eighteen months, a company I was with in Bristol, sent me to America but in between I'd met Keith, my husband. So I still went to America but then he persuaded me to come back. And that was it. And I worked in England ever since.

And how did you come to be in Reading?
Keith was working in Wargrave, and my company was in Reading. So, just up at the Shire Hall, when it was still called Shire Hall, the council had rented out one floor because they couldn't fill it, having built it. It's a very lovely bulidnng actually, very lovely, lovely air conditioning. So we moved, and within a year, Keith had changed job and was working in London, and my office had moved to Swindon, but we decided to stay here.

And what was your first impression of Reading as a place?
Dreadful.

So what was it like when you first came to live here then, in 19-, would that be eighty some ... ?
1988. What did it look like it looked very much like Bracknell, very much post war, functional. The biggest thing about it was the train to London every five minutes.

What about the people in Reading?
The nearest town we'd been to before been frequented was Oxford. So Oxford and Reading was like chalk and cheese. Oxford was interesting and Reading, didn't seem that, that vibrant. Didn't seem that, even The Hexagon wasn't interesting. And that was it for the theatres. But then when we looked a bit

harder and found that the theatre on Mount Pleasant, and the one near Shire Hall. You could find everything you needed if you looked but it wasn't, handed to you on a plate like it was in Oxford.

So you'd had your first child, and you were still at work, and you settled in Reading, and you didn't like Reading much, but how long have you been living in Reading now Janet?

Oooh, eighteen years. Eighteen years last August, this August just gone.

And ... Why did you stay?

It just felt we'd been chasing, we'd moved three times in five years, and we just needed to stop and settle and try not to change 'cause once we had Nassali our daughter, things like who's going to look after the child, what happens if you get a burst pipe, it's just the you need the support network around, and when it's just the two of you you could just pack your bags and move on, but, with a child, it's what about school, and nursery school, how do you find out about it and so on and so, we stayed here because it would be more stable for, for Nass.

And how did you find it having a baby, a young child without the family around you and the support of, your quite large family?

Sometimes it was very lonely, very lonely especially if she was ill. So ... but Keith's parents helped us an awful lot, especially after they retired. They would drive down and come and help, even though it was eighty miles. They would just jump into the car and come and help. It was wonderful, and ... my sisters who were then quite a bit older, they would come down from London.

So in the meantime you have another, a son, and your mother comes to visit and ... how old is your mother now?

Seventy-six.

She still lives in Uganda?

Yes.

But her family are ...

So four of us are here, and two of us are in Uganda, so my sister and my brother are in Uganda.

So where, you've been eighteen years in Reading now, and quite a long time in the UK, where do you think of as home?

Home ... That's, er ... I don't know. When I go to Uganda I feel, that's home. If my mother wasn't there I don't know that I'd feel quite the same. I don't really have a sense of home. It's just where the family is.

So, would you ever move permanently back to Uganda?

Probably not, not unless there was a big change. But certainly would we have a base there, yes. It depends, I mean we've still got a few more years before our son stops being dependent.

So how do the children feel about their Ugandan heritage?
Nassili, the eldest, she feels quite, stongly about it. She's made an effort to
keep in touch with my family there, and two years ago she visited on her own
… completely on her own, catching a flight, and changing in Amsterdam and
going off and then changing in Nairobi, so she's done that. My son isn't so
sure, I think he's just happy to be where his parents are, so he's happy to visit
but not on his own. I think he feels he's more of a Reading lad.

Uganda

*The Republic of Uganda is a country in East Africa, bordered on the north
by Sudan, on the south by Tanzania, on the east by Kenya, on the west by the
Democratic Republic of Congo and on the southwest by Rwanda. Although
it is landlocked the southern part of the country borders Lake Victoria. Most
of the nation's important cities are located near Lake Victoria. Its largest and
capital city is Kampala. Uganda has a tropical climate, rich soils, plentiful
rainfall and rich mineral deposits of cobalt and copper. Agriculture is the
mainstay of the economy with coffee production being a rich source of income.
Like many African nations Uganda has a colonial history having had contact
with Arab traders in the 1830s and then contact with British explorers who
were searching for the source of the Nile in the 1860s. These first colonial
contacts brought Islam and Christianity to Uganda (Protestant missionaries
came to the country in 1877 and Catholic missionaries soon followed). It was
ruled as a protectorate of Great Britain from 1894 and took shape as Uganda
in 1914 (it was previously a collection of tribal kingdoms; Mpororo, Buganda,
Toro and Bunyoro). In 1962 Uganda achieved independence: Edward Muteesa
(King of Buganda) became President and Milton Obote was named as Prime
Minister. In 1966 Obote scrapped the constitution and named himself as
President. This led to a succession of coups and counter-coups which persisted
until the mid-1980s. In 1971 Idi Amin seized power in a military coup whilst
Obote was at a Commonwealth summit in Singapore. Amin's rule was a
bloody one – it has been estimated that 300,000 Ugandans lost their lives
because of his actions. Obote's supporters were persecuted, military leaders
who had not supported the coup were executed and much of the country's
intelligentsia were killed or forced into exile. His reign also saw much sectarian
violence: the Acholi, Lango and other ethnic groups were persecuted as were
Christians. Amin was a Muslim and under his rule the number of Muslims
grew. Before Amin came to power there was a small Jewish community in the
country (known as Abayudaya) numbering around 3,000 people: but Amin
outlawed Judaism, destroyed all the synagogues in Uganda and by the end
of his rule they numbered about 300. In August 1972 Amin issued an edict
commanding the expulsion of Uganda's Asian population (numbering about
50,000) within 90 days. Amin's rule didn't just have a human cost; actions like
the expulsion of the Asian population had a detrimental effect on the country's
economy. Amin forged relationships with the PLO, Libya and the Soviet Union
whilst refusing to acknowledge the existence of Israel, actions which further
deepened Uganda's international isolation. He also made aggressive overtures*

toward neighbouring Kenya, southern Sudan and Tanzania. Amin thwarted an attempted coup by Obote (launched from Tanzania) in September 1972 but his invasion of Tanzania in 1978 led to counter attacks by the Tanzanian military and Ugandan exiles which eventually led to his deposition in April 1979.

Chaudhri Riaz

Born: 10th June 1946
Nanka Kohana, Pakistan
Date of Interview: 25th May 2006

Pakistan

Nanka Kohana,
Pakistan

Reading, UK

Mr Riaz Ahmed Chaudhri

Can you tell me when and where and when you were born?

I was born at a village in Pakistan in Punjab. The village name was Nanka Kohana. It is near Faisalabad and that is in the centre of Punjab. That's where I was born and I was born in 1946, the tenth of June.

Can you remember what were your earliest memories of your childhood?

Well we had the large family system and I would say really it was very relaxed sort of environment. I had all my cousins around and basically we belonged to a land-owner or farming family whereas you did not have to worry about your bills and food and all that because that was all at the farm. I was lucky to be born in a sort of middle-class family so, from the financial point of view and my fees were paid and I was sent to school. The transport was there [laughs] and whatever I needed. So I would say that I was one of those lucky people who had very sound ... pleasant and enjoyable childhood

I had wonderful loving parents ... I consider my mother to be a saint and they give me a lot of love and I was raised in accordance with some basic values and fundamental moral and ethical principles. And that is one of the reasons that I never ... actually sort of broke my contact or you know link with you know my place of birth. I always, you know I visited them on a regular basis. And then obviously I went to school there, I went to college, university and you know, that was wonderful.

What was your father's profession?

My father use to work for Inland Revenue. He was their officer ... before then he was in Police and as I said this is why I was lucky because my father also owned, my grandfather was one of the largest landowner in the area. So due to that reason my father inherited the land [laughs] which we have a reasonable income from. And so we had double income. One was from my father's salary and the other one was actually from the land.

OK and what was your mother's profession?

My mother was a housewife basically and ... she was always busy together with the assistants, the ladies which she had who used to cook at home because we used to have a lot of guests. So this is why even now here, you know since you have been here, the tea is going out and all that. [interviewer laughs] So this runs in our family it is in our blood you know. Any time anyone can come and we will entertain them. So at our home we had a special room where obviously the guest will come and sit. There will be one domestic employee whose job will be to welcome the guest and, you know accommodate the

Chandhri Riaz at home in Reading 2006

guests and then take the food and tea and coffee and whatever they want
to eat or drink. Not alcoholic drink though.

So you know my mother was always busy with the other ladies actually
to make sure that there is plenty of food for everyone who comes in to visit
my father or anyone else. The rest of the time she used to spend in praying,
because as I said, I consider her to be a saint and she used to spend a lot of
time in prayer and [emphasised] a lot of time in worrying about other people
and praying for them. You know if someone is sick my mother will pray to
God and she will spend hours in praying. 'Oh God ... you know, you know
... give him a ... you know, health.' And likewise if anyone got any problem
people used to contact my mother and she will pray for them. For I must say
here that that was all voluntary, voluntarily and you know for charitable basis.
She will not charge a single penny to anyone. Whosoever comes, whosoever
used to come, my mother used to give them food, tea, milk, whatever. And she
used to actually look after a lot of people, usually poor people from the area,
vicinity and village, the ladies and all that they used to come to me, you know
and my mother will give them free milk and sometime what meat we have got
actually for ourselves. My mother would [laughs] simply take some of it and
say 'OK, go home and cook it and eat' because as you know, not everyone
could afford meat ... and so many other things.

So my mother really I think she was an angel. She was a wonderful lady and
she has lived all her life for other people. She was never bothered about how

Jobs

Community

Family Values

Family Values

Education & Training

much money you have got and how much property you possess. She was not interested in money and property. She was interested in serving people and she used to tell actually that, I have quoted that in my speeches. She used to train me, she said 'Look, rivers and seas don't drink their own water. They provide it to the people who are thirsty and for the people actually to the farmers to cultivate their land, for their irrigation purposes. And a lot of people eat food from there and they don't charge anything and the rivers don't demand any reward. And she said, the fruit trees they provide their fruit to the other people to eat, they don't eat it themselves. For people respect the fruit trees, people respect the river because they need it.' And she said 'Likewise, if you are useful for other human beings, then you will be respected and God will like you.'

So I was raised in such a way that I had [with emphasis] to serve the human beings [laughs] but I think this was probably which brought into me the spirit of service, serving human beings. And his is how well I'm very pleased to have heard people say that I am a people's mayor and basically I think all I did was just to … acted upon my mother's, you know sort of … guidelines and served the people of Reading during my mayoral year. And thanks God people have liked that, they have liked it, and so that's what she was to me, doing all her life.

And what about your father?

When he used to come home he was a loving father and he still is. He will be ninety-three next month, by the way and … you know he had a stroke but he's still in good health because my father was one of the best athlete, and he had very good health. Even now at the age of ninety-three he walks about forty-five minutes a day … with his stroke …

And then when he used to come home he used to listen to people's problems and you know if they had any argument or dispute between themselves the people of the area, village they used to come to my father. And my father would listen to both the parties and decided for them whatever he thought was the best. And then help people and assist them with you know if they had any problem … You know if someone was being unfair or they had … For example if someone was sick because as you know yourself in third world or developing world are sick the government can't give them much facilities so people have to make their own arrangement. If someone is sick my father will provide the transport and make sure that they are being taken to the hospital or a doctor … and if they can't afford the medicine my father will pay for the medicine and help them. And likewise in the village if people didn't have wheat or flour or you know some other financial assistance, if they needed any financial assistance my father will assist them.

When he used to come home he used to teach me as well. He was one of the best mathematician in our town. He used to be first in the whole city, in all the schools and he was given actually a prize by then Director of Education who was an English chap. And the name of the book which was given to my father as a prize together with some money was "The Schoolboys' Stories." And we've still got it in the family.

Family Values

What was the significance of being a landowner there ... in the community?

Well first of all obviously if you own land you've got crops of your own, wheat, flour and all that ... You know, grain, all that, vegetables, fruits and all that ... milk ... butter. So I think it gives you a little bit financial soundness because you don't depend on other people, you don't have to worry about where you are going to eat. So that's for number one.

Number two obviously give you a little bit ... you know, you get respect, people respect you because you help them out, and you get some sort of job satisfaction that you are in a position to help the other human being. And of course it gives you a reasonable status in the society because you are on the giving end rather than on the receiving end. And as a person I would say that it gives you confidence because you are never desperate and you know you don't have to compromise. I mean you are nice, you are polite, you know you accommodate people, but you don't have to compromise because you are not dependent on other people.

What about the rest of the family, your brothers and your sisters?
Two brothers.

Two brothers?
And it was important. As a matter of fact let me tell you here something. I had admission here because I wanted to be an accountant. And I had admission in 196 ... 7 or late of '66. And my parents did not allow me to come and I did not come here until 1970. It took me over three years to get permission for visa from my parents. Forget about British High Commissioner or [inaudible, laughing]. I was not worried about that because that was a secondary thing. I had to get the permission from my parents. And my father's and my parents' their argument was 'Why you want to go?' And I said I want to go for higher education. They said 'Look. You've got a Master Degree which is a good education. Now start your practical life.'

I came here basically actually because I wanted to see Europe and all that. And I had no plan to stay here you know, because it took me three years to get my parents' permission. And I only got it by giving the undertaking that, 'Look, I'll be back in four years' time after my study.' [laughs]

But once I completed my training as an accountant I was advised by my principal who used to be Mr Jones, actually Jones and Son, chartered accountant at 66 Queens Road, I still remember that basement where I used to sit there during my training. He said 'Why, to get some varied experience, go to some other firms and then go back.' Now here I am getting the varied experience. You know, so then obviously you get stuck with that because then I started my own practice in 1975 so I have completed thirty-one years of my practice as an accountant.

Mind you I was only because I was the first ... you know, number one son. And I only had one brother and he had to stay with my parents because he had to look after them and he stayed there.

Education & Training

Jobs

Family Values

Why was it important for you … to get permission from your father. Couldn't you just have gone?

Well in those days people used to have some values. And I'll tell you something that if my parents hadn't allowed me I wouldn't have come here. I was so respectful to my parents and I loved them … my father would never say no if someone wants to get further education. He will finance … and he will do anything for him for facilitating, he is a go-ahead for education because he thinks that knowledge is a virtue and one should possess it. And how you get knowledge? By education.

Our family name is Aulakh and when you asked my name I said Riaz Ahmed Chaudhri. As a matter of fact it is Chaudhri Riaz Ahmed Aulakh.

You have spoken about your brother. How many sisters did you have?

I don't have any sister. My mother, my parents adopted one of my cousins who I consider to be my sister and who is living with my parents.

What in particular do you remember about your schooldays and your early childhood?

Well I remember that I was beaten up by my dad because once I think I got ninety-four percent or ninety-five percent marks out of one hundred in maths. And my father hated anyone who didn't get a hundred percent. [Both laugh] So I was beaten up when I was at school. He said 'Why on earth they are not a hundred percent?'

And once actually I didn't go to school … you know I shouldn't have told you that but I'll be honest with you. I went out … I was going to school and I met some of my friends. And there was some funfair going on and we decided that we'd go to funfair, and instead of going to school. And the headmaster said to my father 'Chaudhri Sahib, Riaz hasn't come to school,' he said 'Oh, didn't he?' He said, 'No.' He said, 'Fine.' So my father came home and I went late because we were enjoying the funfair without telling them and when I came back my parents hated someone you know who will tell lies. And he said, I said … I came back and I said 'Salaam aleikum' which means Good Afternoon and all that. And I was pretending to be all tired and exhausted because after school day, you know. And I think I was about seven eight years old then, you know in those days maybe nine. And my father said 'OK, how was the school today?' I said 'Fine, dad.' And he said 'So it went very well.' I said 'Yes.' He said 'OK. So you got the homework from school?' I said 'Yes.' He said 'Come on tell me what it is. Let's do it together.' And he caught me. He proved that I was telling lies so.

And that was the day I can never forget. And I salute my father because I was beaten up quite … in a good way. And he said 'I can tolerate anything but not lies. I can tolerate anything but you know not the wrong statement. So you've got to be honest, you've got to be straightforward. If you don't go to school … number one, you shall never miss the school even if you haven't done the homework. Bear the punishment.' But I can assure you since then I have never ever missed the school and college and the university. And I used to go and say 'I'm sorry sir I haven't done my homework today.' [laughs]

Because I think that one day put me right and I'm quite open and I'm quite straightforward now. I mean if I haven't been able to do something I'll tell people. 'Look I haven't been able to do that ... or I can't do that, I don't know it. I'll come back to you later.'

What about your secondary ... and your university life?

Our teachers were so devoted and wonderful teachers that I think it will be unfair if I don't pay tribute to them. The Persian teacher was brilliant. The maths teacher was brilliant. They were born teachers ... OK, they used to give us extra time near the exam. And not only I, a lot of people used to get very, very high marks in those days. I did my O Levels which we used to call Matriculation. And that was in physics, chemistry, math, English, geography, history, Urdu, you know ... and geometry ... quite a few subjects. And then I went to college and I did my A Level, in economics, political science, history and English.

And then I went to graduation which as you know we call it ... they call it here under-graduation. That was in economics, political science and English, and Persian option. Then I went to university for post-graduation which is Master and that was in politics. And my favourite subjects in that, that was a wonderful time, was international law and international politics. And at that's where I think I got attracted into the international sort of world rather than the local one.

Why are you called Riaz Chaudhri instead of the ... Aulakh?

Well quite honest speaking, when I sent my degrees here, one of my friend, who was an accountant, he got my admission and because as in Pakistan in those days there was no concept of surname, you know you will just put your family name at the end if you want to. But I didn't even bother to put that. I used to just write Riaz Ahmed, you know. But then obviously because if you are landowner and you know that background then people will call you Chaudhri. Chaudhri was basically used for the people who used to own quite a big bit of land and who could actually assist other people. It was a little bit of distinguished position to be in. But basically my surname, my family name is Aulakh because Aulakh is my family. And you see here people who are Sikhs, you know Sikh ... from India, they are Aulakh because they are from the same tribe. My family Aulakhs, they used to own seventeen villages in Amritsar in India and they still do.

Now because that chap you know he was filling in my form for me and they said 'Surname' and he put Chaudhri because he used to call himself Chaudhri. This is how Chaudhri was given to me and then he wrote to me and he said 'Look. There's a system of surname in England, so because I have put your surname as Chaudhri, make sure that your passport is under Chaudhri and everything is under Chaudhri.' So since then I'm stuck with bloody Chaudhri. [Both laugh.] I'm not really, I'm not that much fond of that.

OK so you went Chaudhri ...

Let me tell you, it doesn't look nice to call yourself Chaudhri, you know, because you are praising yourself. [Interviewer: OK] You know, the way I was raised we didn't used to praise ourselves so obviously. That chap he put it there, so I had to call that because I had to write it out again. But now I have put my surname which is original surname, family name, I would say, Aulakh. Even in the mayor book, you know, in my diary it says: Chaudhri Riaz Ahmed Aulakh.

OK, so your name Chaudhri is actually a title?

It's just a title like Mister. So when you call me Mr Chaudhri actually you are calling me 'Mister Mister.'

OK [Laughs]

As a matter of fact I should be Mr Aulakh. [Interviewer: OK] And anyone from Indian subcontinent, Pakistan, India, they call me Mr Aulakh, they don't call me Chaudhri.

Which was the name of the university that you attended?

Punjab University.

And what were your impressions about Britain before you came?

Well [clears throat] there's no doubt about it that because there was British rule in Indian subcontinent. You saw those buildings ... and also I have studied about British constitution and you know so as I said my education medium was English medium so I was familiar with the setup government and system of government and democracy and all that. And my impression was that Britain was one of the old-established democratic system, and I think today, being British, and being a Mayor of Reading and being you know in Britain for thirty-six years, I'm very proud of that. But my impression then was that Britain was one of the ... you know best place for education because my uncles came here for education eighty years you know ago which was about fifty-six years before I came here. [pause] And I knew so many other people, my cousins and relatives they came here for education.

Which university did you study in, in Britain when you came in?

To do accountancy you didn't have to go to university. I used to go to Reading University Library regularly because I was living only three hundred yards away, four hundred yards away. I was in, I was living in London Road which is called Foley Hall. The great, a wonderful lady Miss Foley, she donated those properties to IFL which is abbreviation of International Friendship League. And obviously you know I was here, I was looking for accommodation and I was told that go to Foley Hall. So I stayed four years while I was student.

The system in those days was that you do, you used to do the articles with a principal who used to be a chartered accountant and you actually learned, get the training there. And then obviously you had the study leave and you go to actually the colleges which used to run the courses like London School of Accountancy.

So I have always lived for the last thirty-six years in the one mile radius of this area because I love this area because I came here as a student. This is why I have always stayed in this ward. And, this is the ward I am councillor of.

OK, when you came to England did your impression change from the one that you had before you came into this country?

Ah [pause] ... yes and no. Because there weren't many people and unfortunately the people who came before me [pause] maybe they didn't give the good impression. I came from a social environment where obviously ... to be honest with you it was considered to be a privileged class, and when you came here obviously the ... most of the people are, they were wonderful and nice, but there were people, and you know you could feel that you know they were ... they had their reservations and you know they thought, 'Oh my God.' You know and that happened when I became an accountant and I started my own practice. When they booked an appointment to come in and they saw, and ... you know, some people who didn't have any experience of dealing with [er] ... Indians or Asian person or Pakistani person ... you know they thought, you know ... the first look that you get you sometimes, not always, some ... it depends what exposure the people had who were dealing with you. And they just assumed probably that either you are incompetent or you are not going to be able to do it, or you will not do it properly ... the job and all that.

But I'm proud to say that I have got clients with me who have been with me for the last thirty-nine years, or twenty-nine years, thirty years. So obviously those people and ... I haven't got more than I think three or four Asian clients. You know, the rest are all local clients. But then I was lucky because I had clients who were American, Dutch, Italian, Portuguese, Australian, African, Asian, you know ... Middle East, everywhere. So I never really ran my practice as an Indian or as a Pakistani or as an Asian. I ran my practice as a professional, you know, who will render the professional services to anyone who comes in. And I'm very proud to say that probably I am now one of the oldest, established practice in Reading because I have completed thirty-one years. You know, my firm Brain and Co is about twenty-six, twenty-seven years, but you know I used to have AA and Co before then and overall my practice is about thirty one years old now.

What were the bad experiences that you had?

Bad experiences? [Interviewer: Yes] Well, I wouldn't call it bad but, yes, it was disappointing. I applied to two hundred and sixty-five people to get the articles and [wry laugh] some of them didn't bother to answer. The others actually sent a regret that four, five others had got the invite too and I didn't get the articles, and I thought, well I'm not that bad. [Both laugh.] I mean, I wouldn't call myself to be Plato or Aristotle and a philosopher... not a Shakespeare and [Interviewer laughs] not a Wordsworth, but at the same time I don't think I was that bad. So probably, you know, I think in those days there was ... probably you know sort of reservations and, you know sort of ... You can call it psychological barrier. You know in crude language you can say discrimination.

And I would say that it was psychological barrier because the people ... I'll give you an example. One of my clients came to me and he rang me. And you know he's realised that I am an Asian. I mean probably when I was younger I would have told him off, you know but now as I said ... you have, you get mature, and you have so much experience you enjoy things rather than being

Racism

Jobs

Jobs
Racism

Jobs
Racism

irritated about it. He said 'Where are you from?' I said 'I am from Pakistan originally.' He said ' I don't like Pakistanis.' And I said 'Look, I didn't ask you that question, so this is unasked for and unwanted for.' So I said 'But again, if you had a bad experience, there's nothing that I can do. If you don't want to come to me, don't come to me. OK. But I think now that you don't like Pakistanis, I would like you to come to me. Don't pay fees, but come and see me because where on earth you got that impression? You know I'm proud to be a Pakistani.'

He came to me, and do you know what happened? He gave me a bouquet and he said 'You are wonderful person. My sincere apologies. It has changed my impression of all Pakistanis.' But probably he must have met someone you know who didn't do good ... you know who didn't behave properly. But I told him. I said 'Look. You go to zoo. You know it doesn't really matter which country you go, you see animals of every colour, every skin, every height, every size, every nature, you know, and ... every character. God has created human beings. You find the human beings. There are wonderful human beings, there are worst ones, there are criminal, there are sick, there are saints. You know there are angels. So really you shouldn't form opinion until you have met the person and you have experienced the behaviour, you know, he is putting forward and presenting.'

Jobs

Anyway I have never had a problem, you know, once the people came in. And as I said, now I have been councillor, I'm happy. My ward people have been wonderful and I was Mayor of Reading as you know just a week ago and it was a brilliant experience. I have enjoyed every moment of it. I was welcomed and never ever even once a single time I felt any discrimination or anything. And I really think so far as the system is concerned, as I said, there are individuals of every type, probably sometimes it's based on ignorance, you know lack of experience ... lack of exposure. But I can tell you that system is brilliant because otherwise I wouldn't have been mayor. And not only me, I mean there are you know seven, eight Asian and Africans who are Members of Parliament, there are members of the House of Lords. The system did not stop me. It encouraged me to go forward.

Community

Family Values

Then I came into politics when the children were grown up and, yes, the credit goes to my wife. She helped me along because she gave, always gave me support. You know, Naeema Chaudhri, the Mayoress of Reading and she is a wonderful girl and, a lady, and she has supported me as the mayoress as well. And she was always willing to actually be in the kitchen and cook the food like you know the part which my mother played there at my home, she has played here. So I made a lot of friends and you know we did wonderfully well and I didn't have any problem with that. I was welcomed in politics, I was welcomed as a councillor, I was welcomed as a mayor. And as I said credit goes to her because you know she supported me all the way now.

I think one thing I missed out which I would like to mention was my father's name and my mother's name. My father's name is Chaudhri Mohammad Sherif Aulakh spelled as M-O-H-A-double M-A-D Sharif S-H-A-R-I-F and Aulakh A-U-L-A-K-H. My mother is [pause] Ayasha Bibi A-Y-A-S-H-A B-I-B-I. And children I have got five.

And how have you maintained contact with people in Pakistan?

Yes, ten days ago or two weeks ago I went back on official tour because I wanted to see the chairman of ERRA because I have started RIPER with Martin Salter, which is an abbreviation of Reading Initiative for, Pakistan Earthquake Relief. So we have decided to take over a project in Pakistan, a primary school which we will be actually funding from here and building that school. There will be a plaque put there in the name of RIPER. So I would say that that would be a wonderful thing, you know. So I went there, I saw the chairman ERRA, Earthquake Reconstruction Relief Authority. And I saw a few other people there, a few other ministers, the Inspector General of Police and all that. Deputy Mayor of Reading Chris Maskell. He was with me as well.

And so, yes I have ... kept in touch, you know, I never broke my link with you know them because I visited them regularly and I see them and you know I got good friends there and my relatives, my friends and yes, I enjoyed it. That's a good way to get away from your normal routine life for a few weeks and relax, recharge your battery and come back again into the pressure life.

OK ...You have been Mayor of Reading ...

Yes ... and Deputy Mayor.

And Deputy Mayor, yes. How did you see your role, as ... as somebody coming from ... a big family in Pakistan and being mayor?

As I said, I think from day one my outlook and approach was ... international ... and multinational rather than actually village or town or a province or a country or a ... you know anything like that. And proof of that is now that I didn't learn English when I came here. I started learning English when I was only nine years old. OK? So when I came here I had studied English for fifteen years. And then when I had a choice either to do my BA or even O-level or A Levels, you know or whatever, and degree basic degree, either in Urdu medium, which was my national language or in English medium, I decided to go for English medium.

I like being exposed to the other parts of the world and that's something. And I can tell you now. As and when I can afford it timewise we would like to actually go away a few days and you know see the world. I can tell you because my outlook was international I didn't have any language problem but I had an added advantage being an Asian, originally because I could speak, can speak Punjabi, I can speak Urdu, I can speak a little bit of Arabic, I can speak a little bit of Persian. I can understand Hindi ... and English. So it was a wonderful experience actually whenever I used to go, if I used to go to Sikh Temple I used to speak Punjabi, their language, their mother-tongue. If I used to go to Hindu Temple I used to speak their language ... OK? If I go to you know other, somewhere else, I will speak their language. So I think as a matter of fact it gave me an advantage and I was in a position to actually put the communities together, bring them closer. And to make them feel at home ... and I felt at home as well because wherever I went I adapted to that because I was familiar with it. So I think it was wonderful and believe you me I was welcomed everywhere I went ... you know, in Reading and I loved it.

I am grateful to my colleagues and my friends. And in particular to the people, like you know my ... particularly in earthquake you know. As you know we collected about hundred and thirty-five thousand pound in Reading all of us, with the other friends and ... you know then ... other people helped me as well and I'm grateful to all of them.

And is your wife working?

She helped me at the phone, here, and most of the time actually she is in the kitchen because we receive a lot of guests. This is part of the culture and part of the family and ... but yes she was actually best athlete at her university. And when we were given you know ... leader of the Council he was doing this vote of thanks. He said he was really amazed the way Naeema Chaudhri has worked as mayoress. You know they were actually really impressed, the way she has behaved, the way, the grace she has introduced and all that, and she has actually done quite a few engagements as the Mayoress of Reading on her own. I was in Pakistan, or I was somewhere else, and she did that. So obviously she's done her job wonderfully well. I'm grateful to her. I wouldn't have been here today if it was not due to her, I would say. Number one due to my mother and number two due to my father and number three due to my wife. These are the three people who have helped me to achieve this.

OK. How do you see your role in the future? Your own contribution to the community of Reading?

At the moment I am still a councillor and I shall be councillor up till 2008, so I've got two years you know, to go and I love my ward and you know probably I would like to serve my ward. I'm never scared of responsibility. I'm never scared of hard work and I'm never scared of challenges. I like challenges because I want to test myself. Forget about other people, I want to test myself. I want to see my limit. I can tell you up to now I'm not disappointed with me and people are not disappointed with me so ... I'm here. If someone wants me to do something I'll do it and nothing matter. I have always been actually asked to do jobs.

I have been the chairman of Reading Islamic Centre, I have been vice-chair of board of governors at a school, vice-chair of Pakistan Community Centre. I have been chair of Asian Community Leaders, chair of Asian Parents' Association, you know education group, chair of Reading Earley Police and mosque and Muslims you know Liaison Committee, where my vice-chair was Chief Superintendent of Police in those days, Mr Webb. And I have done so many jobs. You know I have taken so many responsibilities. I was chair of Pensions Working Group.

In conclusion ... What, what would you ... say to fellow immigrants like you that have come to this country?

I'll say: Opportunity doesn't knock at your door all the time. You've got to go and open the door. It's a good system. Don't be put off, don't be discouraged and disgusted and disappointed by one two bad experiences. Keep on fighting. When going gets tough, the tough gets going. So work hard, be committed, be honest with yourself and to your community and to your nation and to your country which is now Britain. OK? Work hard. If I can do it so can you. Sky is the limit. And believe you me, this system, they don't look at your colour. Once obviously you can prove that you are worthwhile and you are capable of doing the job, they'll give you the job. No-one is stopping me because I am a Pakistani. I'm a ... Quite honest speaking I wouldn't accept that you know because I'm there to serve. Why should people stop me from serving the humanity and human beings. I'm proud to be a servant of human beings.

And I'll read here ... you know ... from a book of a famous poet Dr, Sir, Muhammad Iqbal, who had his PhD and barrister-at-law from Cambridge. And he says: [recites in Urdu]. I have said it in Urdu so that if someone hears it who knows Urdu they know what it means. But I have translated. He says: 'There are lot of, thousands of people who call themselves people of God. You know, like they say we are very noble. But I'm not interested in that,' he said. 'I will become slave of that person who serves the human being, who loves the human being. Who loves the people of God, who loves the, you know, mankind.' So what he's saying, his message is: love the mankind. Help the mankind. Assist them. Salve them. That is the real achievement in life.

And then there is a famous, you know, philosopher in Persian and Sheikh Saadi, he said [quotes in Persian] [Clears throat] 'If you want to be served or you want to be leader, learn to obey. OK? So whosoever obeys, is obeyed. So if you want command, obey first.' [Quotes in Persian] 'Whosoever, who serves... [quotes in Persian] he will be served, he will command.'

Also, [Quotes in Persian]. 'God has created the human being to care about the others, to feel the pain about, the, others. To look after them , to assist them, to serve them. Because he says, if He just wanted the human being to keep on praying in the mosque, in the temple, you know, in churches, in synagogues, wherever, He could have created more angels and asked them to keep on doing that. It means He wants you to do something different. Be useful to them, like my mother said. Serve them, look after them. Care about them, OK? And that ... they'll care about you and there will be a wonderful society, because everyone is the neighbour of somebody.'

So my message ... to the immigrant ... and to everyone, local and immigrant is: don't think about impossible things. Everything is possible. It depends how many hours, how many efforts you put into them. OK? That's my message.

Pakistan

The Islamic Republic of Pakistan is located in South Asia and stretches into the Greater Middle East. It shares borders with India to the east, the People's Republic of China to the far northeast, Afghanistan to the northwest, Iran to the southwest, and a coastline with the Arabian sea to the south. It is the sixth most populous country in the world (the second most populous Muslim country) and is home to the second most populous city in the world (Karachi). Islamabad is the country's capital city. Pakistan covers a land mass roughly the size of France and the United Kingdom combined. It has a varied geography with sandy beaches, lagoons and mangrove swamps in the south, and the peaks of the Himalayas and Hindu Kush to the north. Because it lies across several tectonic plates Pakistan is prone to earthquakes, the most recent of which occurred in Pakistan-administered disputed region of Kashmir. Since Pakistan's independence in 1947 it has experienced times of significant economic and

*military growth as well as times of instability (especially the secession of East
Pakistan, now Bangladesh). The name 'Pakistan' was coined in 1933 by
Choudhary Rahmat Ali as an acronym for the Muslim homelands of western
India – P for Punjab, A for Afghania, K for Kashmir, S for Sindh and TAN for
BalochisTAN. The I was added to the name because 'istan' means 'land of' and
'Pak' means 'pure' in Urdu, so it literally means 'land of the pure'. After the
partition of India there was an exodus of millions of Muslims from India to the
new-formed Pakistan, there were also many riots across both nations. There
were disputes over some of the princely states including Jammu and Kashmir
which led to the First Kashmir War (1947) and ended with both Pakistan and
India holding large parts of the state. Between 1947 and 1956 Pakistan was
a Dominion in the Commonwealth of Nations. It declared itself a republic in
1956 but this was stalled because of a coup d'etat by Ayub Khan. Ayub Khan's
time as president was marked by internal strife and the second war with India.
Yahya Khan became president in 1969 and had to contend with a cyclone
which caused 500,000 deaths in East Pakistan. Dissent in East Pakistan
eventually led to civil war and the Indo-Pakistani war of 1971 eventually saw
its secession as the independent state of Bangladesh. Pakistan briefly returned
to civilian rule under Zulfikar Ali Bhutto until he was deposed by General Zia-
ul-Haq (Pakistan's third military leader). Under Zia-ul-Haq Pakistan adopted
the Islamic Shariat legal code and the previously secular state saw growing
religious influence in both the civil service and military. In 1988 Pakistan
had its first female prime minister, Benazir Bhutto (daughter of Zulfikar Ali
Bhutto). During the next decade she alternated power with Nawaz Sharif – this
political instability led to a worsening economic and political situation. After
further conflict with India in 1999 General Pervez Musharraf took to power
and became president in 2001.*

Anne Morris

Born: 29th October 1942
Dublin, Ireland
Date of Interview: 20th July 2006

Ireland

● Dublin, Ireland
○ Reading, UK

My name is Anne Morris

When and where were you born?

I was born on the twenty-ninth of October 1942; I was born in Dublin, in Ireland.

And what are your earliest memories from that time?

Well I grew up in Ireland and ... didn't leave Ireland until the fourth of June 1960, but I was educated in Ireland in Newtown Forbes Convent, that was in County Longford, and we, our family lived in County West Meath and we emigrated in 1960. My parents emigrated in March. Those days in Ireland the economy was not good. I was still at the convent boarding school and the term didn't finish until June so I followed them on the fourth of June.

Have you got brothers or sisters?

I have got four brothers and three sisters.

And what are your memories of Ireland?

Well yes I grew up there well I ... we had a ... it was lovely really growing up in Ireland but, as a child you probably weren't aware of perhaps the economic difficulties that, you know, the adults had. It was lovely and free and, I was educated at a convent which was very strict, very, very strict in comparison to these days. Yes I suppose we all say that the school days are the best days of our lives but, not really, because I used to miss my parents desperately when I would go back at the beginning of term. My best subject at school was Music. I did my, which will be familiar to Irish people, my Intermediate Certificate in the secondary school and I did Music as well. So I, Music was my best subject and I did extremely well at piano. I didn't stay on to finish my education in Ireland because my parents had emigrated so I came over here when, as I say, I was eighteen and, came to England and it was, I have to say, a complete shock to me. It was nothing as I had expected it would be.

I imagined from my History and my Geography that England would be all industry, houses absolutely everywhere not a, you know a sign of any green fields. And my parents had actually settled in a little village, Whitchurch in Pangbourne. I remember my father and mother picking me up and we drove back to Whitchurch near Pangbourne and I could not believe, the country is so beautiful I was really, you know, amazed. And the next morning I remember going down, walking down from Whitchurch down into Pangbourne, which was just about five minutes, and you had to walk down, and there was a toll bridge, which is still there, and it was so pretty, the bridge goes over the Thames. It was absolutely beautiful and I really couldn't believe the beauty

Childhood

Education & Training

Jobs

Old Reading

of the place, it really was amazing. And I was expecting just factories and its just your, you know your perception of things really, isn't it? But I was, I was amazed and it was beautiful. Having said that, when I look back now, I think if my parents weren't there I wouldn't have stayed here but having your family around you it was very comforting and very reassuring.

But when I came over here I just couldn't wait to get a job; I was so anxious to get a job to earn money obviously and I remember getting the, what was it called the Reading Chronicle then, I used to get it and look for jobs. I always remember my father saying to me, 'Anne, don't be in such a hurry to get a job, because once you start working Anne you will be working for the rest of your life' and he's quite true, he was so true. Eventually I did get a job, there was a job advertised in a company called Underwood's Typewriters in Station Road, Reading.

In Reading?

In Reading, yes, in Reading. Quite amusing really, I was very shy, very shy in those days, [laughs] you know, very, very shy, no confidence at all, and I remember this interview. I went in as an office junior. The office isn't there any more, I think it's a burger shop, but I remember my father came with me for the interview, I mean in these days with my children, you know there is no way anybody, young people, their parents or family would go. I remember my father came with me for this interview, it wasn't that I'd said come with me, you know, it was like it seemed the most natural thing to do. And it was this little office in Station Road and the man, the boss there, was a Scotsman and I think he spoke, I think his name was a Mr Grey, and I think my father and him had great chats and I got the job.

I got the job as this office junior and I was paid four pound a week, but after tax I took home three pound fourteen and four pence. But I got the job and my job really was to answer the phone, it was a company that repaired typewriters, which of course they don't do anymore do they.

I remember the first day I had my job in Reading, so at lunchtime I thought I'd just pop out, and I popped out went down towards the lights and then I crossed the road and I was down into Queen Victoria Street and I hadn't a clue where I was. I was totally confused and had to ask somebody, 'Can you please tell me where Station Road is?' and I got back then. That was fine.

Yes, so I worked there for probably about six months and as I say I took home three pound fourteen and four pence, and used to get the bus in from Pangbourne every day. And every week I would go to Martin Fords - which is not in Reading anymore - I would go down to Martin Fords and it was real, we are talking about cheap and cheerful clothes, because obviously I didn't … I had very limited wardrobe to put it mildly, and I would go into Martin Fords and spend all my wages on absolute rags really, I shouldn't really say that but, you know cheap stuff, and I would go home with them having spent all my wages. And my father, he was a gem, 'and why wouldn't you,' he said, 'and why wouldn't you,' he would never tell me off, and for the rest of the week he would be giving me bus fare in and out to Reading.

I was there probably for about six or eight months and then I saw a job advertised at the BBC monitoring station up in Caversham. They were looking

Old Reading

Jobs

for a copy typist and I arranged to have an interview there. So I had an
interview in the afternoon and this lovely lady, a Miss George, I think her name
might have been Hilda, anyway Miss George her surname was, she interviewed
me for the job. And she was from Ireland, I think she was from Northern
Ireland, but she was the loveliest woman out. Now my typing was very ... I'd
done a little typing at school but it wasn't a priority, so I thought there's no
hope I'd get the job, but I got the job. Now the only reason I think I got the job
was because this woman that interviewed me probably felt quite sorry for me
and I was so quiet and shy.

But I was there for ... how long was I there for ... I don't know, maybe a
year or something. And I think meanwhile I had applied to work, I had always
wanted to work in a bank, I don't know why, I just like counting money I
think, and I had actually applied to the bank and I had a letter come through
to say, that was it I had to go for an interview, and the interview was in
London and this was the Nat West bank at the time. And I had to go up to the
head office for this interview, and went up on the train and had an interview,
and then they said to me they'd put me on the waiting list. Now this would
be unheard of now now-a-days as they have a job to get staff now-a-days.
So I was on this waiting list and I had a letter - while I was at the BBC - I
had a letter saying there was a vacancy in Wallingford in the Nat West - the
Westminster Bank it was called - in Wallingford. So I left the BBC and went
to work in Wallingford. I was actually there for four years in Wallingford and
then my parents had moved from Whitchurch into Caversham in Reading,
and I thought it would be much easier and less expensive if I could get a job in
the bank in Reading, so I applied for a transfer to Reading and worked in the
Market Place.

And then during that time I met my future husband, and we got married
in 1965 in St Anne's Church in Caversham, and then we lived in Tilehurst. I
carried on working in Reading for about six months or eight months after I
was married, and then I became pregnant with my first child. So yes, that was I
suppose my early working life stories and I went on and had four children and
what else ... I didn't work then for a long time. I went back to work in 1978.

How did you get involved in the Irish Eye Programme?

I was working in Reading during this time ... I often thought when I listen to
the radio ... I love music and as I said it was my best subject at school. I used
to think, 'I wish there was a programme for the Irish community,' meaning like
a programme of Irish music on local radio, and I the time I'd turn on the radio
and there was like Asian programmes and different nationalities, programmes
that catered for them, and I thought well why can't we have one for the Irish
community, so this was in 1995 now.

In June 1995 I rang up the local radio station, which was Radio Berkshire,
and asked to speak the boss his name was Henry Elford, he was head of the
Radio Berkshire, I suppose at the time, and I said to him have you ever thought
about having a programme for the Irish community? And he said, well we have
sort of, he said that he didn't think there would be a demand for it, obviously
they have to have a demand for things or they won't do it. And I said there's
a lot of Irish people around, and its not just Irish people ... my husband was

English and he loves Irish music ... and I've got lots of friends that are different nationalities and they love Irish music. So we had a long chat about it and the sort of programme it would be etcetera and he, you know, what, who would present it and everything, and I said well the thing is you want somebody to present this programme that's easy to understand; you don't want a definitive Irish accent say from the very north, or the very south, or the west, that people would have difficulty understanding. So it was sort of left like that, and you know he said about the numbers, who it would appeal to, and I said well leave it to me and I'll find out some information for you.

So I then rang up the Irish Embassy and very shortly after that and said I was trying to find out the numbers of Irish people in the sort of broadcasting area of radio Berkshire, Oxfordshire, Hampshire ... and I don't know what ... just all the local counties. And anyway they sent me a chart which was, I can't remember what year the census was taken, a chart of the map of England, Scotland and Wales, and the numbers of Irish born people in each county, the counties that would be relevant to the programme. And when I added them up there was about 38,000 Irish-born people in this little group of counties that would actually be able to listen to the programme - and that didn't take in considerations second generation Irish. So I then rang Henry Elford again and I gave him this information. So he said well you know leave it with me etcetera, that was as I said June 1995.

September 1995 I went into work in Reading as usual on a Monday morning and manager there was lovely lady, she said to me, 'Anne, I heard a lovely Irish programme on the radio yesterday,' and I said, 'Oh yes,' and she started talking about it, and I suddenly thought well that's, that was my idea, the little devils, why didn't they tell me. But I was very excited at the same time so I thought 'I'll have to ring,' this is on Monday, 'I'll have to ring Henry Elford.' Didn't have time to ring him till the Wednesday, and I rang him on the Wednesday and he said, 'Anne, yes we lost your name, we lost all your details, and in fact if you looked in the Reading Chronicle this week you'll see a little piece.' He said, 'We contacted Jo Wise, who is a reporter, and he's done a little piece,' and the heading was, 'Hunt for Mystery Radio Critic.' Well Henry said we really wanted you in on the first programme. I said Henry, 'I will be there for the second.' [laughs]

So the second week the Irish programme went out. I went in. I was so nervous because obviously I'd never spoken on the radio before in my life. I was really nervous, I was very excited just in my own mind, that something I'd suggested had actually taken off. So I went in and the presenter of the programme then was Kieran McGeary, he's a Waterford lad, he was a professional journalist, lovely guy, and I went in and the programme then had started the week before, and it was programme that ran for four hours from six until ten on every Sunday and it was broadcast ... I was trying to think where the studio was ... it was down off near Richfield Avenue, down that direction, they had a studio.

So I went in and I used to answer the phones and I thoroughly enjoyed it. To be honest people say, 'Oh how could you do that without getting paid,' but life is not all about money; I know we all need money and its lovely and we could spend it on wonderful things, but some things you know we get such delight out of. The fact that you've made a difference to a lot of people's lives because they can hear this lovely music, it's something to listen to.

I really enjoyed it and so we were running for maybe a couple of months and at that time, there was a group of us in the process of setting up, in the process of discussing the lives of the older Irish people in the community, and so I had this idea I said to Kieran who was the presenter, I said, for an idea for the programme why don't we ask people to send in a favourite Irish recipe, I said it would be very interesting. And I said the plan would be we would collect them all and we'd put them in a book and then we could sell it and make money for our charity was called the Hibernian Society. So the aim really was that with these recipes we would compile a book and sell it, and the funds would go to the charity ... the aim of the charity being to really improve the quality of life of the older Irish people in the community.

So this charity is linked to the radio?

No, no, no; the charity as I said it is a separate thing. The radio was totally voluntary, I wasn't being paid, and obviously the radio wouldn't, wouldn't what would you say sponsor the charity, because this BBC is totally different. It was just with all these things in my mind, my mind, was to try and do something to improve the quality of life of the older Irish, the older people in the community. Now I've had comments, obviously everybody has different opinions, but some people have said to me why just for the Irish? And I said to them well the thing is, if we all did something for the people we understand, and for our own community, if we all did something to improve the quality of their lives, wouldn't it be a wonderful place. You know you can't expect, you

Anne at convent school in Ireland (Third row from left)

Guinness pudding with whiskey sauce

100g/4oz sultanas	1x5ml tsp ground cinnamon
100g/4oz raisins	1x5ml tsp baking powder
100g/4oz currants	**Sauce:**
2x5ml tsp grated orange rind	100g/4oz butter
100ml/4 fl oz orange juice	50g/2oz demerara sugar
225ml/8 fl oz Guinness	50g/2oz golden syrup
100g/4oz whiskey	2x15ml tbsp whiskey
300g/11oz wholemeal breadcrumbs	225ml/8 fl oz single cream
3 eggs, lightly beaten	whipped cream or ice cream to serve
100g/4oz plain flour	

Method

Place sultanas, raisins, currants, orange rind and juice, Guinness and whiskey in a bowl, cover and leave to stand overnight.

Grease a 3lb capacity pudding steamer (or two smaller ones) with melted butter. Fold breadcrumbs through fruit mixture and leave to stand for 5 minutes, stir in eggs, then sifted flour, cinnamon and baking powder.

Spoon into prepared pudding steamer, lower into boiling water and steam for 2 hours. Leave to stand for 15 minutes before turning out of steamer.

To prepare sauce

Place butter, sugar and golden syrup in a heavy-based pan, stir until sugar dissolves, cook for 1 minute then add whisky. Stir through cream and remove from heat. Pour sauce over hot pudding. Serve with whipped cream or ice cream. Serves 4–6.

This recipe is sponsored by:

The Battle Inn

Late night licence, disco music, pool and darts

For more details contact:
Brendan Healy: Reading (0118) 959 0417

(88)

Broth & Barney recipe book

Community

know, the DSS or the government here to sort of take care of the world and its mother, I think it's up to all of us to do what we can and if we don't succeed, so what? At least we've tried. It's no good waiting 'till we're dead and then thinking I wish I'd done that. And I don't mind if I fail, because I think, you've got to go along, have the courage of your convictions, really, you know.

Then the idea was obviously, it would be a nice feature on the Irish programme if we had an Irish recipe every week, it would be interesting for the listeners, but then the idea with the material we'd get, we would compile a book. We called the book 'Broth and Blarney: The Irish Eye Cook Book.' The radio programme is called *Irish Eye*, so it was great publicity for them, and we did the recipes from mostly the listeners.

Have you got any famous people sponsoring recipes?

Oh the recipes, oh yes, we've got Val Doonican, and Gloria Honeyford, and Bishop Emms, the prime minister of Northern Ireland, you know, the Church of Ireland man. We've got loads of people. And ordinary people as well. Sometimes the ordinary people's are nicer, you know.

How long was the process from the idea … ?

It took probably eighteen months, probably, I'm just trying to think, about eighteen months. But the thing is, my philosophy is, if you really believe strongly in it, you go for it, even if it doesn't succeed, at least you tried. It's great fun when it succeeds. So that's the story of the book. Meanwhile the Irish programme was running, doing very well, and it's been running now for, since 1995, the Irish Eye programme on local BBC, and of course people can pick it up now on the internet, and we have listeners all over the world, and people in Ireland, not just local people. It was great fun.

Getting back to our charity, our aim was to do something for the older people in the community. Now of course you can't do much without money, and it's very hard to raise money, I mean the book sells for just under a fiver, that doesn't make a huge difference to be honest, but we're very lucky in that we're supported by the Ireland Fund for Great Britain - they give grants out - we've had a grant from them for the last three years, and that helps.

The first thing we've done, and we're hoping to move on and do something more now, is three years ago, actually after I retired, is to set up a weekly lunch club. We hired a hall at the English Martyrs Church at Liebenrood Road. We hire that church there every Wednesday. We have a hot lunch, the first week we had it we thought we'd have a glass of sherry for everybody, it was so exciting to have this lunch. So we had a glass of sherry and juice and a hot meal, and then people had a raffle and then a game of bingo … So obviously we do charge, we charge £2 for lunch, but after three years we've just put it up to £2.50, but for that you have a glass of sherry, a glass of orange juice, some lovely crusty bread, fresh flowers on the tables, proper table cloths, proper china. Somebody said to me one week, 'Why don't you use paper plates? I said, 'I wouldn't give my mother her dinner on a paper plate. Why would we use paper plates? Why shouldn't our generation have proper ... why should we settle for second best?' All these people have worked hard all their lives. I mean, I wouldn't want to eat my dinner off a paper plate. I always have this nice Irish CD in the background, nice music.

We then organise outings, we have trips to the theatre. It's more actually, it's not just the fact that people can have their lunches, it's really not about food or drink, it's more about people coming together, people of the same generation, and meeting their friends - that's really what it's all about. It's a bonus if you have a nice lunch on top. Why should they be forgotten, because, I think they are quality, they've worked hard, and they deserve the best.

And you said about your impressions, back a little bit, of England that was totally different, you were imagining grey and things ... What about the people? How was your impression of the people in England when you just arrived?

My impression of the people in England, I think they're so tolerant, and so polite. They are really, to me so tolerant. That's my general impression. Now other people say differently perhaps, but that is my impression.

And after you moved, have you ever considered coming back to Ireland, after you moved to England?

Well, my parents are both dead now and they died actually, well my father died in England, and then my mother moved back to Ireland, and she died in Ireland. For a long time, I used to think ... I think actually a lot of it is, certainly with me, I think, it's where your parents are, you sort of gravitate towards, and my parents were in Ireland, and, I mean, I still love going to Ireland. I go to Ireland quite a few times during the year. My mother is dead now so, I suppose the one thing about Ireland, it's a little bit different once your parents aren't there. Now for years, I used to think I'd love to go back and live in Ireland, and in fact my husband is English, he used to think the same, and we thought that for quite a long time. And I suppose three or four years ago we were in Ireland, and just, I thought to myself, well, no, because I have children now, and grandchildren, and they are in England, and I think home really is where your children, your family are. It's lovely, I still refer to 'going home,' to Ireland, and I still like to go home to Ireland, because it's lovely - lovely country, lovely people. But my family really are everything to me, as I said to somebody, probably they wish we were miles away, but I just, I think family is all important, is everything.

Food

Racism

Community

Okay, Anne, so would you like to say anything else about your immigration, contribution for the society, for Reading, for England, how do you see that? Anything you would like to comment?

Well, basically, I think, as I say, I think it's a very tolerant, this is a very, they are very, English people are a very tolerant nation. It's wonderful how, you know, people from different countries can come here, and they can, you know, you can ... there are opportunities there. I mean, you don't want to be too, shall we say pathetic, and expect people to roll the red carpet out for you, because after all, I think you're in a different country. That's how I see it. You're in somebody else's country, but the opportunities are there, and don't get all pathetic if people do make a comment, which, human nature being what it is, you will get some people that will make a derogatory comment about you. But so what? You've just got to have a life, haven't you? You're bound to, with the variety of people here. Not everybody is going to be welcoming and smiley, but I would say the majority of people are. And if you get on with your life, and work hard, you know, try and live a decent life, there's no reason why anybody can't prosper, if you don't mind work, and not get all fragile and pathetic. In the early days when Irish people came, in the early days, shall we say before we came, of course when I came I had my parents here, but it was very difficult to get accommodation. They used to have signs up, 'No Irish' or 'No blacks' 'No Chinese' and all this sort of stuff. That was a fact.

Where?

I know in Birmingham there was, and it was very difficult. I can't speak for other nationalities. I can't say I have ever had any derogatory ... I might have had maybe a few over the years, but it's no big deal. That's life, isn't it. There's all sorts of people. Human nature is such a mixed bag, isn't it. So I think, I'm quite happy here. And with the help of God, I shall continue to stay here, and enjoy what I am doing, as I said, my big thing is, is to try and make a difference. And I'm not being all pious and goody-goody, or anything like that, I feel, I think I just want to make a difference to other people's lives. If I don't succeed, I don't succeed. If you do, you know, life is short, isn't it. If we're given the gift of communication, whatever it is, and I think I've got a bit of a gift of communication, because I can talk for England, Ireland, Scotland and Wales. [laughs] So that's it really. Can't think of anything else to say.